D1064691

The Complete Book
of
Gymnastics

THIRD EDITION

Newton C. Loken

*Gymnastic Coach and
Associate Professor of Physical Education,
University of Michigan*

Robert J. Willoughby

*Associate Professor of Physical Education,
Eastern Michigan University*

PRENTICE-HALL, Inc. Englewood Cliffs, New Jersey 07632

Library of Congress Cataloging in Publication Data

LOKEN, NEWTON C
   Complete book of gymnastics.

   Bibliography: p.
   Includes index.
   1. Gymnastics.   I. Willoughby, Robert J.,
joint author. II. Title.
GV461.L6   1977   796.4'1   76-56434
ISBN 0-13-157172-9

Printed in the United States of America

10 9 8 7 6 5 4 3 2

Prentice-Hall International, Inc., *London*
Prentice-Hall of Australia Pty. Limited, *Sydney*
Prentice-Hall of Canada, Ltd., *Toronto*
Prentice-Hall of India Private Limited, *New Delhi*
Prentice-Hall of Japan, Inc., *Tokyo*
Prentice-Hall of Southeast Asia Pte. Ltd., *Singapore*
Whitehall Books Limited, *Wellington, New Zealand*

This book is dedicated to the enthusiastic and loyal gymnastic participants, coaches, teachers, and fans who have supported the revival and growth of the sport of gymnastics to its rightful place alongside the other fine sports of our schools, clubs, and colleges throughout the country.

Contents

Foreword

During the past twenty-eight years I have had the pleasure of observing the teaching of the authors. Both have demonstrated that they are genuine students and master teachers of gymnastics. Newt Loken and Robert Willoughby have learned their gymnastics as performers, teachers and coaches. The former was honored by his colleagues in the coaching field by being elected President of The National Gymnastic Coaches Association and Coach of the Year both in 1963 and 1971. Their experiences and writings attest to their qualifications. It is only logical that their combined talents could be channelled into writing a useful compendium in the field of gymnastics. I take pleasure and pride in commending to teachers and coaches this work, *Complete Book of Gymnastics,* by Newt Loken and Robert Willoughby.

PAUL HUNSICKER
Chairman,
Department of Physical Education
University of Michigan

Preface

With the nationwide surge of interest in physical fitness there has been a campaign for the inclusion of more gymnastics in our physical education curricula. It has been found that development of the upper body has been inadequate and that gymnastics makes a unique contribution toward overcoming this lack. With this is mind, many schools throughout the country are exploring the possibilities of including gymnastics in their total physical education programs. But they have found that many instructors are not qualified to teach this activity.

Nearly everyone has seen acrobats perform in circuses or in films. Many have witnessed competitive gymnastics as performed by accomplished gymnasts. Few, however, realize all that has transpired to produce this high level of performance. All of these expert performers had to start at the elementary level and be taught solid fundamentals by an instructor, either in an organized class or informally in small groups. Certainly every physical education instructor is not expected to be a gymnastic coach and produce experts, but he or she should know how to teach the beginning and intermediate levels of this activity. This then is a challenge to all teacher-training institutions to provide basic instruction in gymnastics.

It is the purpose of this book

1. To cover adequately gymnastic instruction for both men and women at the beginning, intermediate, and even advanced levels of gymnastic skills.
2. To include in one book a wide range of gymnastics, plus such allied activities as rope skipping, rope climbing, exhibitions, and flexibility training.

To do this, we have not exhausted all of the stunts that can be performed in each event, but instead have selected the ones which we feel adequately cover the various skill levels. In doing this we have tried to present the material in a manner suitable for class instruction.

Good luck, good spotting, and good performances!

ACKNOWLEDGMENTS

We are indebted to many individuals who have contributed greatly to the development of this book. Those who contributed specific material used in the first edition were: Dr. James Baley, Herb Loken, Gordon Hathaway, Jess Meyers, Bob Sullivan, and Erna Wachtel.

Sincere appreciation is expressed to the Athletic Institute for the use of many of the pictures throughout this book that came from several films produced by that organization. The *Athletic Journal, Scholastic Coach,* and the *Journal of Health, Physical Education and Recreation* very graciously allowed us to use pictures from their files.

Our deepest thanks to Dr. Elmer D. Mitchell for his encouragement and support throughout our work on the initial edition. Appreciation is extended to Ray Chinn, Ed Gagnier, Marv Johnson, and Connie Riopelle for their thoughts and opinions regarding description and selection of stunts.

A special note of thanks to the many fine performers who are pictured throughout the book, many of them national and world champions. In the first edition these included: Ed Cole, Dick Kimball, Nino Marion, Richard Montpetit, Jim Brown, Bill Skinner, Tom Francis, Tony Turner, and Carolyn Osborn. In the second edition these included: Mike Henderson, Gil LaRose, Dave Jacobs, Wayne Miller, and Gary Erwin. In the third edition these include: Terry Boys, Carey Culbertson, Bob Darden, Richard Bigras, Harley Danner, Rupert Hansen, Bob Loomis, Pierre Leclerc, Bruce Medd, Jerry Poynton, Joe Neuenswander, Monty Falb, Jim Scully, Toby Towson, Dave Willoughby, Jim Willoughby, and Rita Kinnell.

For the third edition appreciation also is extended to Linda Morton and Ginger Robey for their help in the chapters on women's gymnastics; to Carl Morton for his photographic skill in taking some of the new women's pictures; and to Lani Loken Dahle for valuable final reading and rewriting of the women's chapters.

Appreciation is extended to Bruce Keeshin for his assistance in the chapter on flexibility training and to Ray Gura for taking some of the pictures. Thanks also to the Nissen Corporation for the use of the double mini-trampoline and to Newt Loken, Jr., for performing the stunts pictured.

N. C. L.
R. J. W.

1

History and Values of Gymnastics

HISTORY

Gymnastics and tumbling, comprising some of our most basic motor skills, also include some of the oldest skills. Their beginnings are somewhat obscure, but can be placed at about 2600 B.C., when the Chinese developed a few activities that resembled gymnastics, particularly of the medical type. However, the actual development of gymnastics began in the early Greek and Roman periods of history. The Greeks first gave great emphasis to gymnastics; in fact, the word itself is derived from the Greek. Systematic exercise was endorsed by the most eminent educators of ancient times, and it became prominent in state regulations for education. In fact, the time spent on gymnastics was equal to that spent on art and music combined. The Spartans were most rigid in providing gymnastic training for their youth, and girls as well as boys were expected to be good gymnasts. The exercises consisted of various tumbling, dancing, running, leaping,

Early Gymnastics Apparatus

rope-climbing, and balance movements.

The early Romans copied the physical-training program from the Greeks but adapted it to their military training program. With the fall of the Greek and Roman civilizations, gymnastics declined; in fact, all forms of physical activity were discouraged. This was true throughout the Middle Ages and in the Renaissance, when a renewed surge of interest in systematic physical activity swept the European countries. Perhaps the earliest

1

contributor to this renewed interest was Johann Basedow (1723–1790) of Germany, who in 1776 added gymnastic exercises to the program of instruction in his school. Johann Guts Muths (1759–1839), who is known as the "great-grandfather of gymnastics," introduced gymnastics into the Prussian schools. He wrote several works on the subject, including *Gymnastics for Youth,* considered the first book on gymnastics. The actual "father of gymnastics" was Friedrich Jahn (1778–1852). Jahn, who is regarded as the founder of the *Turnverein,* conceived the idea of combining gymnastic training with patriotic demonstrations. This was well received by the government, and thus the program grew rapidly, involving huge playgrounds, with whole families participating. Jahn invented several pieces of equipment, among them the horizontal bar, parallel bars, side horse, and vaulting buck. Later, when threat of war subsided, Jahn's motives were misunderstood, and the authorities had him jailed for planning to overthrow the government. The *Turnverein* societies then moved into closed buildings for protection where they still function in Europe and in the United States.

Adolf Spiess (1810–1858) is responsible for introducing gymnastics into the schools of Switzerland.

Pehr Ling (1776–1839), of Sweden, was the first to appreciate the corrective value of gymnastics. He simplified exercises for the individual. Ling invented the equipment known today as Swedish apparatus, including the stall bars and the vaulting box.

Franz Nachtegall (1777–1847) started the first school for training gymnastics teachers at Copenhagen.

The development of gymnastics in America began with physical education programs patterned after European programs. This European influence was felt greatly through the Turnverein movement. When the Turners organization needed training instructors for its numerous clubs, it established in 1866 the Normal College of American Gymnastics in New York City. For years this college produced superb instructors in gymnastics and related activities.

One of the first American contributors to gymnastics was Dr. Dudley Sargent. While still a student he became a teacher of gymnastics at Bowdoin College. Within two years he had developed the activity as an official part of the regular college curriculum. He later served at Yale before moving to Harvard, where he became Director of the Hemenway Gymnasium. During his life Dr. Sargent invented many pieces of apparatus, including pulley weights and leg and finger machines. He also developed a system of anthropometric measurements for determining the physical condition of the student.

The YMCAs also made a notable contribution to the gymnastic program in the United States with their encouragement and inclusion of the activity in their programs. They installed apparatus in their gymnasiums and provided instruction in gymnastics at their training school at Springfield, Massachusetts. One of their early leaders who became prominent in the movement of physical training along educational lines was Dr. Luther Gulick.

Renewed emphasis on gymnastics and tumbling in World War II physical training programs resulted in increased growth of that activity in our schools after the war. Within the last two decades there has been a phenomenal surge of interest in the sport. Old gymnastic centers like Philadelphia, Minneapolis, and Los Angeles are still active, and many new areas produce an energetic flow of top-notch gymnastic coaches, teams, and fans. This is especially true of the Chicago suburban area. Clinics have sprung up throughout the country, highlighted by the annual Sarasota (Florida) Clinic, which began in 1951. Several clinics now being held annually are: Western National Clinic at Tucson, Arizona; Eastern National Clinic at Ft. Lauderdale, Florida; National Summer Clinic at East Lansing, Michigan; Northwestern Clinic at Seattle, Washington; and Northern California clinics.

The active and functional National Association of College Gymnastic Coaches was formed in 1950 by a small group of gymnastic coaches led by Chet Phillips. Past presidents of the Association have been Phillips, Charles Pond, Lyle Welser, Tom Maloney, Charles Keeney, George Szypula, Newt Loken, Hal Frey, Gene Wettstone, Bill Meade, Jake Geier, Hubie Dunn, Otto Ryser, Frank Wolcott, Eric Hughes, Karl Schwenzfeier, Don Robinson, and Art Aldritt. In 1955, the NACGC adopted a policy of honoring one person each year who had made an outstanding contribution to gymnastics over a period of twenty-five years or more. The ones so honored have been: Max Younger, Hartley Price, Roy E. Moore, Leslie Judd, Leopold Zwarg, Gustav Heineman, Charles Graves, Louis H. Mang, Ralph Piper, Erwin Volze, Henry Smidl, Gus Kern, Cecil Hollingsworth, Alfred E. Bergman, Lyle Welser, William Matthei, Charles A. Pease, Rene J. Kern, Chet

Phillips, Eugene Wettstone, Tom Maloney, Newt Loken, Frank Cumiskey, and Joe Giallombardo.

In 1959 a committee headed by George Szypula completed plans to have gymnastics represented in the nationally famous Helms Hall of Fame. Since that time, many gymnasts, coaches, and contributors have been cited.

In the past few years tremendous growth has taken place in the sport of gymnastics on all levels, instructional as well as competitive. A corollary of this renewed interest is the adaptation of apparatus to younger children in the elementary and junior high schools. The innovation of portable riggings for rings, high bar, and so on, has increased the use of this equipment. Also, much of the equipment has been redesigned to provide easier handling, moving, and storage. Competition throughout the United States has become more standardized in events and in scoring because of the influence of the FIG (International Federation of Gymnastics).

Obviously a great deal is happening in gymnastics. It is being rediscovered that with proper supervision and instruction gymnastics can be one of the most popular and exciting activities in the school program.

GENERAL VALUES

What are some of the contributions that gymnastics makes to the development of the individual? Past studies involving physical fitness indicate that gymnastics should be a vital activity in physical fitness training. The movements in this activity are fundamentally big-muscle movements and will develop greatly the muscle groups in the arms, shoulders, chest, and abdomen. These areas of the body are often neglected in other sports. Tumbling and trampolining also develop the musculature of the legs. Besides building strength and power, gymnastics also contributes to other factors of physical fitness, such as agility, flexibility, coordination, and balance. A general improvement in posture also can result from this type of activity.

Gymnastics has special meaning as a sport. Emphasis is on coordination and skill, with stress on the execution and perfection of the performance. Students whose capabilities and size may not fit them for contact sports can find in gymnastics the satisfaction of competition and the thrill of accomplishment in skillful physical activity.

In addition to these physical factors, gymnastics also develops such mental qualities as alertness, daring, and precision. Many of the stunts call for quick thinking and split-second timing is necessary. Because gymnastics is an individual sport, the gymnast is the only person who can make himself or herself overcome fear in learning new moves. By repeating moves, the gymnast develops the ability to make definite decisions and to perform actions that must be correct for the successful completion of the stunt.

Such character traits as self-confidence, perseverance, and self-discipline are developed from gymnastic activities. If the gymnast works to make progress, he or she quickly learns to develop perseverance to the highest degree. Self-discipline and force must be applied, and the same stunt must often be tried repeatedly until mastery is finally accomplished. Because gymnastics is a self-testing activity, each individual may progress at his or her own speed. A gymnast who is challenged by a particular advanced stunt or routine is not prevented from trying it by the lack of progress of fellow gymnasts.

Creative ability has unlimited opportunity in the sport of gymnastics. Great pleasure is derived from working out possible combinations and routines. This develops an understanding of symmetry, continuity, coordination, balance, and timing in the gymnast. It also develops an understanding of the need for strength and endurance in order to complete some of the routines created by the gymnast.

Another value is the fun and enjoyment received from participating in the activity. The joy of successfully completing a stunt is outstanding. The elation of learning a handspring, kip, or giant swing is indescribable. To see children laughing and shouting with joy and pride as they successfully complete a stunt is indeed rewarding to the gymnastics instructor.

International competition, including the Olympic games, has stimulated interest in gymnastics in America. Television coverage and tours by teams from other countries have brought a high caliber of skill before the eyes of many people. In efforts to improve the position of the U.S.A. in international competition, some competitive rules have been instituted to provide training and development along the lines of the Olympics, such as the scoring system (FIG), compulsory routines, and the stress on the all-around competitor.

Winning a single medal at the level of Olympic competition is the mark of greatness. The record of Larisa Latynina of the U.S.S.R. stamps her as one of the greats of all time. Competing in the Olympics of 1956, 1960, and 1964, Latynina won 9 gold medals, 4 silver medals, and 4 bronze medals for a total of 17. A similarly outstanding record is held by her fellowcountryman Boris Shakhlin who during the same time period won 7 gold medals, 3 silver med- als, and 3 bronze medals for a total of 13. In the last few Olympics, men's gymnastics has been dominated by the Japanese and women's by the Russians. The following table gives the results of Olympic competition for the past several games.

RESULTS OF GYMNASTICS COMPETITION IN THE OLYMPIC GAMES

Year	Place	Gold	Silver	Bronze	Place of USA
			MEN		
1924	Paris	Italy	France	Switzerland	5th
1928	Amsterdam	Switzerland	Czechoslovakia	Yugoslavia	7th
1932	Los Angeles	Italy	U.S.A.	Finland	2nd
1936	Berlin	Germany	Switzerland	Finland	10th
1948	London	Finland	Switzerland	Hungary	—
1952	Helsinki	U.S.S.R.	Switzerland	Finland	—
1956	Melbourne	U.S.S.R.	Japan	Finland	6th
1960	Rome	Japan	U.S.S.R.	Italy	5th
1964	Tokyo	Japan	U.S.S.R.	Germany	7th
1968	Mexico City	Japan	U.S.S.R.	East Germany	7th
1972	Munich	Japan	U.S.S.R.	East Germany	10th
1976	Montreal	Japan	U.S.S.R.	East Germany	7th
			WOMEN		
1928	Amsterdam	Netherlands	Italy	Great Britain	—
1932	Los Angeles				—
1936	Berlin	Germany	Czechoslovakia	Hungary	—
1948	London	Czechoslovakia	Hungary	U.S.A.	3rd
1952	Helsinki	U.S.S.R.	Hungary	Czechoslovakia	—
1956	Melbourne	U.S.S.R.	Hungary	Romania	9th
1960	Rome	U.S.S.R.	Czechoslovakia	Romania	9th
1964	Tokyo	U.S.S.R.	Czechoslovakia	Japan	9th
1968	Mexico City	U.S.S.R.	Czechoslovakia	East Germany	6th
1972	Munich	U.S.S.R.	East Germany	Hungary	4th
1976	Montreal	U.S.S.R.	Romania	East Germany	6th

2

Tumbling

Tumbling is a basic motor skill that covers extensively the mechanics of rolling, turning, springing, and twisting. From watching children at play, one can see that it is a natural activity to include in a physical education program. Besides the aspect of fun, it serves as a fine background for apparatus work and also as a carry-over activity for other sports. It is challenging and exciting to develop tumbling skills, whether they are elementary or advanced.

Tumbling is generally done on tumbling mats in a gymnasium, but there is no reason to avoid performing stunts outdoors on a suitable area of grass or beach.

Mats are available in several different sizes. The more common sizes are 4' x 8', 5' x 10', and 6' x 12' and range in thickness from 1 to 3 inches depending on the type of material used. There are also a variety of landing pads from 4 to 12 inches in thickness. Many instructors prefer the 6-foot width because it pro-

vides more space for working across the mats. Longer mats or a series of mats offer the opportunity to perform combinations of stunts, which increases the variety and difficulty of a tumbling program. Some mats are paneled, which allows them to be folded for ease of carrying and storage.

VALUES

The specific values of tumbling activities are:

1. Tumbling develops coordination and timing.

2. Tumbling develops agility and flexibility because of the nature of the movements involved. Much bending, tucking, and twisting is required to perform the stunts well.

3. Because of the running and springing necessary in tumbling activities, strength is developed in the legs. This is

somewhat unique in that most other gymnastic activities tend to neglect the legs.

4. Courage and determination are developed in some of the more daring and difficult tumbling stunts. More advanced stunts involve movements performed with the body completely in the air.

5. Learning to control the body in basic tumbling skills has great carry-over to the other sports.

6. The art of falling correctly, as learned in tumbling, is of great importance in many sports as well as in normal daily activities. A relaxed rolling fall often prevents or reduces injury and enables a person to regain his feet quickly after a fall.

7. Because tumbling is a natural activity, it is self-motivating and provides a great deal of fun and enjoyment for its participants.

ORGANIZATION

Area and Equipment

Beginning tumbling can be taught in a small area. However, when more advanced stunts are taught or combinations of stunts are put into routines, a run is helpful to build up momentum.

Tumbling is best taught using mats. The mats can be put in a small area if used by a squad only or they can be put end to end in a row for mass instruction. For a large class, more than one row of mats may be required. In order for the instructor to see all of the pupils and for the pupils to see the demonstration, a horseshoe pattern would be advantageous. A circle formation is also possible, but it doesn't enable the instructor to view the whole class as well.

Teaching Methods

Perhaps one of the major pitfalls in teaching a tumbling program is to let one pupil work and the remainder of the class stand in line and observe. Too many instructors line up the entire class at one end of the gymnasium and have them perform individually. This type of class organization leads to discontent and will kill the fun element, with consequent discipline problems.

Beginning tumbling lends itself well to the mass method of teaching. Have the class line up along the length of the mats and work across the mats on the command of the instructor. After the class executes one stunt, have them do an about-face and return in the opposite direction while performing the same or another stunt. You will find that the students will not only get more activity out of this type of teaching, but they will also have more fun. It is not uncommon to see the students trying to outdo each other, consequently creating a healthy atmosphere of competition. For most beginning stunts, a maximum of three people can work on a 5' x 10' mat, although two is preferable. More can be accommodated by using shifts of pupils lined up one behind the other.

If the number of mats is insufficient for the whole class, tumbling can also be taught by the squad method. This method combines some other activity or activities with tumbling, and the squads are rotated during the period. Keep in mind that other gymnastic activities probably will require mats also. As the students become more advanced, they will require more space for tumbling and will need more rest between turns. Thus the squad method may be more advantageous for advanced work than the mass method.

Balancing activities can be combined well with tumbling instruction. Both require the same equipment and are organized and conducted in much the same manner. There is some advantage in changing periodically the type of movement; balancing and tumbling provide a good combination for this. After performing two or three rolling movements such as are found in tumbling, it could be restful to execute two or three of the stationary movements found in balancing, and so on. Also, the two activities complement one another. For example, it is helpful to be able to do a forward roll before learning the roll-out ending of a head balance. Similarly, being able to perform a head balance is helpful in learning a headspring.

Evaluation of tumbling probably is best done by use of a stunt chart; this serves to motivate the students as well. For more advanced classes, evaluation could be based on competitive routines.

Safety

Tumbling is a relatively safe activity; however, certain safety procedures should be practiced to minimize the risk of injury:

1. Always use mats for tumbling wherever possible. A grassy area or beach could be used for selected stunts.

2. When using more than one mat in a row, one is well advised to secure them together. This will prevent the mats from slipping and leaving "holes" in the tumbling area. Similarly, guard against overlapping of mats, which will cause ridges on which one may turn an ankle.

3. When placing mats, be sure to maintain adequate clearance from walls and obstructions.

4. Inspect the mats to see that there are no ripped places in them where a performer could catch a toe.

5. To make the mats last longer always carry rather than drag them.

6. It is very important that the neces-

Spotting

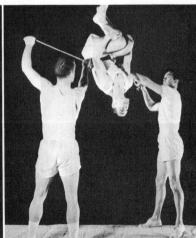

sary progression be used in learning tumbling skills. No one learns to run before he or she can walk. By the same token, somersaults cannot be learned before the basic fundamentals can successfully be performed. Too many instructors try to push the class too rapidly. This could result in the development of bad habits as well as injury. Fundamentals cannot be stressed too heavily.

7. Students should be encouraged to perform stunts with good form inasmuch as this teaches and indicates control of a stunt as well as adding to the beauty of it.

8. No student should be allowed to perform a new or intricate skill without a spotter until he or she is capable of doing so without danger. Encourage the students to learn the spotting techniques so that they can help each other.

9. The recent development of thick landing pads adds to the safety of the program; they should be used often.

There are two main methods of spotting: with the hand and with a safety belt. For hand spotting, one spotter gets close to the performer to assist in doing the stunt if necessary and to act in preventing injury if the situation arises. For some stunts two spotters are desirable. A common mistake of spotters is to stay too far away. A person falls quickly, and unless they can step in and catch him or her the spotting is useless. However, the spotter should also be cautioned about standing so close that the performer is hampered. The performer should be watched closely while going through the move so that conditions leading to a fall can be seen as early as possible. Spotters are simply to break a fall and ease the person to the mat, not necessarily holding him or her clear of the mat. The best

position for the spotter varies with the stunt. In general, try to figure in which part of the stunt the fall is most likely to occur or where the most help is vital and then station the spotter accordingly. When spotting is particularly important, special directions should be given along with the description of the stunt.

For advanced moves spotting is best done with a safety belt. Generally, two people are required to assist by lifting up on the belt. For stunts involving a twist of the body, the ropes must be crossed around the performer in the opposite direction of the way in which the twist is executed unless a twisting belt is used. A traveling overhead belt is very helpful in learning some of the advanced moves.

PROGRAM OF INSTRUCTION

The following moves are recommended for learning in the approximate order in which they appear.

1. *Forward Roll.* From a squatting position place the hands on the mat about shoulder width apart. Place the chin on the chest and lean forward, pushing with the feet and bending the arms. Allow the back of the shoulders to touch the mat first as the roll is executed and continue rolling on over the back. When the shoulders touch the mat, take the hands from the mat and grasp the shins, pulling the body into a tight tuck. Roll forward in this small ball up to the feet and then straighten to a standing position. The forward roll can also be done with the knees on the outside of the arms. For some pupils, this technique facilitates learning, but the correct and final roll should be done with the knees between the arms.

Forward Roll

After learning the technique of doing a roll from a squat, try it from a standing position. More of a forward lean will be evident when going to the mat from a stand. Be sure that the weight of the body is caught by the hands and arms rather than the head or back of the shoulders.

2. *Backward Roll.* Start from a squatting position with the hands on the mat and the knees between the arms. Lean forward slightly and then backward into the roll. Push with the hands, sit down, and start to roll onto the back. Place the hands above the shoulders with the fingers pointed back and the palms up. Keep the chin on the chest throughout the roll. Roll over the top of the head and onto the hands, keeping the knees tucked into the chest. Push with the hands and continue the roll to the feet. Finish in a squat position.

A preliminary move for this stunt is the rocker, which consists of rocking back and forth on the back with the knees in a tuck position and the chin on the chest. Keep the hands over the shoulders, with thumbs toward the head, and rock partially on them during the rocker. Repeat this rocking motion until you have the feeling of rolling smoothly across the back, and then on one backward roll simply continue on over to the feet. This constitutes a modified backward roll.

After learning the technique of doing a roll from a squat position try it from a standing position.

3. *Side Roll.* Start from a hands-and-knees position and then place the forearms flat on the mats, assuming a "doggie" position. Roll sideward across the

Backward Roll

back, holding the knees in toward the chest and continue on over to the hands, forearms, and knees position.

4. *Shoulder Roll.* Stand at the edge of the mat with the feet spread slightly. Lean forward and throw the left arm toward the mat, looking between the legs as the arm is thrown. Strike the mat

Shoulder Roll

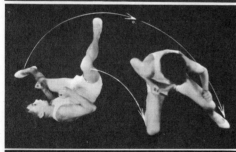

at the elbow first and roll up the arm, across the shoulders and back, and end up on the feet facing sideward. The performer can use the right arm to push up to the feet. After doing this several times, the stunt may be done from a run, simulating the fall that occurs in some games, but in a relaxed and non-injurious way.

5. *Roly Poly.* Start by sitting in a straddle position with the legs flat on the mats. Grasp the ankles with each hand. Keeping the arms and legs straight, roll sideward across the back to a sitting position again.

6. *Back Extension.* This is a variation of the backward roll, in which the performer momentarily passes through a handstand position and snaps the legs down to the floor. As you push with the hands, you fully extend the arms and shoot the feet upward to a momentary handstand. When in the handstand position, bend the knees slightly and snap the legs down from the waist. As the legs are snapped down, push with the hands so that the whole body will be completely off the mat. Finish in a standing position.

Back Extension

To practice the snap-down, kick up to a momentary handstand and repeat the last part of the back extension.

7. *Cartwheel.* The cartwheel may be performed either to the left or to the right. It is here described to the left, but may be done to the right by reversing the instructions.

Cartwheel

Start with the left side facing down the mat with the legs and arms outstretched and apart like the spokes of a wheel. Rock to the right side by placing the body weight on the right leg and lift the left foot off the ground. Then rock back to the left by placing the body weight on the left leg. With the momentum established by this rocking motion, bend to the left side at the waist and place the left hand on the mat about 2 feet to the side of the left foot. Force the right leg overhead and simultaneously push off the mat with the left leg. As the feet approach the handstand, place the right hand on the mat about shoulder width from the left hand. It is important here that the arms be kept straight and the head tilted back so that the eyes are trained on a spot about 12 inches in front of, and between, the hands. At this point, the body is in a handstand with the legs held straight and apart and the back arched slightly.

As the body passes through the handstand from the side, bring the right foot down on the line established by the left foot and hand by bending to the right at the waist. The left foot will follow to the mat, and one finishes facing the same direction as at the start.

In the event of difficulty in learning the cartwheel, several corrective measures can be taken. First, practice kicking up to a partial handstand, landing on the opposite foot from the one that was last to leave the mat. This simulates the proper hands-and-feet coordination. The handstand may be increased in height, and a turn could also be added as proficiency is increased. Next, mark spots on the mat with chalk to show correct placement of each hand and foot, then try the cartwheel in the other direction; many times this will correct the difficulty. If this does not work, start the cartwheel from a squatting tuck position. From there place the left hand on the mat about 1 foot from the left foot. Simply jump and execute a cartwheel, keeping the hands on the mat as described above. Land facing the same direction as at start. Progress by carrying the feet higher overhead until the stunt is done with the body held straight.

If you encounter trouble landing, practice the back end of the cartwheel separately. Kick up to a handstand and bring the right foot down close to the right hand. After the right foot strikes the ground, execute a quarter turn counterclockwise and land with the feet about shoulder width apart. When this can be accomplished successfully, try the cartwheel from the beginning.

8. *One-Arm Cartwheel.* In executing the one-arm cartwheel lean in the direction of the stunt and place the inside

One-Arm Cartwheel

hand down and do a cartwheel without using the other arm. At first the stunt may have to be done on a small arc basis just as in learning the two-arm cartwheel. As skill progresses it may be done correctly with the legs extended straight overhead and the body straight.

9. *Cartwheel with a Quarter Turn.* Execute a regular cartwheel and, as the first foot strikes the mat, turn the body a quarter twist, bringing the other foot to the mat with the toes pointing in the direction of the momentum. This stunt

is an excellent lead-up for a front handspring.

10. *Roundoff.* The roundoff is considered an important key to tumbling because it is used to start the majority of the backward tumbling exercises. The purpose of the roundoff is to change the forward motion of running into backward motion so that backward tumbling stunts may be performed. This stunt may be executed either to the left or to the right, but in this chapter it will be explained to the left.

Take a good run, skip on the right foot, and bring the left foot forward. Place the left foot on the ground, bend forward at the waist, and place the left hand on the mat about 2 feet in front of the left foot. Kick the right foot overhead followed by the left and place the right hand on the mat in front and slightly to the left of the left hand. As the stunt progresses the hands and arms pivot in the same direction and the body turns. The fingers of both hands are pointing toward the edge of the mat. When the feet pass overhead, execute a half turn. Snap the feet down from the waist and simultaneously push off the mat by extending the shoulders and flex-

Roundoff

ing the wrists. Land on both feet, facing in the direction opposite from the starting direction. When the feet strike the ground, bound off the balls of the feet. It is important that the eyes be trained on a spot about 6 inches in front of the hands during the entire trick. Placing chin on chest will mean loss of relative position and inability to complete the roundoff.

The roundoff should be learned from the cartwheel. The two skills are essentially the same, with the exception of the landing. Perform the cartwheel, and instead of facing sideways on the landing, execute a quarter turn more and land on both feet simultaneously.

Partner Assisting Neckspring

11. *Neckspring (Snap-Up, Kip, Nip-Up)*. From a straight sitting position roll backward, bringing the legs overhead to a pike position, and place the hands on the mats behind the shoulders with the fingers pointing toward the shoulders and the thumbs by the ears. From this position on the shoulders roll forward and at the same time: (a) whip the legs forward at about a 60° angle and arch the back; and (b) push off the mat with the hands and back of the head. Continue the whip of the legs until the body lands in a squat position on the feet.

Before trying the kip in its entirety, first try a bridge position on the shoulders and feet. This will give the feeling of lifting the hips. Then go to the bridge from the kip position on the back of the shoulders using the kipping action. When this can be accomplished successfully, try the neckspring as described above. A technique using a partner to learn this stunt is as follows: Have one person sit on the mats with the knees flexed, the hands behind the hips, and the feet flat on the mats. The person

trying the neckspring lies on the mat with his head between the spotter's legs and his shoulders resting on the lifting partner's feet, grasping the partner at the inside of the ankles with the thumbs. The performer rolls backward, lifting his hips with his legs coming near the partner's head. From this position he should then execute the neckspring technique of whipping the legs upward and forward while the assisting partner lifts his legs, thus pushing the performer's shoulders upward, which helps the completion of the neckspring. See illustration.

12. *Headspring.* Take a slight run, hurdle, and land on mat with both feet at the same time. Place both hands on the mat with the top of the head about 6 inches in front of the hands as though doing a headstand. Push off the feet, keeping the body in a deep piked position with the legs straight. The hips are carried over the head until the body weight falls off balance down the mat. Whip the legs overhead from the waist and on toward the mat in one continuous arc, simultaneously pushing with the hands. Land on the feet with the knees bent slightly, depending on how high the

Headspring

this point whip the feet overhead from the waist and then down to the mat in one continuous arch, simultaneously pushing with the hands. Land on the feet. Once mastered from a mat roll, the stunt can be performed on a level mat as described above. The same bridging technique used in learning the neckspring is suggested in learning the headspring.

The spotter sits on the mat roll. As the performer places his or her hands on the rolled-up mat, the spotter grasps the performer's upper arm with one hand, places the other hand under the upper back, and assists him or her through the stunt.

headspring is executed. This skill is not done by kicking or pushing the feet from the knees but rather by snapping or whipping the legs out of the piked position from the waist.

The headspring should first be learned from a rolled mat and with the use of a spotter. First try the headspring from a standing position. Place the hands on the near side on top of the rolled mat, with the head on the far side as though going to a headstand. Move the feet close to the mat roll, keeping the body in a deep pike position until the body weight is off balance down the mat. At

13. *Front Handspring.* Take a good run, skip on the right foot, and bring the left foot forward. Place left foot on the mat, bend forward at the waist, and place both hands about 2 feet ahead of the left foot. Kick the right foot overhead, followed by the left. As the feet are being carried overhead, the arms should be held straight and the eyes trained on a spot about 6 inches in front of the hands. As the body passes through the handstand position, push off the mat

Headspring with Spotter and Rolled Mat

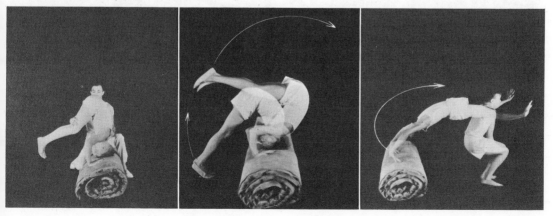

with the shoulders and wrists without bending the arms. Continue on over to the feet and land with the knees flexed.

Like the headspring, the handspring should be learned with a mat roll and with the use of spotters. Start from a standing position. Place the hands on the mat in front of the rolled mat, and with the aid of spotters kick up to a handstand. Arch over the rolled mat. Two spotters should assist the performer throughout this arch. Do this arch over the mat several times to establish the feeling of turning over, with the arms straight, back arched, and so on. Then try the stunt with a small run and execute a front handspring over the rolled mat. The position of the spotter is to sit straddling the rolled mat or kneeling in front of it. As the performer places his hands on the mat, grasp the upper arm with one hand and place the other hand behind his shoulders. As he overbalances, assist him to a landing position on the feet.

Another method of learning the handspring is to walk up to a landing pad that is about 12 inches thick and place the head and hands on the pad. Then kick up into a headstand position but carry the legs over into an arched wrestler's bridge position. The coach should emphasize that the performer should not touch any part of the back or shoulders until after the feet have landed. At that time the body may relax and drop to the back. Do several of these and then try it with a small run and a little stronger kick of the lead leg and push of the hands so that the body springs lightly up and over onto the feet prior to falling back onto the back side of the body. After many of these attempts with continued strong emphasis on the arch, the performer should finish on his or her feet in a standing position. The final skill is done without the head touching and with a good run, a strong whip of the leg, and a forceful push of the hands.

Some students may learn the front

Front Handspring

handspring more easily by using the following technique with a partner:

Have one person stand on the mat facing the performer. The performer kicks into a handstand with the partner catching his legs at the calves. This is repeated several times with a stronger kick each time, with the partner catching the legs surely with each kick. After this has been done several times, the partner then grasps the performer by the hips and allows the performer's back to ride slightly over his shoulders. With confidence the partner will eventually lift the performer slightly from the mats but always place him back to his hands in the direction from which he came. This develops the feeling of kicking the legs upward with the arms straight and the back slightly arched, essential parts of a good front handspring. After the above has been done several times, the performer attempts the handspring with the spotter (or spotters) stepping to one side and simply lifting him over as he executes the stunt.

Variation: A variation of this handspring is to finish on one leg with the other following. This makes for easy access into stunts in sequence.

14. *Tinsica.* Start by taking a good run, skip on the right foot, and bring the left foot forward. Place the left foot on the mat and by bending forward from the waist, place the left hand about 2 feet in front of the left foot, simultaneously kicking the right leg overhead followed by the left and place the right hand on the mat about 6 inches in front of, and about shoulder width from, the left hand. The arms should be held straight, and the eyes should be trained on a spot about 18 inches ahead of the

Front Handspring Walkout

hands. The legs pass overhead and the right foot lands about two feet ahead of the right hand, with the left foot following and landing about 18 inches ahead of the right foot. When this trick is completed the performer should be facing in the same direction as the starting position.

The tinsica may easily be learned by using the cartwheel as a lead-up stunt. At the completion of the cartwheel as the left foot nears the mat, execute a quarter turn and come to a standing

Tinsica

position facing down the mats. Repeat this until the quarter twist comes easily.

15. *Forward Somersault*. Take a good run, skip on the left foot, bring the right foot forward, simultaneously raise both arms overhead, and land on the mat with both feet at the same time (hurdle). It is important here that the hurdle be short and fast so that the forward motion established by running may be directed upward. Throw the arms upward, forward, and downward and place the chin on the chest while lifting the hips. Continue the circular motion with the hands by grasping and pulling the shins into a tuck position. The chest should be close to the knees and the heels close to the buttocks. After completing the somersault, shoot out of the tuck and land in a standing position on the mat.

The forward somersault can easily be learned by stacking mats on top of each other to a height of about three feet. Take a good run, hurdle, and lift into a forward roll onto the stack of mats. Continue this action until the roll becomes easy. Progress by taking the weight off the hands until the roll can be completed without touching the hands to the mat. From here try the front somersault to· a sitting position on the stack of mats. When this is completed successfully, take the mats away one at a time and try to finish standing on the feet after completing the somersault. Another method of teaching a front somersault is to provide a rolled-up mat over which the performer executes a front somersault with the spotter sitting on the mat assisting throughout the stunt. The trampoline can also be used effectively to teach the fundamentals of a good forward somersault.

Still another method of learning a front somersault is with the use of a tumbling belt and two spotters. The spotters simply run alongside the performer and help him through the stunt by lifting up on the belt as the somersault is executed. A springboard trampoline can also assist the performer if spotted by this method.

When spotting this stunt without the use of a safety belt, the spotter stands at the take-off point, placing one hand beneath the performer's head or shoulders to insure a good tuck and to lift him if needed. The other hand should grab the upper arm to prevent an overspin.

Variation: Forward Somersault—Russian Technique. Prior to taking off from the mats, swing the straight arms downward and backward past the hips, keeping the body erect with the chest up. After the arms have swung past the hips, duck the head toward the chest and begin the somersault. Grasp the underside of the thighs, pulling the knees tightly into the body. Continue the somersault to the feet.

Forward Somersault

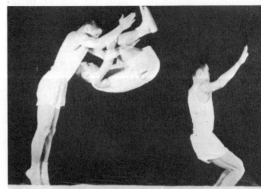

Forward Somersault, Under Arm Technique

of the body. Swing the arms downward, simultaneously bend the knees, and sit back as though sitting in a chair. As the body falls off balance backward, swing the arms upward overhead, simultaneously forcing the head backward. Straighten the legs and push off the mat with the toes. As you push off with the feet, force the hips upward and make a big circle with the hands. As the hands land on the mat with the fingers turned in slightly and the arms bent a little, the body is approaching a handstand position. From this position with a little hollow of the chest, snap the legs down from the waist, pushing with the arms, and land in a standing position. It is important that you continue to force the arms over in the arc until they finally reach the mat.

When spotting by the hand method, the two spotters should take a position on the knees or simply standing on the mat at the side of the performer. Have the performer do a back bend and assist by supporting his body weight. When he is in the back bend position, have him keep his arms straight and force his head back so that he is looking at a spot about 12 inches in front of his hands. Carry his feet overhead so that he passes through the handstand position. Have the per-

16. *Tigna.* A tigna is a type of front somersault following a tinsica in that the take-off is from one foot. The body somersaults in a semituck position.

17. *Back Handspring.* This is one of the more advanced tumbling stunts and should not be attempted without a spotter.

Start from a standing position with the feet about shoulder width apart and with the arms held straight out in front

Back Handspring

former then come to a stand on the mat by bending down from the waist. Repeat this several times until he gets the idea of turning over. Progress by having him try the back handspring in its entirety.

To hand spot the back handspring in its entirety, place the right hand in the small of the performer's back and use the left hand to assist him in turning over. This may be accomplished by lifting him behind the thighs with the left hand as he starts the back handspring and flipping his feet overhead. When using this method of spotting, it is important to stand close to the performer because it may be impossible to support his body weight at arm's length.

A tumbling safety belt may also be used for spotting purposes in first learning this stunt. Two spotters may then assist the performer through the backbend action as mentioned previously.

After learning the handspring from a standing position, try it from a snapdown. This involves kicking into a momentary handstand and snapping the feet down vigorously while pushing off from the fingers. This brings the per-

former back into a standing position with the momentum already started for a back handspring.

Back Handspring

Back Handspring from Snap-down

A good technique for teaching a back handspring that follows in line with a roundoff back handspring is as follows: Have the performer stand on the mats with knees slightly bent, back straight, and arms overhead. Two spotters, one standing on each side, grasp hands behind the performer's back, with the free hands prepared to lift the legs. The performer then slowly leans backward, placing his hands on the mat, and the spotters hold the performer off the mat and at the same time lift the performer's legs through the back handspring movement. The performer, after passing through the handstand, snaps the feet downward to the mat to finish in a standing position. In succeeding attempts, the performer should obtain more spring from the legs and throw his head and arms backward more vigorously, which in turn will make the completion of the back handspring easier. After successfully completing one back handspring, the performer should try two or more in sequence.

18. *Back Somersault.* The standing back somersault should not be attempted without a spotter. Start from a standing position with the feet about shoulder width apart and the arms hanging in a natural position at the sides. Bend the knees, swing the arms downward, and jump up, swinging the arms overhead as though catching a horizontal bar. Throw the head and arms backward hard,

Back Somersault

simultaneously bringing the knees up to the chest. Circle the arms sideways to grasp the shins, pulling the body into a tight tuck. It is important to pull the knees to the chest hard, continually forcing the head backward. Land on the feet in a standing position.

Before trying the back somersault in its entirety, first attempt the jump tuck. From a standing position, jump into the air and bring the knees up to the chest. As the knees strike the chest grasp the shins and hold the tuck position. It is important here to bring the knees up to the chest rather than the chest down to the knees. Shoot out of the tuck and land on the feet. Do not throw the head and arms backward when practicing this lead-up stunt as it can cause partial turnover and possible injury. A spotter may assist here by standing behind the performer and simply placing a hand on his back to prevent overspring. After this jump tuck has been tried several times, try the back somersault with the use of a spotter or two.

In spotting this stunt, it is suggested that two spotters be utilized, one on each side of the performer. As the performer tries the back somersault the spotters should assist by supporting the performer in the small of the back, holding him up. At the same time throw his legs over into the back somersault with the other hand. Spot very carefully during the early stages of this skill.

19. *Roundoff—Back Handspring.* Take a good run and execute the roundoff as described earlier. It is important here to push off the hands on the roundoff so that the entire body is in the air at one point. As the feet are snapped downward, they should be pulled well under the body to impart back motion. Before

the feet land on the roundoff, the back handspring should be started. The hands should come off the floor during the roundoff and be carried as though making a big circle. Keep the arms straight and continue the circle so that the hands will be forward of the center of gravity of the body when they reach the mat. Snap the legs down from the waist, as in doing a snap-down, and come to a stand on the mat.

Do not attempt this trick without a spotter. The method used in spotting may again be determined by the size of the performer. A small boy or girl may successfully be hand spotted. Larger individuals should be spotted with the use of a safety belt and two spotters. It is important that the spotters be experienced; otherwise injury may result.

20. *Roundoff—Back Somersault.* Take a good run and execute a roundoff as described earlier. It is important that the feet *are not* pulled through on the roundoff but are instead kicked out backward so that the backward motion established in the roundoff can be directed upward. The arms should move off the mat directly from the roundoff and be carried upward and overhead. As the feet leave the mat, bring the knees up to the chest (tuck) and simultaneously throw the head backward. As the knees are forced up to the chest, the arms complete a small circle and grasp the shins. When one revolution is complete, shoot out of the tuck and land. The back somersault should be taken high and spun fast to give more time for the landing. In order to increase the rate of spin, think about kicking the chin with the knees as the tuck is made. While in the tuck, pull the knees up tight to the chest and force the toes overhead.

The roundoff—back somersault should not be attempted without spotters. It is suggested here that the safety belt and two spotters be used for this stunt.

21. *Roundoff—Back Handspring—Back Somersault.* Take a good run and execute a roundoff and back handspring as previously described. Snap off the hands on the roundoff and pull the feet under

Side Somersault

the body for the back handspring. The landing on the handspring is very important because it will determine the height of the back somersault. With a long, low back handspring the legs are extended back so as to effect a blocking action, and the arms are lifted upward very swiftly into the back somersault. If the handspring is high and no block is made with the legs, the back somersault becomes low and long. As the feet leave the floor, bring the knees up to the chest into a tight tuck and simultaneously throw the head backward. Complete one somersault and shoot out of the tuck for the landing.

The roundoff—back handspring—back somersault should not be attempted without a spotter. The hand belt, with two spotters running alongside the performer, should be used when this skill is attempted.

Twisting Tumbling

For the purpose of continuity, all twisting moves will be explained from the roundoff and handspring, and to the right. These moves should not be attempted until the roundoff—handspring —back somersault can be completed successfully and should be attempted only with a spotter. The twisting belt should be used in learning all twisting moves.

1. *Half Twisting Backward Somersault.* Start by taking a good run and execute a roundoff—back handspring. It is important here that you kick out on the back handspring so that the half twister is carried high. As the feet land on the back handspring, carry the arms overhead and force the hips high as though doing a layout back somersault— with the body completely straight. Carry

the head backward and then to the right side, simultaneously dropping the right shoulder and arm and bringing the left arm across the chest. Complete the back somersault with one half twist and land on the feet. It is important that the head and shoulders are forced over the body on landing. Failure to do this will result in underturning the somersault, causing a sit-down landing.

2. *Full Twisting Backward Somersault.* As the feet land on the back handspring carry the left arm upward and over the right shoulder, simultaneously carrying the right shoulder and elbow backward and downward. The head moves backward and to the right, looking over the right shoulder. For best results the mat should be seen over the right shoulder as the twist starts and remain visible throughout the twist. The body is in a layout position with the head remaining in one spot and acting as an axis around which the body rotates. After the initial throw, bring the arms into the chest to increase the rate of spin. On completing one revolution, force the arms away from the chest to stop the spin and land on the feet.

Another technique used on back twisting is to lift upward swiftly with the arms but place the body in a hollow-chest layout position with the head slightly forward and chin down. This will tend to place the body in a straight line and increase the efficiency of twisting. Lift the body straight up and in twisting to the right after both arms reach upward, the right arm is dropped toward the right shoulder and the left arm drives across the body, activating the twist. The head remains downward and looks in the direction of the right armpit. Keep the body straight and taut.

ROUTINES

Innumerable combinations are possible and there is much value in allowing the performers to put together their own combinations into a longer routine. Some suggestions follow:

1. Alternating diving rolls with low tight rolls.

2. Forward roll—cross legs into backward roll.

3. Alternate two-arm cartwheel with one-arm cartwheel.

4. Series of cartwheels.

5. Cartwheel into a roundoff into a back extension.

6. Handspring to headspring into a forward roll.

7. Series of headsprings.

8. Series of cartwheels with a one-quarter turn.

9. Series of tinsicas.

10. Front somersault—forward roll—headspring.

11. Roundoff—two or three back handsprings.

12. Tinsica—roundoff—back handspring—back flip.

13. Roundoff—back handspring—back somersault—back handspring—back somersault.

14. Roundoff into successive back somersaults.

DOUBLES TUMBLING

Doubles tumbling consists simply of two persons executing tumbling feats together. This activity can be a great deal of fun and extremely rewarding. It does require close cooperation between the two performers, however, and it is also suggested that at least one and possibly two spotters should assist the performers. Some of the doubles tumbling stunts include:

1. *Doubles Forward Roll.* Start with one partner lying on the mat with his feet in the air while the other stands at his head in a straddle position. The partners grasp each other's ankles. Then the top person dives forward into a forward roll taking the bottom person's feet down toward the mat with him. The roll brings the bottom performer up onto his feet and he in turn dives forward. Then the other is on top again and they continue in a steady roll down the mat.

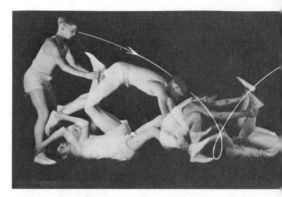

Doubles Forward Roll

2. *Doubles Backward Roll.* Start in the same position as the doubles forward roll. The top person sits down, pulling the bottom person's feet back with him. The bottom performer executes a backward roll, pushing up vigorously with his hands. Thus, the positions of both performers are now reversed, and the stunt may be continued in a steady roll backward down the mat.

3. *Log Rolls.* Start with three persons kneeling on the mat parallel with one another. The middle performer rolls sideways to the left and at the same time the left outside person jumps sideways over the rolling body to the center position. On landing he immediately rolls sideways to the right, and at the same time the outside right man jumps sideways over the rolling body into the center and then proceeds to roll sideways to the left. At this time the outside left person will jump sideways to the right and then roll. This log roll action can be repeated for as long as desired.

4. *Triple Rolls (Monkey Shines).* Start with three persons standing on the mat with the outer persons facing the middle and the middle one facing the left outside person. The middle person performs a tight forward roll toward the outside person, who in turn straddle-leaps over the rolling body to the center position; on landing on his feet he immediately squats into a tight forward roll in the direction of the right outside performer. At this moment the right outside performer straddle-leaps over the rolling body, landing on his feet in the center

position, and then proceeds to do a forward roll to the outside, whereupon the outside man straddle-leaps over the rolling body into the center position. This action can be repeated for as long as desired.

5. *Knee and Shoulder Spring.* The bottom person lies on his back with his knees raised and slightly spread. The top person approaches toward the other's feet and with a short run places his hands on the bottom person's knees. As the top person performs a headspring motion the bottom one assists him by placing his hands on the shoulder blades of the top performer. The top person continues over and lands on his feet just beyond the head of the bottom person.

6. *Back to Back Toss.* In this stunt one person tosses the other person over his back. Start standing back to back with the hands clasped over the shoulders. One person bends his knees, then leans forward and proceeds to lift the other person over his back. The thrower, or bottom person, should be sure to dip slightly with his knees so that the top person's buttocks rest against the lower

Knee and Shoulder Spring

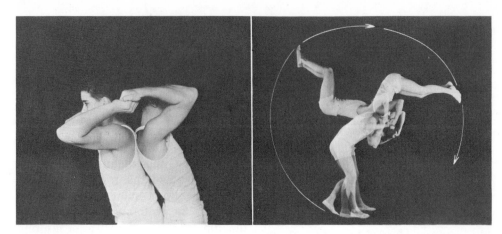

Back-to-Back Toss

back of the bottom man. The thrower should stop his forward lean and raise up as he feels the top person rolling off his back. The top person should continue to pike the body until ready to land. Be sure to have a spotter available throughout the early learning phases of this stunt.

7. *Front Flip Pitch*. Start with both performers standing, facing the same direction. The flyer bends one knee and places his shin and instep into the thrower's hands. Both performers then take a small dip in their knees and then the flyer proceeds to lift for a forward somersault, with the thrower lifting hard under the top person's shin and instep. The flyer, with the aid of the lift, should then execute a forward somersault.

8. *Side Leg Back Flip Pitch*. The flyer places his straight leg into the thrower's hand and places his right hand on the thrower's shoulders. The thrower lifts the leg up into the air and with the aid of the other hand on the flyer's back throws him into a back flip. The

Front Flip Pitch

Side Leg Back Flip Pitch

flyer should keep the lifted leg taut so that the thrower will have a solid means of lifting him into the air.

9. *Back Flip Toe Pitch.* This is done by the flyer placing his hands on the thrower's shoulders and setting one foot in the thrower's hands. The flyer then straightens upward and backward into a back somersault pitch. The thrower lifts upward into the air and throws the flyer into the somersault. Be sure to use a spotter in learning this stunt.

10. *Doubles Cartwheel.* This consists of two persons executing a double cart-

Back Flip Toe Pitch

wheel with one person's legs on the ground while the other's are in the air. One person stands with his legs slightly bent in straddle position with the arms to the side and front of the body. The other performer approaches from the side of the standing person and thrusts his head between the person's legs with the shoulders resting on the top side of the thighs. The hands grab the back side of the standing person's legs. At the same time the standing person circles the top person's waist in preparing to execute the double cartwheel. The top person should swing the forward foot around to the ground as quickly as possible in order to lift the standing person over into the second cartwheel. The two should hold tightly to each other; this will insure the completion of the double cartwheel. The spotter should stand behind and assist by lifting each performer's waist.

11. *Assisted Back Flip Over Arm.* The thrower should place one arm across the waist of the performer and the other

hand under the back side of the knees. The performer grasps the top arm of the thrower and prepares for the back flip. The performer kicks both legs and knees upward and around the arm of the thrower, in a manner similar to kicking

Assisted Back Flip Over Arm

Doubles Cartwheel

over a bar in the playground. The thrower lifts and turns the performer around his arm as pictured.

12. *Back Flip Off Partner's Feet.* One person is in a supine position with the legs elevated. The other person stands in a straddle position over the bottom person's legs and hips, facing away. The bottom person places his feet in the small of the back of the performer as the performer leans backward into an arch position. The bottom person grasps the performer's shoulders as he leans backward, and when the shoulders are over the bottom person's face and his weight well over the bottom person's feet, the top person then continues over in a flip action to a stand on the other side of the bottom person's head. Do slowly at first, like a slow arch backbend (handspring technique), until the timing is learned, and then more of a flipping action can be incorporated into the stunt. A good push with the bottom person's legs gives height and excitement to the stunt.

13. *Wheelbarrow Pitch to Forward Somersault.* The performer assumes a push-up position with the body elevated from the mat by straight arms and with the legs extended backward into the thrower's hands. With a beat consisting of an extension of the performer's waist and a slight dip in the thrower's hands, the flyer then whips his hips upward and over and then ducks his head and commences the forward somersault. The thrower lifts vigorously with his arms (hands under the performer's feet) and thus assists the performer in the forward somersault to his feet. The performer must be sure to wait before beginning the forward somersault turn until the thrower has had an opportunity to lift

forcefully upward; with this waiting time, success is sure to occur. Another version of this stunt is done with the performer in a handstand position; he then falls down into the thrower's hands and does the forward somersault.

Wheelbarrow Pitch

14. *Ankle Pick-Up.* The performer lies on his back and extends the legs straight up, placing the hands on the mat behind the shoulders. The thrower steps in close to the performer's hips and grasps the uplifted ankles with the thumbs on the inside of the ankles. The performer bends his knees slightly and then ex-

Ankle Pick-Up

tends them upward; at the same time the thrower lifts forcefully upward and then activates a throw of the feet over and beyond the flyer's head. The performer continues this back extension action on over to his feet. With proper timing, a good lift by the thrower, and a good push by the performer, the ankle pick-up can be executed at a fascinating height, particularly if the thrower is taller than the performer. This stunt can be done from a handstand position, with the thrower standing behind the performer grasping the uplifted ankles. From here the performer simply ducks his head and lowers his shoulders downward into a partial forward roll. When the performer reaches his back, he bends his knees slightly and then proceeds back upward into the back extension action with the thrower lifting him upward and over to his feet.

15. *Sitting Assisted Back Flip*. The thrower sits on the mat with his legs in

Assisted Front Somersault

straddle position and his hands flat on the mat, palms upward, while the performer stands on the thrower's hands. As the thrower lifts upward with his hands, the performer executes a backward somersault. The thrower gives an assist to the performer in the completion of the backward flip. A spotter should stand at the side to assist the performer.

16. *Assisted Front Somersault*. The performer stands between two spotters, and all face the same direction. The inside hands of the spotters grasp the wrists of the performer, and the outside hands grip the performer's upper arms. Then after a few steps the performer jumps into a forward somersault, and the spotters, lifting on their respective arms, assist the performer in the completion of the flip. Be sure the spotters do not lift too fast or too high, because this prevents the performer from turning into the somersault action. Also, the spotters should continue to lift the performer even after the somersault has been completed. This will allow for a soft landing on the feet instead of slamming into the mats.

Sitting Assisted Back Flip

3

Balancing

We all have seen children in the playground, front lawn, or sandy beach kick upward into a momentary handstand, and each second that the balance is held is a moment of joy for them. It is great fun and a matter of warm pride to accomplish a balance of some sort with a moderate degree of proficiency. Besides this aspect of fun, balancing does contribute a great deal to the physical development of the growing boy or girl. Very little equipment or space is required; the regular tumbling mat is satisfactory for all degrees of balancing stunts. Surely an activity that offers so much return on so little investment of equipment and space should be given serious consideration in the physical education program.

Balancing as such does not lend itself to organized competition, although it plays a large part in other gymnastic competitive events, such as floor exercise and parallel bars.

VALUES

The specific values of balancing activities are:

1. Balancing develops coordination and agility. The ability to maneuver the body in an upside-down position and to land correctly on the feet requires a great deal of coordinated action from the entire body.

2. Strength and endurance are developed by many balancing stunts. Many balances call for holding the body in positions that depend on muscular action for support, particularly of the abdomen and shoulders. Presses often depend on strength in the arms and shoulders.

3. Balance and a sense of relocation are essential in balancing stunts and are gained through consistent practice. Poise and orientation can be developed through balancing activities.

31

4. Balancing develops confidence and sureness in the ability to handle the body. This is a value that all growing boys and girls should experience.

5. In executing the doubles balancing stunts, a certain degree of teamwork is necessary. This value is developed as one performer depends on another to do his or her part of the stunt.

6. Balancing is fun and enjoyable because it is a natural and self-motivating activity.

7. Balancing provides a chance for the small boy or girl to gain needed recognition. Very often the smaller person has an advantage in balancing over the larger person, making balancing different from many sports.

ORGANIZATION

Balancing needs little equipment. Tumbling mats and space are about the only essential requirements, and even if tumbling mats are not available the activity can still be conducted if handled with close supervision and caution. Any area can be used, including a gymnasium, classroom, school corridors, and playgrounds. The important item in this respect is to provide ample space for each student.

There is little difference in the organization and conduct of tumbling and balancing. Only the differences will be noted here, and the reader is asked to refer to the preceding chapter on tumbling for the general plan.

Balancing can be taught by the mass method or by the squad method. Unlike tumbling, it requires no more space for advanced stunts than for beginning stunts. Balancing work requires a lot of practice for most people, so enough time should be allotted for it. However, variety is also needed to maintain interest. Tumbling and a mixture of singles and doubles balancing can make a good contribution to variety. It is not necessary for singles balancing to precede doubles balancing. Both can be presented in the same lesson.

For singles balancing, the students should work in pairs, with one performing and the other spotting. For doubles balancing, groups of three or four are best, with two students performing the stunt and the other students spotting.

Students should be encouraged to perform stunts with good form inasmuch as this teaches, and indicates control of, the stunt as well as adding to the beauty of it.

PROGRAM OF INSTRUCTION

The following stunts are recommended for learning in the approximate order in which they appear. The singles work will be presented first followed by the doubles balancing stunts.

Singles Balancing

1. *Squat Head Balance.* Start this stunt from a squat position with the hands on the mat and the inside of the knees resting on the elbows. From this position lean forward and place the head on the mat. Lift the toes from the mat so that the balance is on the head and hands, thus placing the performer in the squat head balance.

Variation: Do a squat head balance; lift the knees off the elbows, touch them together, and then place them back on the elbows. (For a challenge, see if the students can do this several times without losing their balance.)

2. *Squat Hand Balance.* This is similar to the squat head balance except the head does not touch the mat and the entire balance is maintained by the hands. Start from a squat position with the arms at shoulder-width apart and the inside of the knees resting on the elbows. Lean forward, keeping the head off the mat, and lift the feet into the balance position. Maintain the balance by working with the arms and pressing with the fingers.

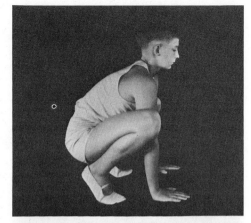

Squat Head Balance

Squat Hand Balance

Variation: While doing a squat hand balance, lift the knees off the elbows, touch them together, and then place them back on the elbows. (For a challenge, see if the students can do this several times without losing their balance.)

3. *Head Balance.* This stunt consists of balancing on the head and hands with the feet straight overhead. One method of moving into the head balance is from the squat head balance position. After reaching the balancing point on this fundamental stunt, raise the feet upward over the head. Do this slowly and

Head Balance

the balance will be maintained more easily. Another method is to place the head and hands in the proper position on the mat and simply kick one leg up, and follow with the other into the head balance position. Be sure to maintain a triangular formation with the head and the hands and keep the back neatly arched. Also, rest the head on the forward part and not the very top or back side of the head.

It is suggested that a spotter be used while learning this stunt. The best position for the spotter is to the side and slightly behind the performer. To come down from this stunt, either duck the head and do a forward roll or return the legs to the mat in the same manner as they were put in position.

Variation: While doing a head balance, lift the hands from the mat and clap them together and then place them back on the mats and maintain the head balance. (For a challenge, see if the students can clap their hands several times before placing the hands back on the mats to maintain the head balance.)

Spotting a Head Balance

4. *Forward Roll to Head Balance.* Do a forward roll, and on reaching the feet remain in a tuck position and place the hands on the mat well ahead of the feet, lean forward, and reach outward with the head before placing it on the mat.

Then slowly move the feet up into the balance position. Rushing into the balance out of the roll will simply cause the performer to fall forward into another roll.

5. *Head Balance, Arms Folded.* Start from a kneeling position with the arms folded in front of the chest and resting on the mats. Place the head beyond the arms and kick upward into the balance position.

attained by placing the forearms on the mat and kicking upward into the balance position without the head touching the mat at all. Keep the upper arms as vertical as possible and the lower arms nearly parallel to each other.

Head Balance, Arms Folded

Head and Forearm Balance

6. *Head and Forearm Balance.* From a kneeling position place the forearms flat on the mat, with the thumbs of the hands almost touching each other. Place the head in the cup formed by the thumb and fingers of the two hands and kick upward into the head and forearm balance. This same stunt may also be done with the fingers interlaced behind the head. In either method be sure that the forearms and head form a good tripod.

7. *Forearm Balance.* From a head and forearm balance, lift the head off the mat and maintain the balance with the forearms alone. The position may also be

Forearm Balance

Backward Roll to Head Balance

8. *Backward Roll to Head Balance.* From a sitting position on the mat, roll backward as in a backward roll. When the back of the head touches the mat, place the hands beside the head and extend the legs upward. Continue the roll to the top of the head, arch the back, and at the same time slide the hands backward to the tripod position to stop the momentum of the moving body and to secure the head balance.

9. *Hand Balance.* This stunt consists of simply balancing oneself in an inverted position on the hands. It is a

fascinating stunt but requires a great deal of practice before final accomplishment.

There are several methods of learning this stunt. One of the most basic is to do it next to a flat surface such as a wall. It is advisable to use a spotter while first learning this stunt, even though support will be received from the wall. Place a mat near the wall and put the hands on the mat, shoulderwidth apart, with the fingers pointing forward a short distance from the wall. With head up and eyes focused on the wall, kick upward until the feet rest on the wall. While kicking into the hand balance be sure to keep the head up to prevent the body from rolling into the wall. From this resting position push gently away from the wall with one foot in order to move slowly into a freely supported hand balance. The action is a back-and-forth motion from a free hand balance to the wall hand balance.

Another method consists of working in an open area with the use of a spotter. Execute the stunt in the same manner

Hand balance

Hand Balance Against Wall

far, move one hand at a time forward a short distance. A constant lean will provide a smooth walk. Avoid taking too large a step with the hands.

11. *Double Elbow Lever.* Start from a kneeling position with the hands on the floor so that the fingers point toward the knees. Lean forward and place the right hip on the right elbow and then the left hip on the left elbow. From this position extend the legs backward until they are straight, then raise them slightly from the mat. The body then will be supporting itself in a double elbow lever position.

12. *Single Elbow Lever.* Start from a kneeling position with the right hand on the floor, fingers pointing toward the knees, and the right elbow inside the right hip. The left hand is on the floor, extended beyond the head. Extend the legs backward, either together or in a straddle position, and raise the feet from the floor, thus placing most of the weight on the right elbow. Gradually shift the entire weight to the right elbow and slowly lift the left hand from the floor. The body will then be supporting itself in a single elbow lever position. (See picture in chapter 5.)

13. *One-Arm Hand Balance.* To learn this difficult stunt, start from an ordinary hand balance. Slowly shift weight from two arms to one arm and at the same time lift the other hand from the floor. Keep the balancing arm straight and strong, with the other hand ready to add support from the floor if necessary to maintain balance. The legs may be kept together or in a straddle position. Practice is the key to the final learning of the one-arm handstand. (See picture in chapter 5.)

and let the spotter grab the legs and hold the performer in a hand balance position. Little by little the spotter can release the legs of the performer and finally a freely supported hand balance will be accomplished. It is most important that the spotter work in extremely close to the performer and safely hold him in position. A safe recovery may be made from an overbalance by turning the body a quarter turn and landing on the feet. In the final hand balance, keep the head between the arms (eyes looking at the hands), back stretched, and hands pointed forward, with fingers gripping the floor and arms straight.

10. *Walk on Hands.* Walking on the hands is sometimes easier than holding a fixed hand balance, although a controlled walk is really more difficult. After getting into a hand balance, simply lean forward, and before overbalancing too

Chest Balance

1. *Chest Balance.* Start this stunt with one partner kneeling on all fours. The other partner slides his arms under the kneeling partner's chest and places his chest on the kneeling partner's back. Then the top person kicks upward as if kicking into a head balance, and finishes in a chest balance position on the partner's back. The arms could also be placed so one is along the kneeling partner's leg and the other along the partner's arm.

Doubles Balancing

Doubles balancing is a very enjoyable activity and can readily supplement a singles balancing program. Many of the stunts are relatively easy, and with a third or fourth person to assist and spot, the activity can become fun and exciting. Some of the stunts could include:

Thigh Stand

2. *Hold Out, Facing Out (Thigh Stand).* Start this stunt by having both persons face the same direction. Then the bottom person squats down, bends forward, and places his head between the top person's legs and lifts him (using the legs and not the back for lifting) into a sitting position on his shoulders. The top person then places the feet on the bottom person's thighs, with toes pointed downward, and the bottom person places his hands just above the top person's knees. The one on the bottom leans backward and removes his head from between the legs and finishes by holding the top person on his thighs with his arms straight. The top person straightens upward and forces a neat arch in the body with the arms out horizontally, head and chest erect. To dismount from this position, the top person simply drops forward to his feet. The spotter should stand in front of the performers in assisting in this stunt.

One may also mount into the position by jumping up onto the bottom person's thighs with bottom person lifting by the hips.

3. *Hold Out, Facing In.* The two partners stand facing each other. The top person circles his hands behind the bottom person's neck while the bottom one

Thigh Stand

places his hands behind the top person's hips. The top person then proceeds to step upward onto the thighs of the bottom person with the toes facing outward, keeping the hips over the feet as he steps up. When a solid balance position

Hold Out Facing In

is reached, each right arm is brought across the other's chest and a sure grip is secured on the other's wrist. From this position, both lean backward slightly and finish up in the hold-out-facing-in position. Some find it easier to grasp right arms as part of the starting position and simply to step up onto the bottom person's thighs and proceed to lean into the hold out, facing in.

4. *Knee and Shoulder Balance.* One partner is in a supine position with the hands and knees raised and the feet on the mat close to the buttocks. The top person places his hands on the bottom one's knees and his shoulders in the bottom person's hands. From this position, he kicks upward into a knee and shoulder balance. Be sure that the top person's arms are kept straight throughout this stunt and that contact is made with the shoulders into the bottom person's hands before kicking upward into the balance. The spotter can stand by the side of the performers to assist in reaching the balance position.

Knee and Shoulder Balance

5. *Front Swan on Feet.* One partner lies in a supine position with the legs and hands raised. The top person faces his partner and places his pelvis on the bottom person's feet, the latter's heels

Front Swan on Feet

angling in toward the stomach and the toes outward. Both grasp each other's hands. Then the top person leans forward into an arched balance position on the feet. He holds the hands until the balance is secure and then releases the grip and lifts the arms gracefully to the side supported by the bottom person's feet.

6. *Back Swan on Feet.* This is similar to the front swan except the top person is balanced on his back. The top partner backs into the upraised feet of the bottom one and leans backward into the back swan on the latter's feet. The bottom person's heels are inward and the toes pointed outward; the feet rest on the hips and the small of the upper person's back.

Back Swan on Feet

7. *Foot-to-Hand Balance.* The bottom person lies on his back with hands beside the head and legs raised upward. The top person stands lightly on the bottom one's hands and grasps the uplifted feet. The top person jumps upward slightly and pushes downward on the bottom one's feet. Simultaneously, the bottom person lifts the hands straight

upward to a straight-arm position. When this foot-to-hand position is secure the top person releases the bottom one's feet and gets up into a comfortable standing position.

8. *Two-High Stand.* The partners stand facing in the same direction. The bottom person's hands rest just above his shoulders, and the top person stands behind him, grasping the bottom person's

Foot-to-Hand Balance

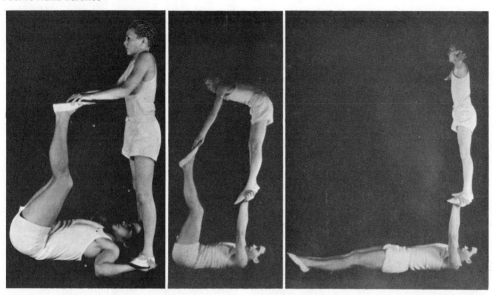

Two-High Stand

hands as in a handshake. The top one then moves to the side of the bottom person, who squats down a little. From this position, the top partner places his right foot on the bottom one's thigh and proceeds to climb upward onto the shoulders. The bottom partner pulls with the arms and keeps both arms firm and strong while the top partner is approaching the final position. When the top person's foot is on the far shoulder of the bottom one, the other foot is removed from the bottom one's thigh and placed on the other shoulder. The hands are still clasped, and after a good balance position is obtained the hands are released and the bottom person's hands are placed behind the top one's knees, just above the calf. The top person's shins should be resting on the back side of the bottom one's head, and the bottom one's hands then in effect pull downward and forward on the top person's legs. This makes for a solid two-high stand. To dismount, the bottom person lifts his right hand, the top person grasps it and proceeds to leap forward, turning slightly to his right as he leaps to the ground. Another method is simply to jump forward off the shoulders to the mat. As skill progresses, the two persons may want to finish the dismount by doing forward rolls after the top person lands on the mat.

Be sure to work with one or more spotters on this stunt. The spotter should be behind the top person while he is climbing up to the shoulders and assist by pushing upward under the buttocks.

9. *Shoulder Balance on Feet.* The bottom person is in a supine position with the hands and feet raised. The top person stands behind his head, grasps the bottom partner's hands, and places his

Shoulder Balance on Feet

shoulders in the bottom partner's feet. The top person then jumps upward in a tuck position and continues to press upward · into the shoulder balance on the feet. Pressure is applied to the hands in order to complete the press to the balance. When the shoulder balance on the feet is secure, the hands are released and the top person places his hands on the lower legs of the bottom one and continues to hold the shoulder balance on the feet. This same balance can be done in the opposite direction, with the top person starting from a position behind the buttocks.

10. *Low Arm-to-Arm Balance.* The bottom person is in a supine position with the arms up and the legs straight out on the mat, while the top person straddles the bottom man's waist, leans forward, and places his upper arms in the bottom one's hands. The top person grasps the back side of the bottom one's arms; he then jumps upward into a tuck position and continues to press into a low arm-to-arm. This position can also be reached by kicking upward with one leg, followed by the other. Keep the head up and grasp the arms firmly for support. This stunt can also be done from a knee and shoulder balance with top person transferring one arm at a time from the bottom one's knees to his arms.

A good combination is to have both partners lying in a supine position, head to head, grasping each other's arms. The top person executes a back extension up to a low arm-to-arm balance.

11. *Low Low Hand-to-Hand Balance.* The bottom person is in a supine position with the arms along his sides. He bends his arms and raises the hands upward, keeping his elbows on the mat. The top person stands straddling the bottom one's head and places his hands

Low Arm-to-Arm Balance

Back Extension to Low Arm-to-Arm

Low Low Hand-to-Hand

in the bottom person's hands. The top person then kicks upward into a hand balance on the partner's hands. A spotter should work closely on this stunt. Remember to allow the bottom person to do most of the balancing by shifting his hands and arms. The top one should simply maintain a rigid position.

12. *Low Hand-to-Hand Balance.* The same as the low low hand-to-hand except that the bottom person's arms are raised straight up from the shoulders. From this position the top person kicks upward into the hand balance position.

13. *High Arm-to-Arm Balance.* The

Low Hand-to-Hand

partners stand facing each other with arms raised, and each grasps the other person's upper arm. The top person then leaps towards the bottom one and circles his legs around the bottom person's waist. He swings down between the bottom partner's legs and then back upward toward the high arm-to-arm position. The bottom person swings the top one up and tries to move under him so that the final part of the stunt can be done with a slight press motion. The top mounter swings freely upward into the high arm-to-arm position allowing the bottom partner to move in and hold him up over his head.

14. *Overhead Back Arch.* The bottom person places his hand in the small of the top person's back and holds the ankle with his other hand. The top person then jumps upward into an arch position while the bottom person lifts her overhead. Be sure to hold the top person's ankle, as this helps to steady the balance position. Have one or two spotters to assist while learning this stunt.

15. *Overhead Swan.* The bottom person places his hands on the hips of the top person and then the top person

Lift to Overhead Back Arch

Lift to Overhead Swan

High Arm-to-Arm Balance

jumps upward into the arch position overhead. Finding the center of balance of the top person is very important in maintaining the overhead swan. At first the top person can hold onto the bottom person's arms while overhead, and as balance becomes secure the hands can be released.

Pyramid

Pyramids

Pyramids

Combinations of balancing stunts can be put together to form pyramids. Because of the great number of possible combinations, no attempt will be made to cover specific pyramids. Instead, general principles will be given and the readers can use their own imagination and creativity.

1. The usual shape of pyramids is either a convex curve with the peak in the center or a concave curve with a peak at each end.

2. The performers may be arranged in such formations as a line or a circle and may utilize apparatus or equipment such as parallel bars, vaulting bucks, ladders, chairs, tables, and flags.

3. For large pyramids the group may be arranged in units, each of which could be a pyramid in itself. In this case the highest unit would be in the center, with the lower units at the sides.

4. If the pyramids are being performed as a part of an exhibition, some attempt should be made to select and arrange the group on the basis of the sizes of the individuals. Ability will be a limiting factor. For example, if a head balance is to be performed on each side of the middle unit, the appearance would be better if two individuals of the same height and build were selected.

5. If the pyramid involves building on top of one another, the stronger and heavier members of the group should be used to form the foundation.

6. Pyramids are usually formed "by the numbers." The group should be lined up in rows with the top people standing behind the bottom people. Then some sort of signal is given for each step or

Acrobats at Work

movement until the pyramid is complete. Another signal should be given for the dismount, which usually is done forward and may include a forward roll when the performers hit the mat. The pyramid need not be held for a very long time. The instructor, through watching the performance, can judge the amount of time that would be most effective.

7. Often a lack of ability may be compensated for by having one person held in a balance position by another person. For example, two performers may do hand balances facing each other and have their legs held in place by a third person standing between them. Also, stunts such as merely standing on a kneeling partner's back or on the backs of two people in a push-up position make suitable parts of a pyramid and require no particular ability.

An example of a pyramid involving simple singles balancing stunts is:

> squat hand balance—head balance—forearm balance—hand balance—forearm balance—head balance—squat hand balance.

An example of a pyramid involving simple doubles balancing stunts is:

> knee and shoulder balance—hold out, facing out—two-high balance—hold out, facing out—knee and shoulder balance.

Pictures of various pyramids are included to help stimulate the imagination of the instructor.

An old art recently revived internationally consists of two, three, or more people performing a balancing and tumbling act such as was used in fairs, circuses, vaudeville, and so forth. This type of performance has now been developed in several nations and has resulted in the organization of the International Acrobatics Association. This Association sponsors meets featuring men's competition, women's competition, and mixed pairs. The performances are choreographed and done with a musical background. Detailed information can be obtained from the United States Sports Acrobatics Federation at 410 Broadway, Santa Monica, California 90401.

4

Trampolining

Trampolín is a Spanish word meaning "diving board" and refers to just that in many of the Latin American countries, Spain, and Mexico. In Germany the word refers to a springboard or to juggling. Little has been written about the beginning and the progress of the sport of trampolining. A French circus acrobat of the Middle Ages, whose name, "du Trampoline," may also be legendary, is said to have first started working on the springboard and leaping board and then visualized the possibility of doing tumbling stunts on the safety net suspended under the flying trapeze acts. He reduced the size of this net and then performed on it, with a unique repertoire of flips, twists, and turns. This net gradually was reduced to approximately its present size.

After this start, the trampoline grew in popularity and soon each circus had its "bounding bed" act.

After this initiation, many YMCA directors, physical education teachers, and gymnastic coaches adopted the main idea of the bounding-bed construction and built them for their gymnasiums and camps.

After some years of research and development, the "Nissen Trampoline" was patented and manufactured in quantity in 1939. At the present time several companies manufacture trampolines and different-sized models have been introduced.

The trampoline consists of a sturdily constructed table-high frame approximately 10′ x 17′, within which is attached, by means of metal springs, a woven webbing sheet that serves as a performing surface. Other size trampolines are 9′ x 15′ and 5′ x 9′.

Trampolining has been an integral part of the intercollegiate program for over twenty-five years and recently was dropped as an event by the NCAA. However, it continues to flourish in interscholastic, USTA, AAU, and international competition. It also remains as an exciting part of a gymnastics unit in a physical education program and serves as an excellent training device in learning twisting and somersaulting techniques used in other gymnastic events and diving.

The high school competitor is allowed to do an eleven-part routine, which is judged as are other events with A, B, and C moves being noted along with appropriate deductions for form, technique, and composition. National and international competition requires a routine of ten parts with the difficulty being determined as follows: a forward or backward somersault is worth .4 points and a full twist is worth .2 points, making a back somersault with a full twist worth .6 points; a double back somersault is rated at .8 points; a barani-out fliffis earns .9 points if done in a tuck position (a pike position adds an additional .1 point); a half in–half out fliffis equals 1.0 points; and a barani-out triffis would be worth 1.3 points. A difficulty judge is assigned the responsibility of determining the difficulty of the routine while four execution judges are concerned only with form, execution, and control. A detailed explanation of this system of judging can be obtained from the United States Trampoline and Tumbling Association at 930 27th St. S.W., Cedar Rapids, Iowa 52406 or the National AAU, 3400 W. 86th St., Indianapolis, Indiana 46268.

VALUES

The specific values of working the trampoline are:

1. More than in any other activity trampolining develops a sense of relocation.

2. The many movements made while in the air display the development of timing, rhythm, and coordination.

3. Trampolining requires and develops confidence and self-reliance.

4. The trampoline, along with tumbling, excels among gymnastics activities in developing the legs.

5. Trampolining is one of the most enjoyed activities in gymnastics. Perhaps the inherent desire to bounce, or the ease with which the bouncing is done, is responsible for the fun in participating in this activity. Enjoyment motivates intensive participation.

ORGANIZATION

Area and Equipment

The trampoline can be used in a class without occupying too much space. Just a few feet of space on each side of the trampoline is all that is needed, although the ceiling should be of sufficient height to allow free bouncing. Depending some-

Trampoline with End Mats

what on the age of the class, the minimum ceiling height should probably be about 20 feet. The area immediately surrounding the trampoline should be clear of obstacles that would hurt a person falling off the device. An additional safety precaution would be to put mats on the floor around the trampoline.

If more than one trampoline is available for the class, it would be advisable to put them a few feet apart and parallel to one another. This would concentrate the activity in one area. Wherever the activity is located in the gymnasium, it should be within clear view of the teacher. Sometimes it is helpful to have a platform between two trampolines the same height as the trampolines. This would allow close supervision of a class involving only two trampolines.

Teaching Methods

If the trampoline instruction is to be profitable, there should be no more than six students working on each trampoline. Any more than that will prevent the students from getting enough time during the class period to practice the stunts. If the class is too large for the number of trampolines, other gymnastic activities could be carried on elsewhere. This would be done best by dividing the class into squads and rotating the squads during the period.

One of the problems facing the instructor is organizing for best use of the trampoline by the class. Too often an instructor will allow one student to monopolize the equipment while the other students only stand and watch. The watchers lose interest and are apt to engage in horseplay. The following suggestions may aid in efficient organization:

1. Make it clear that those standing around the trampoline are spotters and have an important job to perform.

2. Plan your schedule beforehand to insure that each student will have some time to practice on the equipment. A system of rotating the students from spotter to performer back to spotter is highly advisable.

3. Practice one stunt at a time. It is much wiser to have all students in your group learn at least one stunt than to have part of the group learn several while the remainder have learned nothing. A good rule of thumb for beginners is to allow no more than thirty seconds per person per turn. In this way you are sure to give everyone a chance to perform.

Demonstrations should progress from the simple stunts to the more difficult. Sufficient time should be spent on each stunt before the student is allowed to progress to the next. However, this may become a problem because some students may have more ability than others and consequently will progress faster. You probably will find it advisable to rearrange the group so that you are teaching groups of equal ability rather than groups of unequal ability. This not only makes teaching easier but creates a better learning situation for your students.

As an instructor, undoubtedly you have some degree of proficiency in trampoline stunts. This should enable you to perform your demonstrations easily, but remember that although it is easy for you to demonstrate, it is not necessarily as easy for the beginning student to follow the demonstration. Accordingly, you should demonstrate the stunt several times until you are sure the students have grasped what you are trying to show them. While this may take a bit more time initially, in the long run it is quicker. After you have demonstrated a stunt, be sure to ask the group if they understand what they are going to try to do. Once the group appears to have grasped the point of the demonstration, give them the opportunity to practice the stunt. Don't start another demonstration —you will only confuse them.

Because trampolining is a self-testing activity, it is probably best evaluated by some form of stunt chart. Attractive, well-kept charts are also good for motivating the students. If checking individual stunts is too time-consuming, well-spaced routines could be used to check achievement and progress. For more advanced classes, it would be possible to judge the students in competitive routines, taking into account form and continuity as well as difficulty.

Safety

If properly used the trampoline is not dangerous; however, instructors should remember that danger can arise when students think they *cannot* be injured on the bed. This attitude might lead to taking unnecessary chances and result in an injury. Showing off can be dangerous. If you closely supervise trampoline activities, however, stunts can be learned with little or no danger.

Good equipment properly maintained is basic to all other safety precautions. Trampolines are sturdy, well-constructed pieces of equipment, built to last for many years, but like all other types of equipment, misuse can damage them. Therefore, it is important that you as instructor take precautions to insure that they are used properly. The following points should prove to be of value:

1. The trampoline should never be left unsupervised. When you have finished with it, it should be folded up and stored away. Too often people have been hurt and trampolines damaged because the trampoline was left out and was used by inexperienced students who thought it would be fun to bounce on.

2. Never allow students to wear street shoes when using the trampoline.

3. Horseplay should never be allowed on a trampoline—it is not designed for such use.

4. Inspect the trampoline before and after it has been used. This not only protects the trampoline from further damage, but is an excellent means of preventing accidents.

As to actually conducting the class for trampolining, here are some basic safety hints that should be adhered to:

1. There should be a minimum of two spotters, one at each end of the trampoline. If more are available, space them around the trampoline.

2. Safety pads should be provided for the metal frame of the trampoline.

3. Mats should be placed on the floor around the trampoline.

4. The progressive order of learning the stunts should be closely adhered to.

5. Teach early how to "stop" the bounce by flexing the knees immediately upon landing on the canvas. This will prevent students from making an uncontrolled bounce off the bed.

6. To prevent possible injury, have participants come to a complete stop

before dismounting and place their hands on the frame for support as they crawl off.

7. Remember that in bouncing, control is more important than height.

8. To prevent losing control the trampolinist should bounce for short periods of time.

9. Horseplay should not be tolerated.

10. Not more than one student should bounce until the students have become proficient at single trampolining.

11. A hand or overhead safety belt should be used in learning the more difficult stunts.

PROGRAM OF INSTRUCTION

Instruction on the trampoline involves three basic steps:

1. *Individual moves.*

2. *Combinations.* As a person learns a new stunt, he or she should be challenged to combine it with another stunt as smoothly as possible. Because a stunt must be learned well in order to combine it with another, the use of combinations in the teaching progression stresses proper execution and increases the safety of performance. In addition, the smaller combinations serve as building blocks for longer routines. Combinations can be suggested by the instructor or coach or can be created by the performer.

3. *Routines.* Ultimately, a pupil should strive to combine stunts into a routine. Competition is based on routines, required or optional. The approach to optional routines is one of problem solving. Certain requirements involving the types and number of movements are presented as a problem for the performer to solve creatively within his or her own capabilities. The instructor or coach and pupil can coordinate their thoughts on the development of a particular routine. For sample routines refer to the end of the chapter.

Before beginning a discussion of the stunts, it is important to understand the basic trampoline activity of bouncing. Bouncing on the bed of the trampoline is similar to bouncing on a spring board or diving board. The feet should be kept about shoulder width apart while on the bed. The legs should be kept together while in the air. The knees should be bent slightly when contacting the bed and the legs straightened while in the air. One should lift with the arms on the upward bounce of the body and drop them when coming down in preparation for the next upward bounce. The body should be kept straight, the head up and the eyes forward.

Some preliminary bounces and lead-up stunts to use before actually attempting the trampoline stunts are as follows:

1. *Half Pirouette.* Bounce straight up into the air and execute a half turn, twist, or pirouette so that the body is facing the opposite direction upon landing. In twisting, place one hand across the waist and the other hand behind the head.

2. *Full Pirouette.* Same as the half pirouette except a full turn is completed.

3. *Tuck Bounce.* Bounce straight up, and when off the bed draw the knees up to the chest and grasp the shins with the hands. This places the body in a tuck or ball position. On the way down release the tuck and land in a standing position.

Half Pirouette

Tuck Bounce

Pike Bounce

4. *Pike Bounce.* Bounce straight up, and while in the air lift the legs so they are parallel to the bed. While in this position the hands should touch the ankles. Remember to keep the legs straight throughout the performance of this stunt. On the way down snap the legs down and land in a standing position. A variation of this stunt is to spread the legs in straddle position while in the air.

These few preliminary bounces and lead-up tricks serve as "feelers" and will aid tremendously in acquiring confidence and courage for the following stunts.

5. *Seat Drop.* Land on the bed in a sitting position with the legs fully extended forward so the entire back of the legs contacts the canvas simultaneously. The trunk is slightly inclined backward from the vertical. Hands are flat on the bed 6 to 8 inches in back and to the side of the hips, the fingers pointed toward the feet, and the arms slightly bent. Return to the feet. In first learning this stunt, try it from a low bounce and spread the legs when landing in the seat drop.

Seat Drop

6. *Front Drop.* Land on the bed in a prone position. Extend the arms forward with the elbows extended sideward and the palms of the hands downward. The following contact points should land simultaneously: palms, forearms, abdomen, and thighs. Try this first from a hands-and-knees position and then from an upright standing position.

7. *Back Drop.* Land on the bed in a supine position with the legs straight and vertically inclined. Place the hands either on the thighs or free of the legs but near them. Keep the chin on the chest. Try the first few by leaning backward from a standing position and lift one leg up to help tip the body into the back drop position.

8. *Knee Drop.* Land on the bed in a kneeling position with the contact points

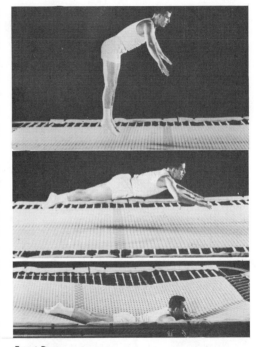

Front Drop

Back Drop

being the knees, shins, and instep. Be sure to keep the body directly above the knees when landing in the knee drop position. In first learning this stunt keep the bounce extremely low and do not allow the back to arch too much upon landing on the knees. An arched back has a tendency to snap the performer forward, which results in strain of the back muscles.

Knee Drop

Half Twist to Back Drop

9. *Half Twist to Back Drop.* Begin as if going into a front drop and on leaving the bed throw one arm across the waist and turn the head in the same direction, thus twisting the body into a half turn. Land in a back drop position.

10. *Half Twist to Front Drop.* Start as if going into a back drop and on leaving the bed execute a half twist of the body by pulling one shoulder back and piking the body slightly. Look over the shoulder and when facing the bed extend the legs and prepare for the front drop position.

11. *Back Drop to Front Drop.* When first trying this stunt it is suggested you do a back drop and shoot forward to a hands-and-knees position. This should be tried several times before you attempt

Half Twist to Front Drop

13. *Basic Routines.* At this stage of your learning program you are ready to try to put a few of these basic stunts into small routines. Some of these are:

a. Seat Drop—Knee Drop—Seat Drop —Feet
b. Front Drop—Knee Drop—Seat Drop—Knee Drop—Front Drop
c. Knee Drop—Half Twist—Seat Drop
d. Front Drop—Seat Drop—Front Drop—Feet
e. Front Drop—Half Twist—Seat Drop
f. Front Drop—Half Twist—Back Drop
g. Back Drop—Half Twist—Front Drop
h. Knee Drop—Seat Drop—All Fours —Front Drop—Back Drop—Feet

14. *Swivel Hips.* From a seat drop landing lift the arms over the head and extend the legs downward. Twist the hips a half turn and swing the legs under the body in a pendulum fashion. After the half twist is finished, flex the hips into a seat drop position and land on the seat. For the first few times do a seat drop and execute a half twist, land on the feet, and then continue on to another seat drop. Do this several times until the "feel" of the stunt is acquired and then attempt the entire swivel hips.

15. *Seat Full Twist to Seat.* This stunt is first done from a sitting position on the bed. The body is rotated in the direction of the twist and the hands are placed on the bed near the hips in the direction of the twist. The hands support the body and the complete full twist is executed and the seat drop position is again assumed. This should be done several times to acquire the feel of the full twist. The seat drop full twist to seat drop is then done from a standing posi-

the final stunt. It is important to obtain a solid landing in the back drop position with the legs up at an open pike position. From this position a kip or kick is obtained by extending the legs forcefully forward and upward. Upon leaving the bed, the shoulders are rolled forward and the legs are tucked under the body. When the body has rolled over to an almost parallel position above the bed, extend the legs backward and place the arms forward and sideward in preparation for the front drop position.

12. *Front Drop to Back Drop.* From a front drop landing, push with the forearms and thrust the body backward by tucking the legs into the chest and forcing the chest backward. Continue on over until in back drop position and then open the tuck and land on the back.

Swivel Hips

Seat, Full Twist to Seat

tion. Drop to a seat drop, landing in a position leaning slightly backward. Extend the body and go into the twist by thrusting one arm across the waist with the other arm behind the hips. Keep the body extended throughout the twist and upon completing the twist, pike the body and land in a seat drop position.

16. *Front Dive to Back Drop*. This consists of diving over to a back drop landing. Remember to keep your eyes

on the bed until about two feet above it and then duck the head and land on the shoulders. Keep the hips forward so that a good back drop landing is obtained.

17. *Half Turntable*. After landing in a front drop position turn in one direction by pushing hard with the arms in the opposite direction of this turn. Upon bouncing off the bed, tuck the knees into the chest, keep the head low, and

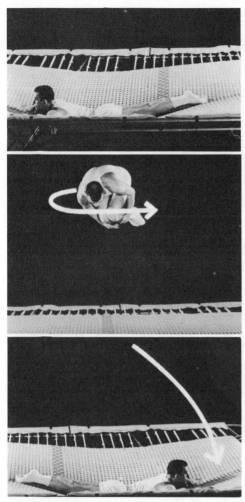

Half Turntable

18. *Back Pullover*. This stunt is a back drop or hip landing and a pull backward into a back pullover to the feet. In first learning this stunt, try several backward rolls from a squat position. Place the hands over the shoulder on the first few tries to assist in pushing the body over the head. After the backward roll has been done satisfactorily several times, the same roll is done from a standing position. The technique here is simply to squat and roll on over into a backward roll. With the standing start the body generally obtains a small bounce on landing on the hips prior to the backward roll. After a few of these have been attempted, try the stunt with a couple of bounces. Land on the hips in a slightly tucked position. From this position pull back under the thighs with the hands and continue on over to the feet. Gradually increase the height of the bounce as the stunt becomes perfected.

This stunt has several variations, including back pullover to a front drop;

Back Pullover

look into the direction of the turn. Upon finishing the half turntable, open the body and land in a front drop position.

Those having difficulty learning this stunt should try a one-quarter turntable and then progress to the one-half turntable. For greater difficulty try a complete turn of the body, executing a full turntable. This stunt involves a good push with the hands and a tight tuck of the body to complete the 360-degree turn.

Back Pullover with Half Twist

back pullover to a back drop landing; and a back pullover with a half twist to back drop.

19. *Cradle*. This stunt is started from a back drop landing, and as the body bounces forward, as if rolling over to a front drop position, one arm is thrust across the waist and the head is turned into the direction of the arm thrust and a half twist is executed. The stunt continues into a backdrop landing. It might be helpful to learn this in two stages: back drop to feet, continuing on forward with a half twist to back drop.

20. *Front Somersault*. Several forward rolls should first be done to acquire the feeling for the somersault. Then the somersault should be tried from an all-fours landing. Simply land in a "doggie" position and duck the head and turn over to the back. Next try it from a knee drop landing. Upon landing on the knees with the arms over the shoulders, throw the arms forward and under and duck the head, turning the body over into the somersault. In executing the front somer-

Front Somersault

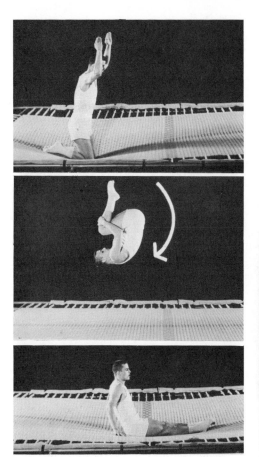

Knee Front Somersault

21. *Back Somersault.* On the take-off, raise the chest into the air and press away from the bed with the legs, at the same time lifting the arms up past the chest and tilting the head backward to look into the back somersault. After leaving the bed, bring the knees up to the hands, grasp the shins, and pull the body into a tight tuck. Continue the back somersault and, when the somersault is near completion, release the tuck and extend the legs downward for the landing.

Hand Spotting

sault from the knees to the feet, remember to lift the arms up and forward as the legs drive down into the bed. Look into the direction of the flip and then grasp the shins with the hands and pull the knees into the chest into a tight tuck. Hold on to the tuck until the somersault is almost completed and then extend the legs downward toward the bed, leaving the arms up and forward of the chest. Next do the front somersault from the feet. This may be accompanied by a spotter, bouncing along with the performer or using a safety belt.

Safety Belt Spotting

A preliminary move for a back somersault is to have a spotter stand on the bed to the side of the performer with the right hand behind the performer's neck and the left hand holding at the hips. The spotter should have the performer lift into the air in a facsimile of a back somersault, but should hold the performer and place him or her back to the bed in the starting direction. The performer goes through the action of placing the head back, with the eyes looking toward the ceiling and the arms and knees up toward the chest. The spotter momentarily holds the performer in this tuck position and then pushes him or her back to the bed in the direction from which the stunt was started, so the performer lands on the feet. After several of these are attempted, the performer should attempt the entire stunt, with adequate spotting.

Another method similar to the one described above is for the spotter to stand on the bed directly behind the performer, with his or her hands on the performer's waist. Use the same technique of holding the performer in the air while he or she has the head back, arms up, knees to the chest, and so on. Again the performer is pushed back to the bed in the starting direction.

22. *Barani.* A barani is a front somersault in a pike position with a half twist. The best way to learn this is by doing a knee bounce and going into a handstand

Back Somersault

Preliminary Technique for Learning Back Somersault

and executing a half twist and continuing over to a knee drop position again. This is somewhat like a roundoff from the knees. After doing this several times, try to finish on the feet. Remember in doing this stunt to get a strong lift of the hips at the start and thrust the body into a good forward momentum movement before executing the half twist. Be sure that the legs describe an arc over the head and not to the sides as is often the case with beginners. Next try the round-off from the knees to the knees without touching the hands, and the stunt will then be a knee barani. Do several of these and then try the barani from the knees to the feet. Finally, attempt the barani from the feet to the feet.

Knee Barani Touching Hands

Knee Barani

Barani

Hand Spotting Barani

There are several other ways that the barani can be learned and these are mentioned here briefly.

One method is to try a front somersault with a half twist using the twisting belt. By doing the front somersault in pike position and then executing a sharp half twist, a barani can be learned. Because this stunt is somewhat "blind," the twisting belt is essential for safety.

Another proven method is for two persons to stand on the bed facing the same direction, grasping hands behind the front person's hips. The forward person then does a front somersault through the arms of the spotter. After the somersault has passed through the arms, the spotter crosses his or her arms, which in turn twists the performer into a half twist or barani action. The performer then continues the flip and finishes facing the spotter.

Another method is to have the spotter stand to the left side of the performer, with the right hand partially around the performer's waist and the left hand behind the neck. After the third bounce, the performer starts into the barani action and the spotter pushes downward with the left hand and holds the performer up slightly with the right hand. After the initial forward barani action has started, the spotter then places both hands on the hips of the performer and actually turns and assists the execution of the barani motion. This should be tried after the performer has tried several knee baranies, touching the hands, and even the two-foot barani again, touching the hands so the general feeling of the forward motion and the twist is established.

23. *Three-Quarter Back Somersault to Front Drop.* This consists of doing a back somersault for three-quarters of the way over and then landing in a front drop. In trying this stunt for the first time, land on the hands and knees instead of the stomach. This will prevent

unnecessary jarring or straining of the back because of improper landing. On the take-off the arms are lifted straight up and the hips seem to slide forward and upward. The head goes back to look into the stunt. Try not to travel and open up flat for the front drop landing.

24. *Front One-and-One-Quarter Somersault to Front Drop.* Try a few front somersaults that are turned a little too far and land on the feet leaning forward. After acquiring the feeling of going a little too far on a front somersault then try the complete stunt. Hold on to the tuck a little beyond the opening point for a front somersault and extend the legs backward and thrust the arms forward in preparation for the front drop landing. It is suggested that this stunt be learned with the use of an overhead safety belt. For more difficulty, a half twist just before finishing will put the performer in a back drop position.

25. *Back One-and-One-Quarter Somersault to Seat Drop.* Execute a back

Front 1½ to Front Drop

somersault and hold on to the tuck a little beyond the point of opening up to the feet. Upon reaching this point, extend the legs forward and place the hands behind the hips and keep the shoulders forward. Land in a seat drop position.

26. *Back One-and-One-Quarter Somersault to a Back Pullover.* Complete a back somersault and continue toward a seat drop position but land on the hips with the body in a semituck position. From this landing, continue into a back pullover to the feet. Pull under the thighs with the hands upon landing on the hips, as this aids in completing the pullover.

27. *Kaboom.* In doing this stunt, land in an extended back drop position with the legs raised about a foot above the bed. Immediately upon landing on the back drive the heels forcefully into the bed keeping the legs straight. The heels bounding into the bed serve to toss the body backward into a flip. Upon leaving the bed, the knees are brought into the chest and the kaboom is completed.

28. *Cody.* This stunt is a back somersault executed from a front drop position. Upon landing on the stomach, get a feeling of sinking low into the bed. The knees should be bent. Push hard with the arms and force the chest up and back. Upon leaving the bed, grasp the shins and pull the body backward into a tight tuck. Complete the somersault to the feet. This can be done more easily after a three-quarter back somersault to the stomach.

29. *Twisting Backward Somersault.* The basic mechanics of the full twisting, double twisting, and triple twisting som-

ersaults are very similar. The take-off for all three twists resembles the take-off for a back somersault layout. As the number of twists is increased (full, double, triple) the somersault should become more stalled. On the take-off, the arms should lift straight over the head, a little further apart than shoulder width. There should be very little bend at the elbows. The straight-arm position will give more force and momentum to the twist when the arms are finally folded into the body. When the arms are extended all the way overhead before a twist to the left, the right arm should be pushed out to the side and swept across the abdomen up toward the chest. The performer should think of keeping his or her elbow straight at the beginning of the sweep, and as the arm reaches across the left side of the body it should be folded into the chest. The tighter the arm is drawn to the chest, the more force the twist will have. Little force is required for the full twisting back somersault.

Simultaneous with the right-arm sweep is the movement of the left arm, which is bent slightly and forced backward and down in the direction of the twist. As the twist progresses, the left hand and arm are folded into a position directly in front of the chest. As mentioned before, a tight wrap-up of both arms will increase the speed of the twist.

Upon completion of the twist, the arms are thrust forcefully from the body, which serves as a means of stopping the twisting action.

It is highly recommended that a twisting belt be used in learning the twisting back somersault.

Remember while twisting to keep the body in a firm position with toes pointed,

Full Twisting Back Somersault

Double-Twisting Back Somersault

legs straight, stomach taut, and so on. A sloppy, loose appearance is undesirable for its own sake as well as for its interference with the performance.

30. *Back Drop Ball-Out to the Feet.* Land on the back and get a sharp kick off the bed by extending the legs quickly. After the initial start, pull the body into a ball and complete the somersault to the feet. For the first few times the performer will land in a seat drop position but will finally finish in a standing position. This may also be done from a dive to a back drop landing and from there into the one-and-one-quarter somersault (or ball-out) to the feet.

31. *Front One-and-Three-Quarter Somersault to Back Drop into Front One-and-One-Quarter Somersault to Feet.* After the completion of the first somersault, continue the spin but attempt to see the bed for just a fraction of a second; then duck the head and land in a back drop position. From the back drop position execute a front one-and-one-quarter somersault to the feet. The last one-and-one-quarter should be tried alone at first, either from a high dive to the back drop and then the stunt, or from a back drop into the front one-and-one-quarter to the feet as previously explained. For safety's sake, the one-and-three-quarter front should first be attempted with an overhead safety belt.

32. *Double Back Somersault.* After a power take-off, lifting the chest and arms into the air with the head up, bring the knees forcefully up toward the chest. The hands then grasp the shins and pull the body into a tight ball. Continue the backward spin until the second somer-

Double Back Somersault

sault is almost completed, then open the tuck by releasing the knees and dropping to the feet. This stunt should be learned using an overhead safety belt. To accelerate the somersault action, bring the head into the chest after the initial revolution has begun. This serves to tighten the ball or tuck, which will increase the speed.

33. *Rudolph.* Start the somersault in a slightly piked position with the arms out to the sides. After the body is well in the air throw one arm down and across the front of the thighs and continue upward toward the chest with the other arm pushing backward. Turn the head in the direction of the twist. The body extends to a straight layout position while it is twisting and then pikes downward to the bed for the finish. To stop the twist, thrust the arms out to the sides after the one-and-one-half twist is completed. This stunt is best done by lifting the somersault almost straight up,

giving the performer the feeling of underturning (or stalling) the somersault. The use of a twisting belt is advisable in learning this stunt.

34. *Randolph.* This stunt is similar to the one-and-one-half twisting front somersault except another full twist is added. Height and a more pronounced stall of the somersault is necessary for the accomplishment of this stunt, along with a tighter pull of the arms into the body for a faster twist.

35. *Fliffis.* A fliffis is a combination of a double somersault backward or forward with a twist added. Because of the difficulty of these stunts it is advisable to use an overhead twisting belt when learning them. Some of the possible combinations follow.

(a.) FRONT FLIFFIS WITH LATE TWIST (Late Fliffis). Do a double front somersault, and on the second flip execute a one-half twist. To learn this in an over-

Rudolph

head twisting belt, try a front one-and-one-half somersault and open up with the body suspended above the trampoline by means of the belt. At this point the one-half twist is executed and the entire trick is then completed. Try the entire stunt by doing a fast one-and-one-half flip and then look for the canvas and at the same time execute a one-half twist to the feet. A slight forward lean into the stunt is helpful. After numerous successful completions in the belt, try it without the belt. The following are some preliminary stunts or progressive steps in learning the stunt:

1. Do several low and fast twisting baranies.

2. Do several one-and-three-quarter somersaults to back drop so that you can see the opening spot for the half twist.

3. Do several back drop ball-outs with barani to feet.

4. Do the stunt with the use of the twisting belt.

(b.) FRONT FLIFFIS WITH EARLY TWIST (Early Fliffis). Execute a barani and then quickly grab a tuck and go directly into a backward flip. This makes for a double front somersault, with a one-half twist on the first flip. Here are some progressive steps in learning this fliffis:

1. Do several baranies.

2. Do several baranies to a back drop into a back pullover. Do this stunt low and hard. Try this several times, and after you have the twisting movement perfected, try the entire stunt in the overhead belt.

(c.) BACK FULL FLIFFIS (Early full twist). This is a double back somersault with a full twist in the first flip. This is

Barani Out Fliffis (Late Fliffis)

done by forcing an overturning full twisting back flip into a tuck back flip to the feet. The progressive stunts are:

1. Do several back full twisting somersaults to a back drop back pullover.
2. Try the complete stunt in the twisting belt.

(d.) BACK FULL FLIFFIS (Half In–Half Out Fliffis). This is a back double somersault with a half twist in the first somersault and a half twist on the second somersault. To accomplish this stunt do an overflipping one-half twisting back somersault followed by another one-half twisting flip of the barani type. In short, this is a half twisting back somersault with a barani out to the feet. The progressive stunts are:

1. Do several overflipping half twisting back somersaults to the stomach.
2. Continue the stunt mentioned above but carry it over to the back.
3. Try the complete stunt in the twisting belt.

(e.) EARLY ONE-AND-ONE-HALF TWISTING FRONT FLIFFIS. This consists of doing a double front somersault with a one-and-one-half twist on the first somersault followed immediately with a back somersault. Progressive stunts are:

1. Do several overflipping one and one-half twisting front somersaults to a back drop back pullover (rudolph to a back pullover).
2. Try the complete stunt in the twisting belt.

(f.) LATE ONE-AND-ONE-HALF TWISTING FRONT FLIFFIS. This consists of doing a double front somersault with a one-and-one-half twist on the second somersault. The progressive stunts are:

1. Do several front one-and-three-quarter somersaults to the shoulders with a barani ball-out.
2. Try the same stunt, but instead of a barani ball-out execute a one-and-one-half twisting somersault to the feet.
3. Try the complete stunt in the twisting belt.

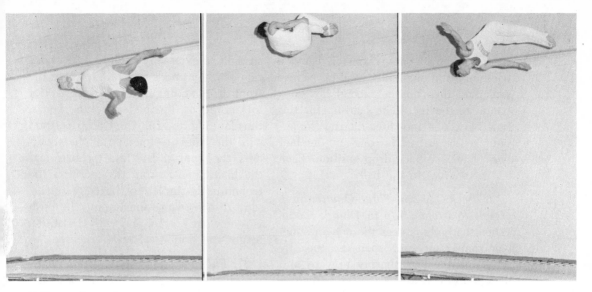

Half In—Half Out Fliffis

Rudolph Fliffis

71

(g.) DOUBLE FULL FLIFFIS. Execute a back one-and-one-half twisting somersault and then on the second flip do a barani to the feet. The lead-up for this is a back one-and-three-quarter somersault with an early one-and-one-half twist; land in a back drop position. Then try entire stunt in the belt.

36. *Back One-and-Three-Quarter Somersault to Front Drop to Double Cody.* When the body is near the one-and-one-half somersault spot open the tuck by extending the legs sharply upward and the chest downward. Keep the body in a straight or even very slightly piked position as it continues to rotate towards the front drop landing on the bed. Just prior to landing on the bed bend the knees, thus landing in a full front drop position with the hands to the side of the shoulders, the stomach full into the bed, and the knees bent. From this position the technique is similar to the cody somersault discussed previously only the push is somewhat harder, and with the added height the double cody is executed.

37. *Full Twisting Cody.* Upon landing on the front drop from a back one-

Back 1¾ to Front Drop to Double Cody

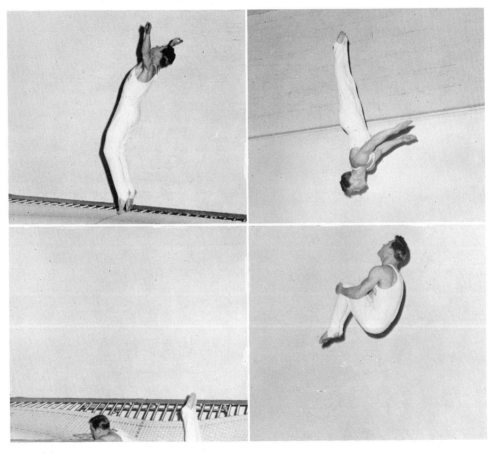

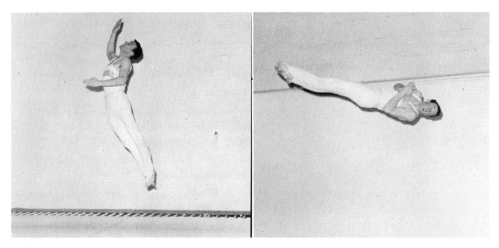

Double Twisting Cody

and-three-quarter somersault, start the cody in a layout position. After the body has moved well into the cody somersault the arm is swung across the chest with the opposite shoulder moving backward into the direction of the twist. Upon completing the single (or double) twisting cody, pike the body sharply downward to the bed. A common fault on the twisting cody is to start the twist too soon, which hinders the somersault action and results in a landing on the face, all fours, etc.

38. *Fliffis with Barani In and Full Twist Out.* Consists of executing a fast barani in the first somersault with the legs in pike position and then continuing the twist into a back somersault with a full twist. It is imperative that the barani and the full twist are done in the same direction. The legs in the full twisting back somersault are drawn up towards the stomach in order to increase rotation of the second somersault. It can also be executed with the legs bent in the barani

and straight in the full twisting second somersault. As skill increases attempt both somersaults with legs straight in pike position.

39. *Fliffis with Full Twist In and Barani Out.* Consists of doing a full twisting front somersault and continuing into a barani somersault to the feet. Lead-ups consist of doing many full twisting front somersaults to either the stomach or the back. After the orientation of the full twisting front one-and-one-quarter somersault is established, try the complete stunt in an overhead belt.

Routines

Creativity, imagination, and resourcefulness can be developed in the sport of gymnastics by the individual's construction and performance of his or her own sequence of stunts. The following are simply suggestions of combinations that certainly can be enlarged upon within the pupil's ability:

1. Knees—seat—swivel hips—all fours—front drop—half turntable—back drop—cradle—feet.

2. Back pullover — feet — seat drop — swivel hips—knee drop—front somersault—feet.

3. Back somersault (tuck)—barani—tuck bounce—half twist to back drop—half twist to feet—straddle leap—three-quarter back layout—front drop—full turntable—feet.

4. Rudolph—back somersault (tuck)—barani—back (tuck)—back somersault layout position with full twist—barani—three-quarter back somersault—front drop—cody (tuck).

5. Fliffis—barani—back somersault—double back — rudolph — back somersault — back with double twist—back—forward one-and-three-quarter to back drop with barani (or rudolph)—ball-out to feet.

Continue the general theme of increasing difficulty as the performer gains in proficiency.

Good luck and finish those routines with top form!

Here are two examples that were required for a recent world trampoline meet:

Compulsory Exercise Men

1. Double back somersault (tuck).
2. Barani to back landing.
3. ¾ back somersault (back pullover, pike).
4. Back somersault (tuck).
5. 1½ twisting front somersault.
6. Back somersault (pike).
7. Back somersault with full twist.

Forward Double Somersault with Barani In, Full Twist Out

8. Barani (pike).
9. ¾ back somersault to stomach (layout).
10. 1¼ back somersault (cody, free).

Compulsory Exercise Women

1. 1¼ back somersault to back (tuck).
2. Forward ½ somersault, ½ twist to back.

3. ¾ back somersault (back pullover tuck).
4. Back somersault (tuck).
5. 1½ twisting front somersault.
6. Back somersault (pike).
7. Back somersault with full twist.
8. Barani (pike).
9. ¾ back somersault (layout).
10. 1¼ back somersault (cody, free).

5

Floor Exercise

The floor exercise event can be one of the most exciting and creative activities in gymnastics. The range of ideas and the scope of imagination connected with this event are unlimited. A performer can execute stunts of great flexibility, of tremendous strength, of soft agility, of keen tumbling and balancing, and of imaginative rhythm. The floor exercise routine should use all of the available space on the 1-inch-thick resilient pad that is 12 meters (39 feet 4½ inches) square. The area is bordered with a 1-inch line either of paint or tape. To leave the area while performing results in a deduction of points from the judge's score. With this in mind it is imperative that the area be properly marked as an aid to the performer.

VALUES

The specific values received from working this event are:

1. The values of floor exercise are similar to those of tumbling covered in chapter 2 in that floor exercise develops timing, agility, and the musculature of the legs.

2. The values received from balancing are the development of a keen sense of balance and coordination. The minute control of intricate balance positions calls for the utmost in coordination and cooperation of all the muscles in the body.

3. The strength movements executed in floor exercise develop power and strength, particularly in the upper body.

4. The flexibility movements develop suppleness to its highest degree.

5. The creativity of the exercise calls for keen imagination and expression not found as readily in the other events.

ORGANIZATION

Methods of teaching the tumbling and balancing moves that make up floor exercise have been covered in the preceding chapters. When these skills have been learned separately, time can be taken from class periods to put them together in various combinations. A basic feeling for the event is thus promoted, and as skill progresses, more difficult moves may be introduced.

Because of the creativity, originality, and individuality that is desired in this activity, the best work can be done with individuals, particularly at the more advanced stages. However, elementary floor exercise can be given by mass instruction methods. Large groups can go through elementary movements together and, with practice, can use such synchronized routines for exhibitional purposes. Such exercises as swinging the arms into a front scale, into a forward roll, to a V seat, or sideward roll can be used for mass work. Be sure to allow ample room between the students.

PROGRAM OF INSTRUCTION

Instruction in floor exercise involves three basic steps:

1. *Individual moves.*

2. *Combinations.* As a person learns a new stunt, he or she should be challenged to combine it with another stunt as smoothly as possible. Because a stunt must be learned well in order to combine it with another, the use of combinations in the teaching progression stresses proper execution and increases the safety of performance. In addition, the smaller combinations serve as building blocks for longer routines. Combinations can be suggested by the instructor or coach or created by the performer.

3. *Routines.* Ultimately a pupil should strive to combine stunts into a routine. Competition is based on routines, required or optional. The approach to optional routines is one of problem solving. Certain requirements involving time and the types and number of movements are presented as a problem for the performer to solve creatively within his or her own capabilities. The instructor or coach and pupil can coordinate their thoughts on the development of a particular routine.

Floor exercise routines generally consist of a mount or starting move followed by the body of the routine consisting of skills of all types, and finally a finishing stunt, often called a "dismount." For sample routines refer to the end of this chapter. Descriptions and learning techniques are given by categories in the following pages.

Balancing Stunts

The balancing stunts consist of any movement that has an element of stationary pose to it. Stunts such as head balance, hand balance, and scales belong in this group.

1. *Front Scale.* Scales are probably the easiest balancing moves that can be learned, but unless they are done gracefully, it is best to omit them from the routine. The easiest scale is done by starting in a standing position and then slowly leaning forward so that the upper body lowers to a position parallel to the floor and at the same time the right leg is elevated to make a straight line with the chest, also parallel to the floor. The arms are held in swan position with the head up and the back arched, or the right arm is held along the side of the body and the left arm extended forward, parallel to the floor. The leg is extended backward in a taut, yet smooth, position with the toes pointed.

Front Scale

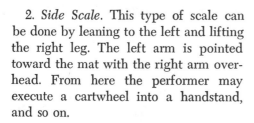

Needle Scale

2. *Side Scale*. This type of scale can be done by leaning to the left and lifting the right leg. The left arm is pointed toward the mat with the right arm overhead. From here the performer may execute a cartwheel into a handstand, and so on.

3. *Needle Scale*. This is done by simply lifting the right leg up into the air to the side of the performer. The ankle of the lifted leg is grasped with right

Side Scale

hand, and the entire leg is pulled in as close to the body as possible.

4. *Knee Scale*. An elementary move is to do a one-knee scale from a kneeling position. Simply lift one leg back and lower the chest parallel to the floor. This is very similar to the forward scale except that the performer is resting on one knee with the shin and instep adding to the support.

5. *V Seat (Balance Seat)*. This consists of merely sitting on the floor with the legs elevated and straight. Thus the body assumes a V position. The hands may be on the floor behind the performer or raised out to the side.

6. *Double Elbow Lever*. See description on page 37.

7. *Single Elbow Lever*. Similar to the two-arm version, except that the weight of the body is on one elbow. Steady the balance with the free hand and then lift it from the floor, holding it straight out in a line with the legs.

8. *Planche*. This stunt is started in a straddle position with the arms between

Single Elbow Lever

the legs and with the fingers on the floor pointing backward. Lean forward slightly and lift the legs upward into the planche position as is pictured. Practice this stunt by placing the feet on low parallel bars

and holding the position momentarily; or, by lifting the legs up into the position and then holding only for a second, and so on. This is a difficult but very impressive stunt once learned.

9. *Hand Balance.* This is probably one of the most commonly used stunts. For techniques of learning an ordinary hand balance, refer to Chapter 3. There are many different methods of moving into the hand balance position, and some of them will be covered in the next section on strength balance moves. For greater difficulty, this stunt may be done with the following variations:

(a.) WIDE-ARM HAND BALANCE. From an ordinary hand balance the arms are moved to a wide-arm position by moving the hands to the sides with a finger-creeping movement.

(b.) YOGI HAND BALANCE. After complete control of the hand balance position is reached, slowly bring the head forward between the arms and allow the hips to move in the opposite direction, with the legs piking downward slightly. This awkward-looking handstand has been named a Yogi handstand because of

Planche

Wide-Arm Hand Balance

10. *L Seat on Hands.* From a sitting position with the hands on the floor at the side of the hips, lift the legs and body upward and hold this L seat with the hands supporting the entire body.

11. *Straddle Seat On Hands.* Sit on the floor with the legs in a straddle position. Place the hands on the floor between the legs and then lift the entire body upward, supporting the weight by the hands and arms alone.

the unique position of head, hips, and legs.

(c.) ONE-ARM BALANCE. From an ordinary hand balance, slowly shift weight from two arms to one arm and at the same time lift the other hand slowly from the floor. Keep the balancing arm straight and strong with other hand ready to add support from the floor if necessary to maintain balance. The legs may be together or spread in a straddle position. Practice is the key to learning the one-arm hand balance.

Straddle Seat

Strength Balance Moves

These stunts are generally called "presses," and as implied they consist of moving into balance position with an element of strength or power required.

1. *Squat Press to Head Balance.* From a squat balance with the knees resting on the elbows, place the head on the floor and slowly raise the hips and legs upward into a head balance.

2. *Bent-Arm Straight Leg Press to Head Balance.* From a kneeling position, place the head on the floor and lift the hips upward, keeping the toes on the floor with the legs straight. From this

One-Arm Balance

pike position slowly lift the legs upward into a head balance position.

3. *Head Balance to Hand Balance.* From a head balance position bring the legs downward slightly so that the body is piked a little. From this position extend the legs upward and at the same time push hard with the arms. Continue upward until the body is in a hand balance position. A spotter can be of assistance on this stunt in lifting the hips upward into the hand balance position.

4. *Bent-Arm Press to Hand Balance.* From a squat position on the floor press upward into a hand balance. At the start of this stunt the legs may be either between the arms or resting on the elbows. In pressing to the hand balance position be sure to move the hips upward and forward to a position above the hands

Straight-Arm, Straight-Leg Press to Hand Balance

and then extend the legs to a full hand balance. A spotter can assist by holding the performer's hips and steadying them as the stunt is attempted.

5. *Bent-Arm Straight Leg Press to Hand Balance.* From a pike position on the floor, with the arms bent, the hips high, and toes resting on the floor, press upward with the legs straight into a handstand position. Be sure to move the hips forward and upward to a position above the hands before extending the legs upward.

6. *Ball Through Arms to Hand Balance.* Start from a sitting position on the floor with the hands at the side of the body. Elevate the body with the hands and then pull the knees into the chest and on through the arms. Continue the movement through and on up into the hand balance. This stunt can also be done supporting the weight on the fingers.

Bent-Arm Press to Hand Balance

7. *Tiger Press.* From a forearm balance position lean forward, shifting the weight toward the hands, and then press upward into a hand balance position. This is a stunt that calls for great strength

Ball-Through Arms to Hand Balance

in the arms. A spotter can assist by grasping the performer's ankles and lifting upward.

8. *Arched Roll to Hand Balance or Head Balance.* Start by lying prone on the floor with the hands at the sides of the body near the hips. Lift the chest upward and from this position roll downward and forward onto the chest and up toward the hand balance. Remember to rock forward onto the hands and with the momentum of the roll push hard with the arms and finish in the hand balance or the more intermediate position of the head balance.

9. *Press to One-Arm Handstand.* Start by placing one hand in close to the forward foot with the other leg elevated toward the handstand position. From here press sideward into the one-arm balance as is pictured and then hold for the required two seconds. Notice the position of the extended arm and the straddle legs to assist in holding the balance. This stunt is very difficult and requires considerable strength and balance for its final accomplishment.

Agility Stunts

This area of floor exercise is one in which an imaginative person can create many new and different stunts of agility that fit in well with a floor exercise routine. These stunts generally arouse much interest and appreciation of participants as well as of spectators.

The following are a few of many stunts that can be done in this group:

1. *Pirouette.* From a standing position leap into the air, turning the head and shoulder to the left and pulling the right arm across the front of the chest, and execute a full turn (pirouette) of the

Straddle Seat Press to Handstand

Press to One-Arm Handstand

body. Keep the body erect and straight throughout the turn. For more difficulty a double pirouette may be executed.

2. *Straight Fall*. This generally follows a tinsica or handspring. The momentum is simply continued, and the performer falls downward toward the floor with one leg elevated. The body is caught with the arms, and by flexing slowly and smoothly, the chest continues downward to the finish position.

3. *One-Half Turn Fall*. From a standing position, fall backward and immediately execute a half turn to the left and continue to fall toward the floor with the front of the body facing the direction of the fall. Catch the weight of the body with the arms and flex them softly with the fall. Finish in the position of a straight fall. This stunt often follows a tumbling stunt such as a back somersault.

4. *Straddle Leap*. Leap into the air, raising legs in straddle position parallel to the floor, and touch the ankles with the hands or place the arms straight downward between the legs.

5. *Tour Jeté*. Take off from one leg and leap into the air and execute a half turn of the body; land on the other foot in a balance position with the arms out to the side and the upper body parallel to the floor, similar to a forward scale.

6. *Single Leg Circle*. Start from a squat position with the hands on the floor in front of the body and with the left leg stretched out to the left side of the body. Bring the left leg forward and around in front of the body, lifting one arm at a time as the leg passes under. Continue the swing of the left leg behind and under the right leg, which is continually flexed, and finish up in the starting position. This stunt is generally done two or three times and thus has a pinwheel action. Be sure to keep the left leg straight, with the toes pointed, throughout the stunt.

7. *Single Leg Circle to Elbow Lever*. Execute two or three single leg circles and near the end of the final one extend the right leg back with the left and drop both hips into the elbows and finish in a double elbow lever.

8. *Back Roll to Straddle*. Execute a backward roll, and when the weight is

Straight Fall

Straddle Leap

Single Leg Circle

on the hands spread the legs and continue the roll, finishing in a straddle stand position.

9. *Front Support with Full Turn.* From a front support position, with the arms straight and legs extended backward, push hard with the arms and at the same time bring one leg up slightly. Support the body on the flexed leg and execute a full turn of the body and land back on the hands again in a front support position.

10. *Wide-Arm Forward Roll.* Do a forward roll with the arms out to the side, keeping them in this position throughout the roll and on up to the feet as is pictured in the three photos. This type of roll has been required for some international competition.

11. *Straight Leg Roll.* This consists of executing a forward roll with the legs straight throughout the stunt. It is important to push hard with the hands as the body completes the roll, because this helps the performer to roll up to the feet. Remember to keep the head and shoulders forward during the latter part of this stunt.

12. *Double Tap Handstand into Forward Roll.* Kick into a hand balance and immediately hop forward, with both hands maintaining the hand balance position, then execute a forward roll, with legs either straight or in a tuck position.

13. *Twisting Handstand into Forward Roll.* Kick up in a cartwheel action to a momentary one-arm handstand. Then turn on the supporting arm, and after a half turn is completed, execute a forward roll. This also can be done by placing the right arm across the body and on the floor with the fingers turned toward the left foot and in front of it. The

Back Roll to Straddle

left arm pulls inside of the right arm in front of the right foot, fingers facing it, and at the same time the body completes a half turn to the left and then a forward roll is executed.

14. *Shoot Through to L Seat*. From a front support position with the arms straight and legs extended backward, lower the hips slightly. Then raise the hips quickly and push with the hands.

Wide-Arm Forward Roll

Straight-Leg Roll

Shoot the legs through the arms and finish in an L sitting position, supporting the body with the arms.

15. *Headspring to Straddle Seat on Floor.* Execute a high headspring and immediately after the whip action has started, pike the body strongly and

Shoot-Through to L Seat

Flank Circles

and hold the handstand position momentarily before going into the forward roll.

18. *Neckspring with Half Twist.* Execute a high neckspring, and immediately after the whip of the legs has started, execute a fast half twist. After the twist, land on both hands with the feet extended to a front resting position. It is important to do the spring high in order to complete a clean half twist.

Double Around to L Seat

spread the legs and land on the floor in a straddle sitting position. Try this stunt several times on a mat before attempting it on the floor. It can also be done to a sitting position with legs together.

16. *Double Around to L Seat.* Start in a front rest position. Flex the hips slightly and then bring the legs around the left arm. Lift the hand as the legs pass under it and quickly drop it to the floor so as to catch the body in an L seat position. This can also be done by straddling the legs on the outside of the arms in passing them forward, landing in an L seat position.

17. *Half Twisting Back Dive to Roll.* Start from a standing position, leap backward, and execute a half turn of the body landing on the hands and continuing into a forward roll. It is important to lift the legs and hips upward as the stunt is executed and then the forward roll can be done smoothly. A spotter can be of assistance by lifting up under the performer's hips during the first part of the stunt.

Variation: Upon completion of the back dive half twist, land on the hands

Half Twisting Back Dive to Roll

19. *Cradle with Half Twist.* Start out as a slow and deliberate back handspring. Upon landing on the hands, tuck the chin in toward the chest and lower the body slowly to the back of the neck and shoulders. At the same time, swing the legs up into a pike position similar to the start of a neckspring. Then whip the legs upward and forward, pushing hard with the hands, and execute a half twist of the body, landing on the hands, the legs and feet extended to a front resting position.

20. *Back Handspring to Hand Balance.* Execute a slow, deliberate and long back handspring, with the feeling of "just making it" to the hands. Stall the feet behind the body as much as possible, and after numerous attempts, the feeling of holding a balance position out of the back handspring will emerge.

Cradle with Half Twist

21. *Valdez.* Start from a sitting position with the left hand placed on the
floor behind the back and the fingers
pointed away from the body. Keep the
right leg straight, with the left leg bent
and the left foot near the buttocks. Raise
the right hand over the head. With a
push off the left foot, a throw backward
of the right arm, and an upswing of the
right leg, the performer executes a quick
back bend motion into a hand balance
position. It is imperative that a spotter
be used while first learning this stunt.

22. *Forward Dive with Full Twist into
Forward Roll.* Run and, after a 2-foot
takeoff, thrust the arms forward and
outward, lifting the heels and back of
the legs upward, keeping the body in a
straight and taut position. Then, pull the
right arm across the front of the body
while the left shoulder is forcibly moved
in the direction of the twist. Upon completing the full twist, place the hands
out in preparation for the forward roll.
This move is best learned on the trampoline by doing full twisting dives from
a knee bounce to the stomach and then
from the knees to the back. Try it next
from the feet to the back with a low
bounce. When first attempting this move
on a tumbling mat, use a thick landing
pad.

23. *Back Dive with One-and-a-Half
Twist into a Forward Roll.* Upon completion of a roundoff, reach upward with
the arms, executing a back dive, looking
slightly over the left shoulder in antici-
pation of the twist. After the take-off,
swing the right arm across the body to
activate the twist and at the same time
force the left shoulder back and look
in the direction of the twist. Keep the
body tight while twisting and don't sag
at the waist or relax the legs. Try this

Valdez

move first on the trampoline by bouncing with the feet partially turned in the direction of the twist. Continue the one-and-a-half twisting dive over to a back drop. As skill progresses, bounce straighter into the back dive. You also may try this move from a mini-tramp onto a thick landing pad. If the mini-tramp is placed near a parallel bar rail, the performer can bounce a couple of times on the mini-tramp, holding onto the rail, and then lean backward slightly into the back dive with the one-and-a-half twist onto the thick landing pad.

Flexibility Stunts

There are several moves that are grouped in the flexibility category, and these skills demand a great deal of looseness and suppleness of the joints and muscles. Many of these moves are not particularly difficult, but they require time and constant practice to accomplish.

1. *Regular Splits.* This simply consists of standing with one leg ahead of the other and slowly lowering the body downward into a split position. By placing the hands on the floor on each side of the body, a slight cushioning effect is produced. This stunt can be done with the following variations:

(a) From a hand balance fall sideward to the split position.

(b) From a hand balance bring one leg through the arms to a split position.

(c) From a hand balance snap the feet down to the mat and then bounce back to the hands, lifting the legs upward. Upon landing on the hands, snap one leg through the arms to a split position.

(d) Back handspring to the feet and then back to the hands and immediately pass one leg through the arms to a split position as in variation (c).

(e) Back handspring into an immediate split position. Upon landing on the arms, bring one leg down quickly and pass it through the arms to a split position.

(f) Back somersault to a split position. Lift a backward somersault as high as possible and just prior to landing on the feet, move the legs apart and drop into a split position, catching the body with the hands.

Regular Split

2. *Straddle Splits.* Splitting action can be done sideward with the legs out to the sides, the upper body forward parallel to the floor, and the arms outstretched. This stunt may be combined very nicely with a front fall. After landing in a front fall position, bring one leg around to the side and twist the body in the same direction so that the straddle split position can be assumed.

3. *Head to Knees.* Start in a standing position and then bend forward and

Straddle Split

place the hands behind the thighs and continue bending forward until the head touches the knees or shins. Constant practice will produce the flexibility necessary for this stunt.

Routines

Creativity, imagination, and resourcefulness can be developed in the sport of gymnastics when the individuals construct and perform their own sequence of moves. The following are suggestions for combinations that can be enlarged upon within the pupil's ability. *

1. Start in corner, do side scale, and move on to cartwheel action into a handstand. Hold momentarily and drop into a forward roll (legs bent or straight). Stand and then run a few steps across area and execute a cartwheel and front handspring to a front fall. Bring one leg up under body to squat position with other leg straight behind and from here execute two single leg circles and then come to stand. Walk along side of area and do a double tap handstand into for-

ward roll to a straddle stand position. Press to either a headstand or handstand, holding momentarily, then do a forward roll with bent knees into a lunge position into corner. Turn and finish with a run across diagonal of area and do a roundoff, bouncing into the air with a straddle leap to stand.

2. Start in corner and jump to handstand, immediately dropping to a chest roll, and then push to a straddle stand, bending forward with the arms outstretched parallel to floor. Press to a headstand or handstand and then do a forward roll to a stand. Along the side do a handspring and then a dive and roll to stand and then a front fall. Bring one leg up under the chest and execute two single leg circles, extend both legs back, resting on the toes, then whip both legs up and snap both feet to floor coming to a stand. Across the diagonal of the square do a front handspring into a headspring to a forward roll to a headspring to a straddle seat. Bring chest forward toward the knees and then sit up straight and execute a partial valdez to a stand on the feet. Do a front scale while in the corner and then turn and finish routine with a run along side and execute a roundoff–straddle leap into air to a stand.

3. Stand in corner at attention position. Swing arms in circular manner crossing in front of body and place right leg to side in straddle stand position with the arms out to the sides and the chest leaning forward parallel to the floor. Press to a handstand (bent arm press) and hold momentarily. Roll forward with legs straight or bent and then run a few steps to a roundoff–back handspring. Execute a half turn and drop to a front

---

* For additional routines consider the Age Group Compulsory Exercises for Boys and Girls published by the United States Gymnastic Federation, Box 12713, Tuscon, Arizona 85711.

fall position. Place both feet back, dip hips slightly, and then whip hips up and over to a forward roll to sitting position. From here execute a valdez on to the feet and then along one side of the area do a front handspring, dive, and roll to a lunge position in corner. Lift one leg and execute a front scale. Place both feet on floor and then turn and face diagonal corner. Run and execute a roundoff–back handspring into a high bounce with legs into straddle position and then drop to a stand.

4. Start in corner and then run across the diagonal and execute a roundoff–back handspring–back flip to a backward roll to a stand in corner. Along the side do a running front somersault to a diving forward roll, stepping into corner, and then execute a half turn to stand facing the center of the area. Place one leg to side into a straddle stand position (or do a split). Press to a handstand and roll forward to stand. Run toward far corner, executing a roundoff–back somersault.

5. Stand several feet from corner and do a back dive with half turn to a handstand position. Roll forward, turn around, and run diagonally and execute a roundoff–back handspring–back somersault–back handspring; snap the feet down and back to a handstand to a forward roll to another back handspring to feet, step toward corner and then with half turn swing into a handstand. Slowly lower the legs into a straddle position on the upper arms. From this position, lift legs back up to a handstand or simply drop back to the seat and execute a backward roll to feet. Along one side, run and execute a diving forward roll (with full twist if possible) and then do a front scale. Then turn and run diagonally to finish with a roundoff–back handspring–back somersault in pike position.

6

Pommel Horse
and Vaulting

Friedrich Jahn is credited with inventing the side horse with pommels in the early 1800s. This apparatus lends itself both to vaulting and to support work. The vaulting phase is somewhat easier and less dependent upon strength and as a result generally precedes the support work.

The pommel horse is a leather-covered cylindrical body about 14 inches in diameter and 64 inches in length. The horse has two pommels or handles near the center that are required to be from 15¾ to 17¾ inches apart (400 to 450 millimeters). The height of the horse may be adjusted from approximately 3 to 5 feet, although the regulation height for competitive purposes is 4 feet 2 inches (1270 millimeters) from the floor to the top of the pommels.

The vaulting horse is a pommel horse without the pommels. In competition, vaulting is done along its length at a height of 4 feet 5 inches (1350 milli-

meters) from the floor to the top of the horse.

Organized competition for men is held in vaulting and pommel horse support work. In the former the gymnast executes a vault lengthwise over the horse. He is judged on the basis of the pre-flight, post-flight, height, and execution with the difficulty of each vault predetermined and listed in the *Code of Points*. The pommel horse support work competition consists of swinging movements, without stops or holding of position, and scissors, forward and reverse (one of these at least twice in succession). All three parts of the horse must be used and double leg circles must predominate.

VALUES

The specific values of working the side horse are:

94

1. Pommel horse work develops strength in the upper part of the body, particularly the arms and shoulders.

2. A person needs agility for the vaulting stunts and develops it from this type of work.

3. Coordination, rhythm, balance, and a sense of timing are all factors developed particularly by support work. The constant shift in weight and cutting action of the legs in a limited space make these values especially important.

4. The pommel horse provides an outlet for activity for many kinds of handicapped people. Because most stunts involve action of the upper body, a person with an impediment in the legs can safely work on this piece of apparatus and receive much joy and recognition from it. Records show that men who have been paralyzed from the hips down have been champions.

ORGANIZATION

Area and Equipment

The pommel horse itself occupies very little space in the gymnasium. Usually two 5' x 10' mats are sufficient to cover the area under the horse, with one on each side. Special platform mats that have cut-out areas for the legs are now available and are highly recommended; however, when vaulting, more mats may be desired at the landing area to cover more space and to give added thickness. Room for a short run must be provided when vaulting crosswise. When vaulting lengthwise, at least 65 feet (20 meters) should be provided for a run.

Several training devices are available for developing the skills used in vaulting and/or support work. The buck is a horse without pommels and is about 24 inches long. The short horse has pommels and is about 29 inches long. The horse-a-roo is a wheel mounted on a single-leg stand. (See pages 126-7.)

Teaching Methods

Only one person may work a pommel horse at one time. Most schools do not have more than two pommel horses, so the activity does not lend itself to the mass method of instruction very well. However, most stunts, particularly the vaults, do not take much time to perform, so that large squads or small classes could be kept busy at one piece of equipment without undue waiting. A vaulting buck, which is a short side horse without pommels, can be used for vaulting and many of the support stunts and is very helpful as a lead-up to the pommel horse itself. A balance beam with mats hung over it can be effectively used as a multiple vaulting apparatus.

Because only one person can work the pommel horse at one time, it is easy to supervise this activity. Thus the squad method of instruction fits in nicely. The pommel horse can be one teaching station of a gymnastic unit with the squads rotating during the period.

A good method of supervising vaulting is to have the students line up and then the instructor can demonstrate the stunt. Following this, the first student in line performs the stunt with the instructor spotting. After one person performs a vault, he spots for the next one in line. In this way the instructor is free from spotting and can make corrections when necessary. Pommel horse work is probably best evaluated by means of a stunt chart, although actual competitive routines could be used in advanced classes. Another method of promoting good pommel horse work is to place the body of the horse on the floor without the legs and practice circles on it. This develops long, stretched flank circles.

Safety

Support work requires little spotting in the beginning stages because missing a move seldom means falling from the apparatus. However, close spotting is necessary for the vaulting skills where it is very easy to catch a foot on the horse, causing a fall. The following are some general safety hints to consider when working the pommel horse:

1. In vaulting exercises set the side horse as low as possible at first and gradually increase its height.

2. Be sure to post a spotter on the far side of the horse and near enough to prevent serious falls by the performer.

3. Learn the proper technique of taking off from both feet before attempting even the fundamental vaults.

4. Be sure to learn the technique of pushing downward with the hands in passing over the horse on the vaults.

5. It is advisable to have a double thickness of mats on the landing side of the horse.

6. Always work in a progressive manner in learning the stunts. Start with the easier vaults and support stunts and progress toward the more difficult as skill is acquired.

PROGRAM OF INSTRUCTION

Instruction on the pommel horse involves three basic steps:

1. *Individual moves.*

2. *Combinations.* As a person learns a new move, he should be challenged to combine it with another as smoothly as possible. Because a move must be learned well in order to combine it with another, the use of combinations in the teaching progression stresses proper execution and increases the safety of performance. In addition, the smaller combinations serve as building blocks for longer routines. Combinations can be suggested by the instructor or coach or can be created by the performer.

3. *Routines.* Ultimately a pupil should strive to combine moves into a routine. Competition is based on routines, required or optional. The approach to optional routines is one of problem solving. Certain requirements involving the types and number of movements are presented as a problem for the performer to solve creatively within his own capabilities. The instructor or coach and pupil can coordinate their thoughts on the development of a particular routine. For sample routines refer to the end of the chapter.

Horse work can be divided into two categories: the vaulting activity and the support activity. Vaulting will be treated prior to the support work, although the two activities are sufficiently different in nature so that one is not dependent on the other. The skills listed under each category are arranged in a progressive order of learning.

Prevaulting Practice

Some fundamental vaulting skills that can be performed on the mats by a large group and serve as a lead-up to vaulting over the horse follow.

1. From a front support position,

spring to a tuck position and then stretch jump to a stand.

2. From a front support position, spring to a kneeling position and then jump to a stand.

3. From a front support position spring to a straddle stand then stretch jump to a stand.

4. From a front support position, spring to a wolf stand (half squat and half straddle) then stretch jump to a stand.

5. From a front support position, spring and swing the legs to the side, landing in a sitting position facing left or right side (rear vault lead-up).

6. Repeat skill 5, but land sitting in opposite direction.

7. From a front support position, spring and swing the legs to the side and under one arm. Land in sitting position facing forward (lead-up to side or flank vault).

8. Repeat skill 7, but swing legs to opposite side.

9. From a front support position, spring to a pike stand and then stretch jump to a stand.

10. From a front support position, spring to tuck position, rock forward to squat head balance, arch over to a bridge position, then straighten arms. Keep the body low during the arch-over.

Vaulting Work on the Pommel Horse

Before attempting the vaulting stunts it is exceedingly important for the performer to learn the art of taking off into the vault. A lead-up for this could be running to the horse and taking off from both feet and reaching for the pommels with the hands. Bounce off the feet, leap into the air, and grasp the pommels with

the hands, flexing the arms only slightly, and let the feet ride upward behind the body. Do not pass over the horse but instead return to the same side of the horse from where the run started. This warm-up stunt will acquaint the performer with such principles of vaulting as: proper running approach, correct hurdle, and the take-off, using both feet. After this has been done a few times the student is ready for the first series of vaulting stunts. When the idea of the vault is gained, it may be done first with a walk approach, then a jogging approach, and finally a run. However, many teachers find that such a gradual progression for each stunt is not necessary, particularly with the first few vaults.

The first three vaults can be done either to the right or left, and it is recommended that the performer learn to do the vault both ways.

1. *Front Vault.* Upon taking off, grasp the pommels with the hands, turn toward the horse, and lift the legs to the left, passing them over the top of the

Front Vault

Some fundamental vaulting skills that can be performed on the mats by a large group and serve as a lead-up to vaulting over the horse are:

1. From a front support position, spring to a tuck position and then stretch jump to a stand.
2. From a front support position, spring to a kneeling position and then jump to stand.

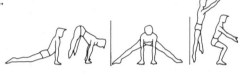

3. From a front support position spring to a straddle stand, then stretch jump to a stand.

4. From a front support position, spring to a wolf stand (half squat and half straddle) then stretch jump to a stand.

5. From a front support position, spring and swing the legs to the side, landing in a sitting position facing left or right side (rear vault lead-up).

6. Repeat skill 5 but land sitting in the opposite direction.
7. From a front support position, spring and swing the legs to the side and under one arm. Land in sitting position facing forward (lead-up to side or flank vault).

8. Repeat skill 7 but swing legs to opposite side.
9. From a front support position, spring to a pike stand and then stretch jump to a stand.

10. From a front support position, spring to tuck position, rock forward to squat head balance and arch over to a bridge position, then straighten arms. Keep the body low during the arch over.

horse toward the other side. The front of the body should face the horse throughout the stunt, and an attempt should be made to force an arch in the body while passing over the top of the horse. As the body passes over the horse and starts toward the mat, drop the left hand, hold on with the right, and proceed to land on the mats with the right side of the body closer to the horse.

2. *Flank Vault*. Upon taking off extend the body to the left and pass over the horse with the side of the body closest to the horse. Land on the mat on the other side of the horse with the back toward the horse and close to the pommels.

3. *Rear Vault*. Upon taking off, grasp the pommels with the hands and lift the legs to the left. Turn the body so that the back side passes over the horse in a sitting position. Release the left hand first and then the right in passing over the horse. After dropping with the right hand, grasp the pommel with the left hand to steady the landing on the far

side of the horse. Finish facing to the left with the left side of the body nearest the horse.

4. *Squat Stand Leap*. Upon taking off, bend the knees and land in a squat position with the hands on the pommels. From this position leap forward by removing the hands from the pommels, lifting the arms and pushing off with the feet. Land in a standing position on the mats.

Rear Vault

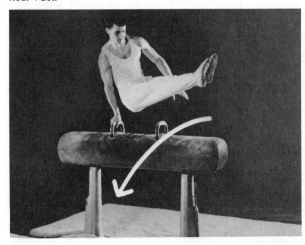

Flank Vault

5. *Squat Vault.* On the take-off, reach with the hands for the pommels, and as the body passes over the horse with the knees in a squat position, push downward with the arms. Land on the other side of the horse upon completion of the squat vault. For more difficulty add a half turn before landing on the mat.

6. *Wolf Vault.* Upon taking off, grasp the pommels and pass one leg in a tuck position between the pommels, with the other leg over the end of the horse in a straight and extended position. Upon passing over the horse, bring both legs together and land on the mat with the back toward the horse.

7. *Straddle Stand, Jump Dismount.* Jump into a straddle stand on the side horse with the feet on the outside of the pommels. Lift the arms and jump forward off the horse and land on the mat on the other side of the horse.

8. *Straddle Vault.* Upon taking off, place the hands on the pommels and push downward forcefully. Release the hands as the legs pass over the horse in a straddle position. Be sure to keep the

head and chest up as the vault is executed. After passing over the horse, bring the legs together and land on the mats with the back toward the horse.

9. *Thief Vault.* This vault is begun with a take-off from one foot. Run at the horse and at a distance of about 3-4 feet from the horse lift one leg up and thrust it forward between the pommels and immediately bring the other leg up adjacent to the lead leg so both feet pass over the horse ahead of the body. As the hips pass over the horse, grasp the pom-

Straddle Vault

Wolf Vault

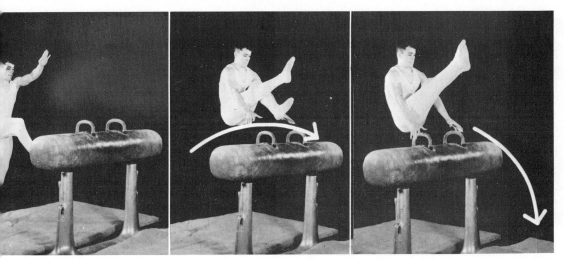

Thief Vault

mels momentarily with the hands and continue the vault by pushing downward, keeping the body in flight as the feet come down for a landing on the mat.

10. *Rear Vault with Half Twist.* Just after passing over the horse in a rear vault to the right push the pommel with the right hand and turn inward toward the horse. Complete a half turn of the body and land on the mats facing the opposite direction from that of passing over the horse. A mass drill for this stunt consists of having all the students stand, facing the same direction, with their right hand by their side as if grasping an imaginary pommel. Explain that all of them should feel they have just passed over the side horse in a rear vault position. Then they all should push with the right hand and execute a half turn in the direction of the right hand. This will give them the feel of the half twist to the right. Do this several times prior to actually attempting the stunt on the horse itself.

11. *Stoop Vault.* Upon taking off from both feet grasp the pommels with both hands and lift the legs and hips high. Then snap both legs downward between the pommels in a straight leg position. Continue the stoop and land on the mats on the other side of the horse. A practice drill for this is to stand on the horse between the pommels and kick into a partial handstand with the hands on the pommels. As soon as the feet are up in the air, snap them down through the arms into the stoop dismount.

12. *Neckspring from Knee Stand.* This stunt is done from a kneeling position with the hands on the pommels. With a firm grip on the pommels, lift the hips into the air and tuck the head back under so that the back of the neck rests on the horse. The body should be in a pike position with the legs extended backward and the hips forward beyond the horse. Lean in the direction of the hips and then whip the legs over toward the mats, push with the hands, and continue the

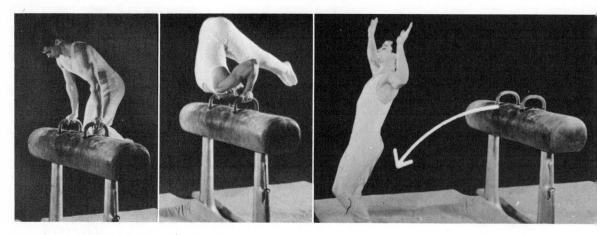

Neckspring from Knee Stand

neckspring to the feet. Land in a standing position on the mat on the far side of the horse. Spotters can be particularly effective in helping the performer by grasping his arms and assisting him through the neckspring. Continue to hold the performer's arms even after he lands on the mat for the first few times. This will prevent overflipping, which would cause a fall on the face.

13. *Neckspring*. This is done in a similar manner to the previous neckspring, from a kneeling position, except it is done from a run. After the take-off, grasp the pommels and leap into the air with

Neckspring

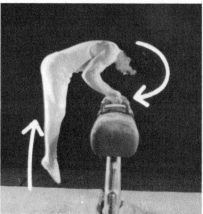
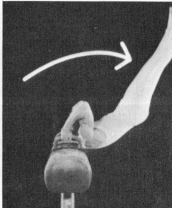

the hips high. Then duck the head and place the back of the neck between the pommels. Allow the body to continue over the horse in a pike position; when it reaches the point where the hips are past the horse and the body feels as if it is off balance, whip the legs sharply over toward the mats. At the same time, push hard with the hands and land in a standing position.

14. *Headspring.* Same as the neck-spring except the top of the head is placed on the horse instead of the neck. It is important to emphasize the delaying of the whip action of the legs until the hips are well past the horse.

15. *Handspring.* Same as the head-spring except the head does not touch the horse and the weight is supported by the arms in a semiflexed position.

Vaulting

Vaulting (Long Horse)

Vaulting is an exciting event in which a performer runs at the horse, lands on a beat board, sails into the air and pushes on the horse with the hands while executing a vault, such as a stoop, straddle, hecht, or handspring.

To prepare for long horse vaulting, simply remove the pommels, turn the horse lengthwise, obtain a beat board for take-off, and the event is ready for action. As mentioned, the vaulting is done from the beat board over the entire length of the horse. Some of the vaults that can be done and techniques of performing them will be described, but before this a few words should be said regarding the proper take-off from the beat board.

One of the most important phases of long horse vaulting is the proper take-off from the beat board. This takes courage, timing, and considerable practice. First the performer places himself at a good distance from the horse and beat board, the exact spot being determined with practice and repetition. From this position the run should start with a couple of trotting steps and, as the horse is approached, should become a fast and confident run. The gaze includes beat board, horse, and surroundings rather than only the beat board. As the board is approached, take off from one foot into a hurdle and then bring the other foot up and proceed to land on both feet. Be sure to land on the part of the beat board that will provide the maximum amount of spring. Land strongly on the board with the body more in an upright position than in a forward-leaning position. Remember that the run will provide the forward force, but it is up to the performer to make sure he obtains a maximum spring upward from the board. Many beginners have a tendency simply to jump over the horse with no thought of obtaining a beautiful lift or flight throughout the vault. Try one of the fundamental vaults such as a straddle vault many times while trying to cultivate style and ease of performance. Proper take-off from the board cannot be overstressed. Remember to hit the board solidly and take off with the thought of obtaining height and lift and not just skimming over the top of the horse. Also try to swing the feet high into the air before executing the particular vault in mind. The landing should also be practiced diligently because this provides the final impression, and an unsure landing can detract considerably from an otherwise fine vault. Try to land solidly in one spot and avoid if possible any additional hopping or jumping around after landing on the mat. Bend the knees to absorb the shock of hitting the mat and spread the arms forward or sideward to maintain balance. When a secure position is obtained, straighten to a position of attention.

Some reminders on good vaulting techniques are:

Speed is essential for good vaulting.

On the run, take short steps carrying the shoulders high and the arms up. This keeps the center of gravity up and on an even keel.

Upon taking off the beat board, reach forcefully forward with the arms and keep the chest in a hollow position.

Land on the horse with the hands ahead of the shoulders.

Block hard with the arms when landing on the horse.

Try vaulting first with the horse sideways to the board and move the board back gradually. Also perform a dive and roll over the horse landing on a soft landing pad. A good vaulting practice drill is to use the trampoline with either the horse at one end and crosswise or a firm piece of padding on the end frame. The gymnast should bounce a couple of times at a low height from one end toward the other. As he gets to the middle of the bed he reaches forward with the hands and lands on the padded frame (or horse) and continues over into the vault. A thick landing pad or piled-up mats should be used for the landing area.

Competitive Vaulting

In normal competition the gymnast performs one vault. In individual finals a gymnast performs two different vaults, with both counting. The vault is judged on the basis of pre-flight, post-flight, execution, and form with the difficulty predetermined and listed in the *Code of Points*. International competition has two zones on the horse, and, if the performer places his hands on the line across the center of the horse, there is an appropriate deduction in the score. NCAA competition also uses the two zones.

Regarding the flight of the body, a deduction is made if the angle of the stretched body with the top of the horse is less than 30° for the far end vaults (except for the hecht, which only requires 20°). For vaults where the hands touch the near end of the horse, the body must be in a horizontal position or a deduction is made.

1. *Straddle Vault*. With the take-off and landing in mind, the vault itself consists simply of landing with the hands

on the far end of the horse and then straddling the legs forward outside of the hands. Continue the straddle until the horse is passed and land on the mat in a standing position. Try to elevate the legs before cutting them downward for the straddle. Upon doing this vault from the croup (near end) place the beat board at a further distance from the end of the horse. Keep the body in more of an upright position and push hard with the arms in order to pass comfortably over the entire horse.

2. *Squat Vault.* Similar to the straddle vault except that the legs are tucked into the chest and between the arms as they pass over the end of the horse.

Scissors with Half Turn

Squat Vault

3. *Scissors with Half Turn (Rear Straddle).* After the two-foot take-off, the hands are placed in a line parallel to the length of the horse at the far end, the right hand ahead of the left hand. The legs start off as in a straddle vault, but the right leg suddenly cuts over the horse to the left side, then the left leg over to the right side. This turns the performer around so that he is in a straddle position, with the rear of the body leading the way. The vaulting body forces the hands to be released as the performer passes over the far end of the horse. Land in a standing position facing the end of the horse. Place the right hand on the end to steady the landing.

To learn the mechanics of this scissors vault, it is recommended that the stunt first be tried from a standing position on the end of the horse rather than with a running take-off from the board.

4. *Stoop Vault.* After the take-off, land on the hands on the far end of the horse with the legs in almost a hand balance position. From this position, pike downward forcefully with the legs, push hard with the hands, and lift the chest so the body is extended prior to landing on the mat. The legs are straight throughout the stunt.

In doing this from the croup (near end) the legs may be either bent or straight at the start. In the stoop vault, with knees bent at start, the legs are straightened after they pass over the point of support of the hands. When

Stoop Vault

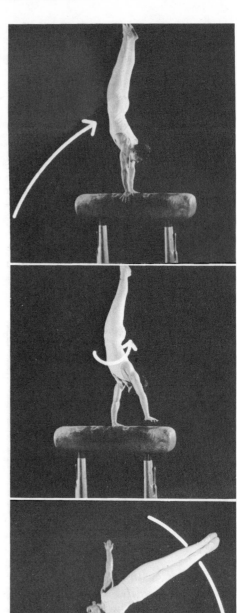

keeping the legs straight throughout the stoop vault from the croup, emphasis is placed on a forceful take-off from the board and a strong push with the arms resulting in an elevation of the hips, which allows the legs to pass over the croup without bending.

5. *Handstand Pivot Cartwheel*. After the take-off, land with the hands together in the middle zone. Continue the swing of the feet up to the handstand position. At this point reach out with one arm, execute a quarter turn of the body, and place the reaching hand on the neck. From here allow the momentum to carry the performer into a cartwheel. Dismount off the end.

6. *Giant Cartwheel*. Similar to the handstand pivot cartwheel except that upon taking off the beat board, the performer sails into a cartwheel position by placing one hand in the middle zone and from there continuing with the other hand so that it is placed on the end of the horse. This provides the giant cartwheel action and will carry the per-

Handstand to Pivot Cartwheel

former over the entire horse in a cart-wheel fashion to a landing position on the mat, sideways to the horse. It is imperative to get a good blocking action with the last arm for a good lift off the horse.

7. *Handspring.* Take off from the board and reach forcefully for the far end of the horse with the hands. Allow the feet to carry upward, extending the body forward, and as you near the end drop the hands and body onto the horse and then bounce off quickly into the handspring. A spotter is essential when gymnasts first learn this vault. For safe progression it is suggested that you try this first from a standing position on the horse, simply kicking into a handstand on the end of the horse and continuing over to the feet. When the move is first attempted over the entire length of the horse, it is recommended that the horse be lowered slightly from its regulation height.

8. *Yamashita (piked handspring).* Use an approach and take-off similar to that used for the front handspring, but try to execute the pre-flight more quickly by swiftly reaching for the end of the horse with the heels coming up forcefully. Get a good block off the horse by landing on the hands with the shoulders behind the hands, keeping the arms strong and tight. This positive blocking action will propel the body upward into a good postflight angle. The piking action is executed by the upper body moving upward toward the legs into the pike position. Then the legs are thrust forward with a resulting extension of the body prior to the landing on the mat. The arms may be out to the sides or along the legs.

Twisting Vaults

It is essential first to try twisting techniques on the trampoline and even off a mini-tramp with an overhead twisting belt rigging. On the trampoline, try to

Hecht Vault

simulate a straight-body front layout somersault in the belt with the arms in front as if touching an imaginary horse. As the straight body continues over into the layout somersault and when the legs are past the ropes (in a vertical position), then pull the right arm forcefully down and across the front of the body and push the left shoulder back into the direction of the twist. Keep the body straight and taut. Upon completing the twist, thrust the arms outward and try to assume a landing position on the tramp, simulating the vault. After using the trampoline, the gymnast may want to try some using a twisting belt in an overhead rigging off a minitramp. Use the same technique as on the trampoline but land on a soft landing pad. Then try the entire move into the landing pad without the belt. It can also be done using the twisting belt in an overhead traveling rigging off a minitramp over a raised horse placed sidewards. For safety, drape a mat over the horse.

A chart of the vaults and their difficulty values follows.*

* Appreciation is extended to the United States Gymnastic Federation for use of the figure men in this section.

Values and Forms of Vaults with Support on the Neck (Far End) of Horse

Vaults A = 7.0 points

1. Straddle   SK I
2. Squat   SK I

Vaults B = 8.0 points

3. Simple Hollander   SK II
4. Squat with ½ turn   SK I

Vaults C = 9.0 points

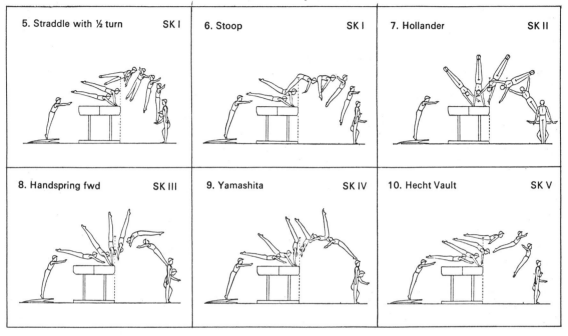

5. Straddle with ½ turn   SK I

6. Stoop   SK I

7. Hollander   SK II

8. Handspring fwd   SK III

9. Yamashita   SK IV

10. Hecht Vault   SK V

Vaults D = 9.4 points

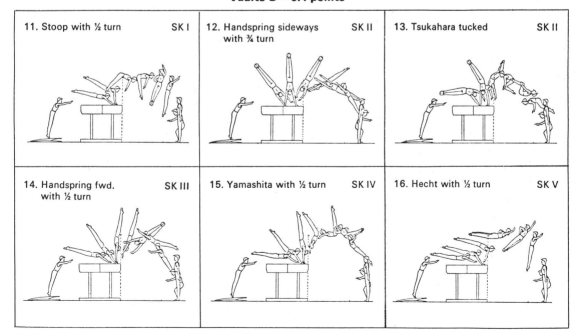

11. Stoop with ½ turn   SK I

12. Handspring sideways with ¾ turn   SK II

13. Tsukahara tucked   SK II

14. Handspring fwd. with ½ turn   SK III

15. Yamashita with ½ turn   SK IV

16. Hecht with ½ turn   SK V

Vaults E = 9.8 points

17. Tsukahara piked SK II	18. Handspring sideways and SK II salto sideways with ¾ turn to cross stand (Kasamatsu)	19. Handspring forward SK III with full turn
20. Jump fwd. with ¹/₁ turn SK III and handspring forward	21. Handspring fwd. and SK III salto fwd.	22. Handspring fwd., ½ turn SK III and salto backward, tucked (Cuervo)
23. Yamashita with ¹/₁ turn SK IV	24. Yamashita and salto SK IV piked	25. Hecht with ¹/₁ turn SK V
	26. Hecht and salto fwd. SK V tucked	

*Value and Forms of Vaults With Support on the
Croup (Near End) of Horse*

Vaults A = 7.0 points

Vaults B = 8.0 points

Vaults C = 9.0 points

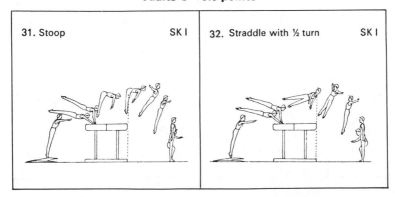

Vaults D = 9.4 points

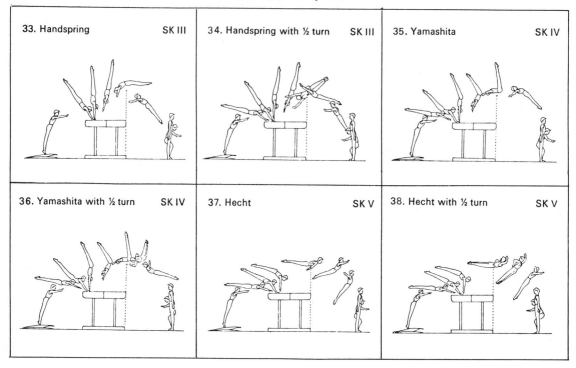

33. Handspring   SK III

34. Handspring with ½ turn   SK III

35. Yamashita   SK IV

36. Yamashita with ½ turn   SK IV

37. Hecht   SK V

38. Hecht with ½ turn   SK V

Vaults E = 9.8 points

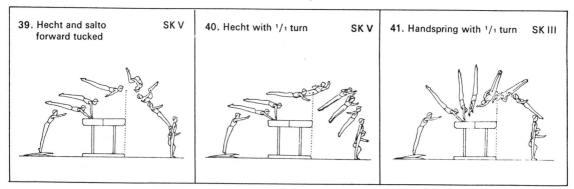

39. Hecht and salto   SK V
    forward tucked

40. Hecht with ¹/₁ turn   SK V

41. Handspring with ¹/₁ turn   SK III

42. Handspring and salto   SK III
     fwd. tucked or piked

43. Handspring with ½ turn   SK III
     and salto backward tucked

44. Yamashita with ¹/₁ turn   SK IV

45. Yamashita and salto   SK IV
     fwd. tucked

46. Yamashita and salto   SK IV
     fwd. piked

Support Work on Pommel Horse

Support Work on the Pommel Horse

Support work is the activity of performing moves while on the horse, with the performer supporting himself by the arms with the hands on the pommels or ends of the horse. This type of work is more difficult than vaulting, but the participation will be as enjoyable as the vaulting phase of pommel horse work if a person progresses effectively.

It is important to remember a few general hints for the successful learning of support work:

1. Be sure to work from the shoulders, thus supporting oneself with straight arms, and keep the chest up.

2. Learn soon to shift the weight from one arm to the other in a rhythmical manner.

3. Learn everything in small parts first and later incorporate the moves into a presentable routine.

Some of the vaults that have been described under side horse vaulting can be used as mounts or dismounts in beginning support work. For mounts, the vault would be done from a stand to a support position, and for dismounts the vault would be done from a support position on the horse rather than from a take-off from a beat board. Vaults such as the front, flank, rear, squat, and straddle are usable.

Basic Swings

Jump to a support position and proceed to swing the body back and forth, shifting the weight from one pommel to the other, by swinging one leg up, and then down, and then moving to the other side with the other leg. This is a method of learning to shift the weight from one arm to the other, maintaining the balance with the hands and keeping the weight over the pommels. Learning to shift the body weight from one pommel to the other is an essential basic requirement for any move and routine, be it elementary or advanced.

Other support stunts are as follows:

1. *Single-Leg Half Circle.* From a front rest position supporting the body with the arms, hands on the pommels, and the front of the body leaning on the horse, swing the right leg over the end of the horse. While the right leg is swinging over the end of the horse, shift the weight of the body toward the left arm and release the right hand. Immediately after the leg has passed over the pommel, the right hand then regrasps the right pommel. Swing the right leg slightly to the left and then pass it backward over the pommel and the right end of the horse. Regrasp the right pommel with the right hand and finish up in the original front rest support position. This move can be done to the left with the

left leg. (Most of the skills described hereafter can be done either to the left or right, although for brevity's sake the instruction for the most part will cover the right only. The understanding will be that the stunt can and should also be done to the left.) A strength exercise for this is to do ten leg lifts sideward and then hold the leg up on the tenth lift. Do the same for the left leg.

2. *Single-Leg Half Circle from Rear Support Position.* Start from a rear support position with the body resting on the far side of the horse and the back of the legs against the horse. Swing the right leg backward across the right end of the horse over the right pommel to a front support position on the other side of the horse. Return the right leg to the starting position. Don't pike the body while doing the half circles.

3. *Alternates from Front Support.* Start from a front support position and swing the right leg over the right end of the horse under the hand to a position between the pommels. Then swing the left leg over the left end of the horse under the hand to a position adjacent to the right leg between the pommels in a rear support position. When the left leg reaches the rear support position, then the right leg is immediately brought backward over the right end of the horse to its original position, and the left leg is swung back over the left end to its original position.

Alternates may also be done starting from a rear support position.

4. *Single-Leg Half Circle Travel.* Start from a front support position with the hands on the pommels and the arms straight. Swing the left leg over the left end and under the left hand to a position between the pommels. Swing the

right leg over the right end but don't cut it under the right hand. Instead, leave it to the right of the right pommel so

Single-Leg Half Circle

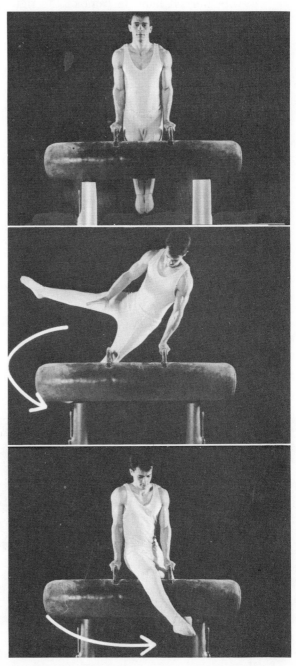

both legs are astride the right arm (right pommel). Then swing the left leg back over the left end of the horse and shift the left hand to the right pommel. Now both hands are on the right pommel with the left hand in front of the right hand. When the left leg reaches the back side of the horse, swing the right leg back over the right end and shift the right hand to the end of the horse so the body is in a front support position supported with the left hand on the pommel and the right hand on the right end of the horse.

5. *Single-Leg Circle.* From a front support position, swing the right leg over the right end of the horse and right pommel. Continue the swing over the left end of the horse and left pommel and then down the near side of the horse to the original starting position. Remember to shift the weight to the left when the leg is passing over the right side of the horse and then to the right as the leg continues the circle to the left side of the horse. This stunt will give the performer a great deal of practice in the skill of

shifting the weight, which is of great importance in pommel horse performance.

6. *Single-Leg Reverse Circle.* From a front support position, swing the left leg to the right between the right leg and the horse, on over the right end of the horse and the right pommel. Continue the circle of the left leg over the left pommel and left end of the horse. Finish with the left leg back at the starting front support position. The secret to performing this stunt is a neat shifting of the weight to the left as the leg passes over the right side of the horse first.

7. *Double-Leg Half Circle.* From a front rest position, swing both legs slightly to the left and then forcefully to the right over the end of the horse and the right pommel. Finish in a rear support position with both legs between the pommels. Return by swinging both legs slightly to the left and then pass them back to the right over the end of the horse and the right pommel and finish in the original front support position.

Single-Leg Circle

Double Leg Circle

8. *Right Feint.* This movement is often used in order to obtain momentum for more advanced stunts and so should be learned thoroughly early in the learning progression. Start from a front rest support position and then shift the weight to the right arm and pass the right leg over the right end of the horse straddling the right arm. The left leg remains behind resting against the horse. Push slightly with the left knee off the horse and swing the right leg back toward the

Right Feint

original starting position, shifting the weight to both arms. As mentioned, this movement helps to obtain momentum for more advanced stunts such as flank circles, dismounts, and so on.

9. *Single Rear Dismount.* Start from a front support position with the hands on the left and right pommel respectively. Feint with the right leg around the right arm, then swing it back across the right end to meet the left leg. Pass both legs over the left end and left pommel in a position parallel to the horse. Continue moving the legs over toward the mat and land on the feet. At the same time have the left hand regrasp the left pommel for a sure standing dismount.

10. *Regular Scissors.* From a front support position, swing the right leg over the right end of the horse and the right pommel. Regrasp with the right hand and immediately shift the weight to the right. Allow the right leg to swing up above the level of the left end of the horse and follow with the left leg in this same direction. When both legs are above the horse, release the left hand and

Single Rear Dismount

Front Scissors

execute a scissors movement by passing the right leg under the left leg toward the back side of the horse, and pass the left leg forward above the right leg toward the front of the horse. For the best scissors movement, swing the top leg high. To finish, the left leg ends in front of the horse between the pommels; the right leg ends in back. Be sure to keep the hips facing forward throughout the scissors action. Don't twist or turn the body in the direction of the scissors.

11. *Reverse Scissors.* Start from a scissors position between the pommels with the right leg in front and left leg in back. Swing both legs slightly forward and then back toward the right hand, shifting the weight to the left arm. Release the right hand and as the legs rise above the horse cut the left leg forward under the right leg and the right leg back in a scissors action. As the reverse scissors is completed and the legs swing down, regrasp the right pommel with the right hand. Finish in a scissors position between the pommel with the left leg forward and right leg back.

12. *Double Rear Dismount.* Start from a front support position as in a single rear dismount. Feint with the right leg

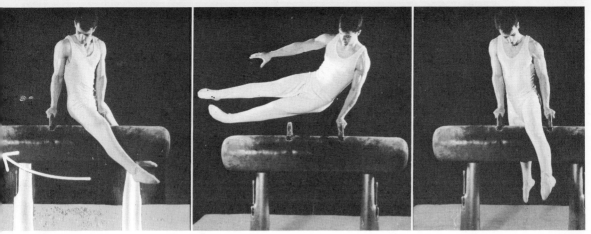

Reverse Scissors

and then swing it back over the right end. Pick up the left leg and pass both legs over the left end and continue moving them on in front of the horse and to the right over the right end into the dismount to the mats. Throughout this stunt the weight is kept on the right arm and the hips remain close to the right arm until dropping to the mat, at which time the right hand is released. A spotter can assist by standing in front of the performer and, after the performer's legs pass beyond him, he can then step in toward the horse and place his hands on the performer's hips in

order to help him through the last part of the stunt.

13. *Triple Rear Dismount (Schwaben-kehre Dismount).* Just prior to reaching the point in the double rear dismount where the performer passes over the right end to the mats, the legs continue to circle parallel to the horse, and the left arm is placed forcefully on the front side of the right end. The legs then complete the triple rear circle by passing over the pommels with the left hand supporting the body and the right hand free. After the legs and body have completed this

Double Rear Dismount

pass, the performer drops to the mat in a dismount stand.

14. *Flank Circle.* Start from a feint position, with the right leg circling the right pommel. Then bring the right leg backward toward a complete circle of

Triple Rear Dismount

the horse. As the right leg starts its circle, push slightly with the left knee and thus extend the left leg out in order to join the right leg in its circle. Pass both legs over the left end and continue moving them across the front of the horse and over the right end. Finish in a front support position. Remember to shift the weight of the body from right to left to right, and so on, as the legs pass over the respective opposite ends of the horse. Don't forget to roll the hips inward slightly as the legs pass over the end of the horse coming from the front to the back. Also, remember that the entire body is involved in the swing and the swing is activated from the shoulders. Push away from the horse in all directions and maintain good extension, keeping the feet at the same height and the shoulders up throughout the entire swing.

15. *Side Travel.* After the legs pass across the front of the horse in a flank circle, shift the body over one pommel and grasp that pommel with both hands. Continue the flank circle while shifting the body on toward the end of the horse. Finish doing flank circles on the end, with one hand on a pommel and the other on the end of the horse. Remember to keep the body extended while traveling to the end.

16. *Double In (Kehre In).* Start with flank circles on the end of the horse. When the legs swing toward the front after passing across the end of the horse in a flank circle, shift the weight toward the pommel arm, keeping the hips in close to the arm. Allow the legs to swing around the front of the horse and over the pommels, with the body executing a half turn. Then place the free hand on the far pommel and continue with flank

Flank Circles

circles. Remember while doing the kehre in to extend the body and try to simulate a flank circle extension as the legs swing over the pommels and around the front of the horse to complete the kehre in action to the pommels. Think of originating the turn from the shoulders.

17. *Double Out* (*Kehre Out*). This move starts with flank circles on the pommels, and, as the legs pass over the end of the horse, the shoulders commence to turn in the direction of the end of the horse and the weight is shifted to the turning arm. Continue moving the legs around with the body extended (simulating a flank circle action) and after the legs have passed across the end of the horse, place the free hand on the end of the horse.

18. *Tramlot*. This move is a combination of a side travel from the pommels to the end and a double in to the pommels again without an intermediate double leg circle. The key is the mastery of the two moves so that the double in can be anticipated while you are performing the side travel.

19. *Stockli*. This move is a combination of a kehre out followed by a kehre in without intermediate circles. It can also be a kehre in from the end of the horse to the pommels followed by a kehre out without intermediate circles. Try to extend the body while executing the kehre out (or in) action. Keep the body as high as possible without bending the supporting arm. Initiate the turn from the shoulders.

20. *Direct Tramlot*. This stunt consists of a side travel from the center of the horse to support position with both hands on one pommel followed by an immedi-

Tramlot

ate double in without touching the end of the horse with a hand. This necessitates a good support position on the one pommel as the immediate double in is performed.

21. *Reverse Stockli*. The stockli backward (reverse stockli) may start from the pommels. After swinging the legs across the front of the horse, turn the body backward, swinging the legs toward the end of the horse and reaching backward with the free hand, the other hand on the pommel. Remember to push with the one hand to help place the body over the end of the horse, keeping the hips away from the supporting arm. Upon reaching the end of the horse, flank circles may be executed (or a reverse stockli into the pommels may be executed).

22. *Moore (Czechkehre)*. As the legs swing backward in a flank circle, start turning the body inward toward the horse and reach back with one hand, joining the other on the supporting pommel. Swing the legs around the end of the horse and then extend the body so the legs pass over the open pommel, turning the body in the direction of the czechkehre, and then regrasp the free pommel and continue flank circles. (Incidentally, by increasing the speed of the last flank circle prior to the czechkehre, the move is made easier.)

23. *Russian Wendeswing*. This stunt consists of a continuation of the Moore movement from the first pommel over the second pommel in a layout position. As you pass over one end of the horse, promptly reach for the other pommel with the leading hand in preparation for the layout movement over the second pommel. A strong flank circle prior to

Reverse Stockli

Moore (Czechkehre)

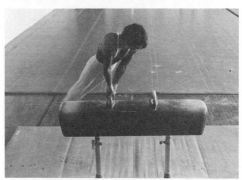

the Russian and a low layout position of the body during the stunt are essential for its accomplishment. Try to place both hands on each of the supporting pommels sooner than on the czechkehre. Balance becomes very important, and it is essential to control the move with both hands sooner and longer.

Russian Wendeswing

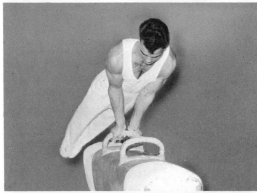

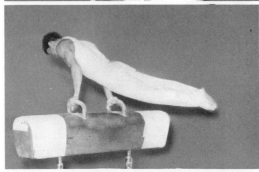

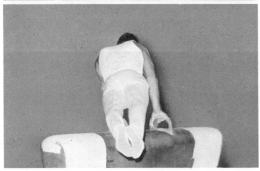

24. *Loop Dismount (Schwabenwende)*. From a support position on the end of the horse with one hand on a pommel and the other on the end of the horse, swing the legs around the end of the horse and place the pommel hand next to the hand on the end of the horse. With the body facing down the length of the horse, continue the loop of the legs around and under the end of the horse and over the top, dismounting to a stand sidewards to the horse. This dismount is usually done from a side travel or double out (kehre out) to the end of the horse. If a quarter turn is executed so the performer's side is facing the top of the horse as he passes over prior to the push-off for a dismount landing with the back towards the horse, the move is then called a *schwabenflanke*. If a half turn of the body is executed with the front of the performer facing the top of the horse as it passes over into the dismount, the move is called *schwaben-wende*.

25. *Double Swiss*. As the legs swing through the back part of a flank circle push with the hands and execute a hop move with a half turn of the body quickly regrasping the pommels and continue the circles facing the other side of the horse.

26. *Back Czech (Direct Stockli A)*. This move is often called a *back Moore* since it is similar to the regular Moore except the move is done with the hands behind the back, and thus the back of the body faces the pommel. Complete a flank circle and then execute a kehre-out action, placing both hands behind the back on the one pommel. Allow the feet to swing around the end of the horse turning the body in the direction of the back czech and after completing the

Schwabenwende

half turn, reach back for the other pommel and continue flank circles facing the opposite side of the horse. This move can be used as a mount by jumping into the back czech (back Moore) position with both hands on one pommel and, after clearing the other pommel with both legs, shift the weight inwards, grasping the far pommel with the free hand, and continue flank circles in the middle of the horse. This is often called a *back Moore uphill* or direct stockli B.

For many more combinations using many of the moves previously described, please refer to the F.I.G. Code of Points.

Routines

Creativity, imagination, and resourcefulness can be developed in the sport of gymnastics by the individual's construction and performance of his own sequence of stunts. The following are simply suggestions for combinations that certainly can be enlarged upon within the pupil's ability.

1. Start at right end with left hand on pommel and right hand on end of horse.

Squat vault through arms to rear support, bring right leg half circle to right, left leg half circle to left. Then bring right leg half circle right and left leg half circle left, but do not cut the left hand. Instead, finish with the legs straddling the pommel. Bring right leg back in a half circle, shifting right hand to right pommel, and then as the left leg is half circled to the left, the left hand is shifted to the left pommel. Execute alternate half leg circles, starting with the right leg, and finish with a front vault dismount.

2. With hands on the pommels, execute a flank circle across the right end, halfway to rear support. Continue the left leg over the left pommel, followed by a half circle back with the right leg to the right. Swing the left leg in a half circle over the left pommel and then execute scissors to the right. Then bring the left leg over the left end to a rear support and continue it to the right by cutting it under the right leg to complete the single leg circle (with the left leg). Continue the swing over the left end to join the right leg in front again. Execute a right leg half circle right and a left leg

half circle left, finishing with a rear vault over the right end of the horse to a stand on the mat.

3. Stand facing the right end of the horse with the right hand on the end and the left hand on the pommel. Jump to a support position with the right leg passing over the end of the horse. Execute a scissors over the left pommel. Leaving the left leg in front of the horse, bring the right leg around the end, turning to the left, and continue moving the right leg over the horse, grasping the far pommel with the right hand, the left hand remaining on the left pommel. From here execute a scissors to the left, then right, and then left. Bring the right leg to the front of the horse, bringing the left leg back, and execute a reverse scissors. Bring the right leg around to a straddle position on the right hand pommel. Then bring the right leg back, turning the body to the right, and place the left hand on the end of the horse. Continue to circle the legs into a single or double rear dismount.

4. Start at right end of horse with left hand on pommel and right hand on right end of horse. Execute a double leg half circle and continue with the right leg by cutting it under the left leg, moving it completely around to join the left leg in front. Execute a double in movement to the saddle (between the pommels) and then circle the left leg back over the pommel to the left. Bring the right leg back over the right pommel and then execute a scissors by bringing the left leg over the end of the horse with the scissors to the right. Bring the left leg to the front of the horse and swing the right leg back over the right end of the horse. Execute a reverse scissors to

the left. Bring the right leg back over the right end and then bring the left leg over the left end in a half circle. Bring the right leg around the right end of the horse and continue over the far end of the horse (left end), executing a single leg circle around it with the right hand placed on the end of the horse. Continue the single leg circle over this end of the horse to a dismount stand on the mat.

5. Start at right end of horse and jump into a flank circle. After one full circle, execute a double leg circle in (double in) to the center of horse and there execute a double leg circle. Stop both legs in back with the right leg continuing over the right end of horse and then into a scissors to the left side

Horse-a-Roo

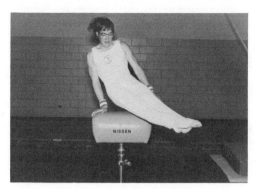

Using the Buck

and then the left leg over the left end to the front of the horse. Then bring right leg around right side of the horse and execute double leg circles. After two circles execute a double out to the left and on the end execute a loop dismount to the mat.

6. Start with loop around end of horse and then do a side travel to the pommels. Continue on to other end and then do a double in to pommels to flank circles. After two circles stop in back of horse and bring right leg around right end and do two regular scissors. Then bring left leg over the left end of the horse to front of horse and bring right leg back and execute a reverse scissors. Then commence regular flank circles and after two circles do a side travel to end and then two loops on end to dismount.

of horse. Then execute a scissors to the right side, bring left leg over the left end of horse, bring right leg back over right end of horse, and execute a reverse scissors over the left end of horse. Bring right leg back over right end of horse

For additional routines consider the Age Group Compulsory Exercises for Boys and Girls published by the United States Gymnastic Federation, Box 12713, Tuscon, Arizona 85711.

7

Rings

The flying and still rings have always had an air of adventure and daring since Francis Amores of Spain invented this apparatus along with the flying trapeze in the early 1800s.

Competition is now limited to the still rings, where greater strength and control is required. The rings are made of wood and are suspended 18 feet 5 inches (5600 millimeters) and placed 19¾ inches (500 millimeters) apart. Adjustable or nonadjustable straps about 27 inches in length are attached to the rings from steel cables, with a swivel attachment at the point of suspension. For competition, the distance from the floor to the lower inside edge of the ring is 8 feet 6½ inches (2600 millimeters). Still-ring work is intended to be done without any swinging of the rings and should combine swinging movements with strength exercises and hold positions.

VALUES

The specific values of working on the rings are:

1. Rings develop strength in the muscles of the arms and chest through the different presses, levers, and difficult balances.

2. Because the rings must be gripped in the hands, strength in the fingers and a good grip are developed.

3. Ring work develops a sense of timing, rhythm, and beat.

4. Stunts involving twisting and turning of the extended arms develop suppleness within the shoulder joints.

5. Due to the nature of the activity, still rings can be worked by certain handicapped people, giving them enjoyment and a feeling of accomplishment. Most stunts on the rings involve the upper body, with the legs only being

swung to give momentum. Those with only partial use of their legs have been known to win championships.

ORGANIZATION

Area and Equipment

Because the rings are in a fixed position, they cannot be moved at will around the gymnasium. Where conditions are not satisfactory for suspending the rings from the ceiling, a portable rigging has been adapted by some gymnastic equipment companies. Adequate padding beneath the rings should be provided for the safety of the performer.

Teaching Methods

Because only one person at a time can work on the rings, and because most schools do not have more than two or three sets of rings, the squad method is best used for instruction. Skills on the still rings are difficult, and the trials will proceed rapidly because generally one stunt at a time is tried.

The instructor or squad leader should constantly stand to one side of the performer while the skills are being attempted. The instructor can then assist performers through the moves and can also catch them in case of a slip or fall.

Evaluation of performers on the rings can be done by means of a stunt chart with competitive routines serving this purpose in advanced classes.

Safety

Because of the height involved, spotting is more difficult on the rings than on other pieces of apparatus. Also, the fact that the full body weight is supported by the hand grip leaves some danger of falling. Many stunts involve a strain on the shoulders, which leaves some danger of shoulder injuries if moves are improperly performed. However, if instruction is carried out using a progressive order of learning and the activity is closely supervised, it is not a dangerous activity.

Some hints for the safe conduct of this activity are:

1. Use an adequate number of mats beneath the rings, anticipating the distance students will swing.

2. Use carbonate of magnesia chalk on the hands before working.

3. Use an overhead safety belt rigging when learning difficult moves and dismounts.

4. Periodically check the rings, straps, cables, and connections for weak spots.

PROGRAM OF INSTRUCTION

Instruction on the rings involves three basic steps:

1. *Individual moves.*

2. *Combinations.* As a person learns a new move, he should be challenged to combine it with another as smoothly as possible. Because a skill must be learned well in order to combine it with another, the use of combinations in the teaching progression stresses proper execution and increases the safety of performance. In addition, the smaller combinations serve as building blocks for longer routines. Combinations can be suggested

by the instructor or coach or can be created by the performer.

3. *Routines.* Ultimately, a pupil should strive to combine moves into a routine. Competition is based on routines, required or optional. The approach to optional routines is one of problem solving. Certain requirements involving the types and number of movements are presented as a problem for the performer to solve creatively within his own capabilities. The instructor or coach and pupil can coordinate their thoughts on the development of a particular routine. For sample routines refer to the end of the chapter.

As suggested, the rings should first be worked at approximately shoulder height. Some of the stunts that can be done on the still rings in the recommended order of progression are as follows:

1. *Chin-Ups.* Grasp the rings and simply pull up into a chin-up position. Repeat.

2. *Chin-Ups with Legs in L Position.* Raise the legs to an L position parallel to the mats and execute a chin-up.

3. *Chin-Up—One Arm to the Side.* Execute a chin-up and while the arms are in the flexed position, extend one

Chin-Up, One Arm to Side

arm to the side, then bring it back and extend the other arm to the side.

4. *Inverted Pike Hang.* Grasp the rings, and bending at the hips, bring the feet up and over the head. Finish in a jackknife position with the knees straight and close to the chest. This is a fundamental starting position for many ring stunts.

5. *Inverted Layout Hang.* Grasp the rings and bring the feet up and over the head. Finish with the legs straight above between the rings with the feet together, body arched, and arms straight. Hold this position for a few seconds and then return to the starting position. At first it may be tried with the legs resting on the straps.

Chin-Up, L Position

Inverted Pike Hang

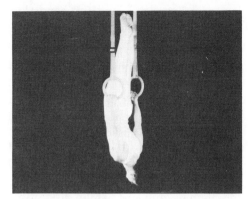

Inverted Layout Hang

6. *Bird's Nest.* Grasp the rings with the hands and pull the feet up and into the rings. Place the instep in the rings

Bird's Nest

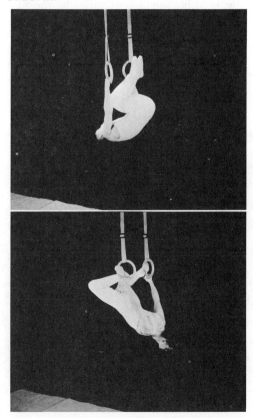

and arch the body so the chest is facing the mat. Hold for a moment and return.

7. *Bird's Nest—One Foot.* Do the bird's nest and remove one foot from the ring, extending that leg straight out behind.

8. *Bird's Nest—One Foot and One Hand.* Do the bird's nest and remove one foot and then release opposite hand and hold the position with only one hand and one foot.

9. *Skin the Cat.* Grasp the rings and bring the legs up between the arms and continue moving them over to an extended position with the toes reaching downward as far as possible toward the mat. Return to original position. Keep the knees close to the chest for better control of the movement.

10. *Single Leg Kip Up.* With the body in an inverted pike hang position, put the right leg across the right arm with the foot outside the ring. Rock forward, pulling with both hands and ending in a position with the head and shoulders above the rings and the right leg resting on the right arm. Return to pike hang.

11. *Single Leg Cut-Off Forward.* With the body in an inverted pike position, swing forward with both legs and at the same time spread them apart so as to cut one leg between a ring and a hand. Release the ring with the hand and allow the leg to pass between and then regrasp the ring. While doing the single leg cut-off, the arms should be in a slightly flexed position, as this will give added control to the stunt. The head and shoulders should be rolled up toward the rings before cutting off for a safer and easier execution of the stunt. This also may be done as a dismount by finishing

Single-Leg Cut-Off Forward

in a standing position on the mats after the cut-off.

12. *Double Leg Cut-Off Forward.* Same as single leg cut-off except that both legs are swung between one ring and hand. Regrasp the ring after the legs pass between it and the hand. The spotter should stand behind the performer for this stunt.

13. *Dislocate.* With the body in an inverted pike position, extend the legs up and backward and at the same time push the arms out to the side and extend the body. With the arms completely out to the sides and the body in a stretched position, dislocate the shoulders and swing the feet on toward the mat. Turn the thumbs outward while dislocating. Allow the feet to continue toward the mat to a standing position or bend the legs and swing on through to the original pike position. Keep pressing the rings—don't relax or flop or jar at the bottom. The instructor can assist in this stunt by lifting up on the shoulders and by holding the legs parallel to the mat until the dislocation of the shoulders is completed.

14. *Inlocate.* From an inverted pike position swing the legs forward, down-

Dislocate

Dislocate

15. *Jump to Straight-Arm Support.* For this particular stunt the rings should be at shoulder height. Grasp the rings and jump upward into a straight-arm support position above the rings. Keep the arms near the side of the body while in the straight-arm support position.

Inlocate

ward, and backward. At the peak of the backward swing turn the arms inward, drop the head forward, pike the body, and inlocate to an inverted pike position. Assistance can be given by lifting up on the performer's legs as he swings into the pike.

Spotting a Dislocate

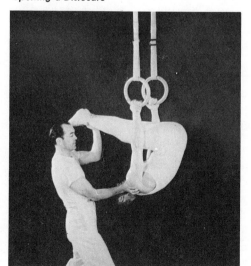

16. *Forward Roll.* From a straight-arm support position above the rings roll forward slowly into a pike position below the rings. Be sure to elevate the hips as the head is dropped forward prior to the roll. Lower the body slowly by keeping the arms flexed as the roll is completed.

17. *Muscle Up.* Grip the rings with the palms of the hands resting above the rings in a false grip, or overgrip. Bring the legs between the arms in a pike position. Flex the arms as in chin-

Forward Roll

Muscle Up

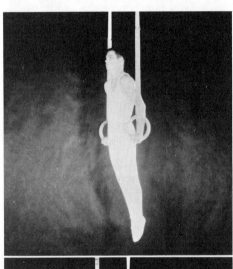

ning and roll forward slowly, trying to get the head and shoulders above the rings, keeping the rings close to the body. When the head and shoulders reach a position above the rings, the arms are then straightened to finish with the legs either in an L position or lowered to a straight position. The spotter may assist by placing one hand on the back and the other hand under the buttocks, lifting the performer as he does the muscle up.

18. *Kip to Straight-Arm Support.* From a pike position under the rings, extend the legs upward and forward and pull with the arms. Continue the kip until the body is above the rings in a straight-arm support position with the shoulders and arms resting against the straps. The spotter may assist by pushing upward under the hips.

Kip to Straight-Arm Support

19. *Back Uprise.* The rings should be elevated to the regulation height of about 8 feet while trying this stunt. Bring the legs up into a pike position and then extend them forward and downward. Continue the swing of the legs under the rings, and as the legs swing backward, pull with the arms and finish above the rings in a straight-arm support position. A forceful downward, backward, and upward swing of the legs is of great importance in executing this move. Remember to use the entire body to swing and not just the hips. Also, tighten the buttocks throughout the swing.

20. *Front Uprise.* This stunt can first be tried on the still rings at the regular elevated height of 8½ feet. Swing the feet back and forth a few times and prior to the front end of the swing, pike slightly and start pulling with the arms. After a quick pike of the body, extend the body by thrusting the hips and chest up toward the rings. Pull hard with the arms and on the way up to a position above the rings, shift the wrists from a hanging position to that of a support

position. Straighten the arms and finish in a straight-arm support position.

Back Uprise

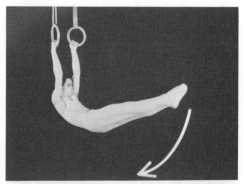

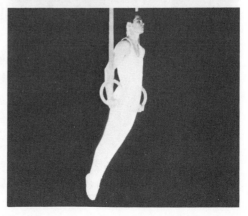

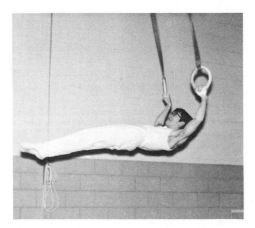

Front Uprise

21. *Shoulder Balance.* From a straight-arm support position bend forward, lifting the hips above the head and flexing the arms so that the shoulder balance position can be reached. Keep the head up and slowly lift the feet upward to a straight shoulder-balance position. Hold an arch in the body and point the toes. The arms should be flexed enough so that the upper arms may apply pressure against the straps in order to maintain

the balance. A spotter should be used in learning this stunt. Also, the feet may be placed along the straps during the learning period.

22. *Reverse Kip.* Grasp the rings and swing the feet back and forth a few times. Finally, as the feet swing forward, continue moving them upward between the straps of the rings. Shoot the feet into the air and attempt to change the grip of the hands from a hanging position to a support position above the rings. In learning this stunt it may be advisable to think of it as a high dislocate. Try to stop the dislocate half way through and catch the body above the rings in a support position. The spotter can assist by pushing upward under the performer's shoulders as he attempts the shoot into the reverse kip. Be sure to finish with the rings in front of the body and not behind the hips.

23. *Muscle Up into Forward Roll.* This is a combination of the muscle up and forward roll above. Try to make the

Shoulder Balance

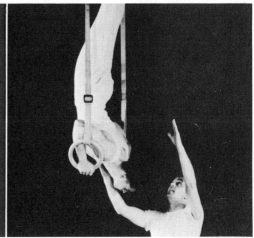

Reverse Kip

action a slow and continuous motion so that the forward roll is at the same speed as the muscle up.

24. *Kip to Forward Roll.* This stunt is similar to the previous stunt in that it is a combination of a kip and forward roll. Be sure that the kip is executed high enough so that the forward roll is commenced with the shoulders above the rings. The spotter should be sure to help the performer so that he does not drop too forcefully into the roll, causing strain on the shoulders and sometimes a loss of grip.

25. *Back Hip Circle.* From a front support position, swing the legs backward slightly and then forward into the back hip circle action. Keep the rings close to the hips, simulating a back hip circle around the horizontal bar. Again the spotter should help the performer throughout the action to prevent him from dropping below the rings too far.

26. *Backward Straddle Dismount.* From a swing below the rings bring the

legs upward above the hands and into a straddle position. Pull hard with the arms and continue the motion upward and backward, releasing the hands and passing the legs outside the rings to finish in a standing position on the mat. At the time of the releasing of the hands, the head and shoulders should be lifted to assist the performer in completing the backward somersault movement to a standing position. After releasing the hands, the body may maintain a layout or pike position in dropping to the mats. As proficiency improves, the height may be increased to a point where the hips rise above the rings. This action is best learned by swinging forward below the rings and shooting upward into a handstand action, with the legs in straddle position, but without the release of the hands. Several of these swings upward toward a handstand position give the performer the feel of a truly high straddle dismount (See picture).

27. *Flyaway.* This is similar to a straddle dismount except the legs are be-

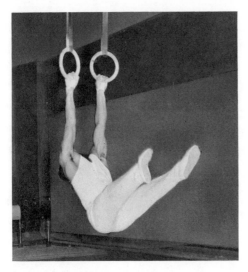

Backward Straddle Dismount

tween the rings and not straddling them. As the body reaches the position where the hands release the rings, pike at the hips sharply to bring the legs downward to the mat in a neat manner. This can also be done in a layout position.

28. *Back Uprise-Back Somersault Dismount from Support.* Execute a strong back uprise. Upon reaching a straight-arm support position bring the legs forward and quickly thrust the body into a back somersault, bringing the knees into the chest with the head back. Release the rings and complete the somersault to the feet.

29. *Back Lever.* Start from a straight body inverted hang and slowly lower the body backward to a position parallel to the mats with the stomach facing downward. The spotter can assist by holding the legs in the desired position.

30. *Front Lever.* Start from a straight-body inverted hang and slowly lower forward to a position parallel to the mats with the back facing downward. The spotter should assist by holding the hips in the desired position. For progression the performer may try this stunt with one leg straight and the other bent with the foot on top of the opposite knee. This may also be tried at first with the arms bent.

31. *Handstand.* From a straight-arm support position lift the hips upward, bending the arms slightly. Continue the movement, and when the hips are over the rings, the legs are extended upward into the handstand position while the arms are straightened. Hold the handstand position with the arms straight and the hands turned sideward so that the palms face each other. In a top-flight performance, the gymnast does not touch the straps with his arms. If the performer overbalances, he should pike the body so as to control the roll into the hanging position. While students first learn this stunt, the legs as well as the

Back Lever

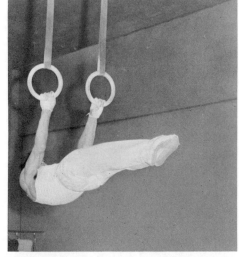

Front Lever

arms may be bent as the performer moves upward into the handstand position.

Handstand

32. *Straight-Body Bent-Arm Press to Handstand.* From a support position lean forward, bending the arms but keeping the body straight; move upward into a handstand position. This stunt requires considerable strength and can be practiced on the parallel bars.

33. *Reverse Kip Back Hip Circle.* This stunt is a combination of a reverse kip and a backward hip circle. Care should be taken that the rings are under control as the reverse kip is completed and the back hip circle begins. This can be done by keeping the rings close to the hips and trying to maintain a constant speed of movement.

34. *Shoot (Streuli) to Shoulder Balance.* From a swing below the rings, pass the legs forward and upward as if performing a reverse kip. As the legs reach a position near the straps, they should extend upward between the straps and at the same time the arms pull and the hands shift from the hang position to a

Straight-Body Press to Handstand

support position as the body moves into the shoulder balance position. The head is lifted upward to control the balance.

35. *Shoot (Streuli) to Handstand.* Similar to a shoot to shoulder balance except the shoot upward is more forceful, the pull of the arms is stronger, and the final position is a handstand. Remember to lift the legs forcefully through the bottom, and by pulling the arms you accentuate the shoot action. Pull the rings backward but not too wide and wait as long as possible before bending the arms. Later, as skill improves, this move may be done with straight arms.

36. *Kip to L Support.* This stunt is a regular kip ending with the body in an L support position with the legs parallel to the floor. A high forceful kipping action along with a powerful arm pull is necessary to execute this stunt. The spotter may assist by pushing upward on the hips.

37. *Crosses*

(a.) STRAIGHT-BODY CROSS. From a support position, lower slowly downward, spreading the arms to the side until the arms are straight out from the shoulders. Hold this position at this point. To come out of this stunt, the usual procedure is to lower the body into a hanging position below the rings, although some stronger gymnasts will push upward into a straight body support position above

Kip to L Support

Straight-Body Cross

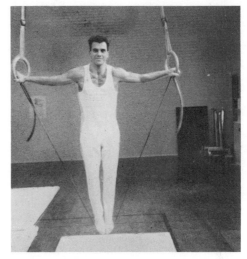

Learning Cross with Inner Tube

the rings. The spotter may assist by standing in front of the performer and holding the feet with his hands, thus taking some of the weight off the performer's shoulders and arms. Another method is to use an old bicycle inner tube that has been cut into one length. Place one end through each ring. Jump to a support position with the hands holding each end of the tube and then place the feet on the hanging part of the inner tube. This will give support as the body is lowered into the cross position.

(b.) OLYMPIC CROSS. From a support position, turn the shoulders so the head is facing one strap. Then lower the body downward into the Olympic cross position.

(c.) L CROSS. From a support position, lower downward into a regular straight-body cross. While in this position lift the legs upward to an L position and hold.

(d.) INVERTED CROSS. From a handstand position, lower downward, spreading the arms until they are straight out

to the sides in an inverted cross position. Hold this position.

38. *Planche (Free Support Scale)*. From a support position on the rings, lift the legs backward to a point parallel to the mats. This places the body in a planche position above the rings. For

L Cross

Planche

ease in first learning this stunt the performer may place his feet slightly higher than his head. He may also do it at first with his legs in a straddle position for a slightly easier approach to the move. Another learning method is to lower downward from a handstand to the parallel, or planche, position. Many performers practice the movement on the floor with the legs in straddle position.

Maltese

39. *Maltese.* This stunt is similar to the planche except the body is down in a position between the rings with the arms to the side. Considerably more difficult than the planche.

40. *Regular Giant Swing (Riesenfelge).* From a handstand position, lower slowly toward the inverted cross position with the arms outward to the sides. As the shoulders near the level of the rings, push the body backward and place the arms forward and swing through the bottom prior to the upward shoot to the handstand. Be sure to keep pressure on the rings throughout the swing. Also, don't arch the body on the way down but instead stretch it out as far as possible. A good progressive move is to try from a support position and after swinging the legs back and forth a couple of times, simply cast backward into a baby giant swing action, constantly keeping pressure on the rings. Try to relate this to the feeling of a dislocate. As skill improves you may want to simulate the technique used in casting off the horizontal bar in executing a regular giant swing bail out. On the rings you simply push the rings straight out in front of you and allow the body to cast straight backward, which obviously gives a tremendous swing throughout the movement. A straight-arm giant swing will result. An overhead safety belt should be used in learning this move.

41. *Reverse Giant Swing.* From a handstand position, lower downward, turning the wrists inward and ducking the head and shoulders to activate the reverse giant swing action. Throw the body forcefully forward to place the rings and body in the same line. Push the hands outward in a manner similar to

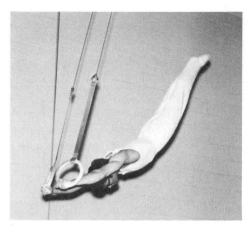

Giant Bail-Out

an inlocate. As you pass through the bottom, drive the heels upward, and not just backward. Press the shoulders down with the head down slightly. Try to arch the chest rather than the lower back. When the heels come above the shoulders, the arms push the body upward into the handstand position. When first learning try it from a shoulder balance position and then fall forward, pushing the rings back, and swing through the bottom up to the shoulder balance position again. Use a spotter while first learning. An overhead safety belt can also be very helpful.

42. *Flyaway with Half Twist.* Start to do a regular flyaway, and just as the hands are released, turn the shoulders and head to the left. Then execute a sharp half turn with the body and land on the mat facing in the opposite direction. The spotter should position himself so that he can grasp the hips as the twist is executed.

43. *Flyaway with Full Twist.* Start to do a regular flyaway, and as the hands are released, turn the shoulders and head to the left. Thrust the right arm across

the chest to complete a full twist and then land on the mat in a standing position. This stunt is best learned on the trampoline with a twisting belt or on the rings with an overhead rigging. Another method of learning this dismount is by the degree method. While a straight layout flyaway is tried, add just a quarter of a twist on the way down. Land in a soft landing pad for safety. As you gain familiarity, add a little more twist—from a quarter turn, to a half turn, to a three-quarter turn, and finally to the complete full twist. It is essential to get a strong pull prior to releasing for the flyaway. On a double twisting flyaway an even stronger pull is essential, and the hands must be released at the same time. Set the body and then wrap up a tight double twisting flyaway.

44. *Double Flyaway.* Swing forward and upward from below the rings. As soon as the legs start the upward swing, bend the knees to start the double flyaway action. Bring the knees up close to the chest and push the head backward. The hands, upon releasing the rings, grasp the shins to form a tight tuck. After completing the second somersault, open smartly to a landing position on the feet on the mat. The mechanics of the double somersault should be tried on the trampoline in an overhead rigging and also on the rings with an overhead safety rigging about the performer. When first learning this move use an overhead belt and try a double skin-the-cat move with the knees in tuck position. Upon completion of the second turnover, drop to the landing pad. This gives an orientation to the two somersaults. Then try it with a release of the hands after the first skin-the-cat rotation and execute the second rotation free of the rings. A strong

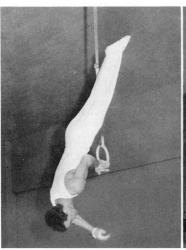

Full Twisting Flyaway

and long pull is essential to a good double flyaway. On the double somersault be sure to have the tucking action upward and obviously not forward. Also, have a feeling of pressing down on the rings, since the double flyaway should be high and inside the rings.

45. *Honma (Whippet).* This move consists of doing a strong forceful inlocate action with hard heel drive and then a quick forward somersault action, pulling with the arms to finish in a support position above the rings. It is important to wait long on the backward and upward inlocate prior to ducking into the somersault action.

Strengthening Sequence

The following is a suggested sequence of moves that will help the performer to increase his ring strength. Do this sequence a couple of times every other day upon completion of the regular workout. Also, use the assistance of a fellow gymnast or coach. The helper holds the per-

former in the various positions and assists in moving him upward into the handstands, crosses, and so on. As strength improves, less assistance is required. It is difficult at first, but within a few weeks it can be handled with comparative ease. *You will miss it if you don't do it regularly.* On lowered rings start in an inverted hang and lower to a front lever (assisted by the spotter); pull straight body up and over to back lever; then up to an inverted hang to a pike to a kip to an L position above the rings; press to a handstand and then come down and do a back roll (felge) to another handstand; then lower slowly through a planche position down to a back lever; then over to a front lever and a quick pull to an L cross; pull up to an L seat and press to a handstand; and then come down and do three crosses up and down.

Routines

Creativity, imagination, and resourcefulness can be developed in the sport of gymnastics by the individual's construction and performance of his own sequence of stunts. The following are suggestions for combinations that can be enlarged upon within the pupil's ability.*

1. On low rings (rings at shoulder height) pull up to an inverted hand layout position, slowly lower legs into a pike position, and then continue on backward to a skin the cat. Bring the legs back to the pike position and execute a single leg cut and catch with the right leg. Return to pike hang, do a single leg cut (left leg), and dismount to a stand, grasping rings with the hands.

2. On low rings (rings at shoulder height) pull up to an inverted hang layout position, lower legs to a pike hang position, and then place the feet into the rings and execute bird's nest (an additional challenge would be to have performer do a bird's nest with two hands and one foot with the other foot free of the ring). Return to pike position and then a single leg cut off dismount.

3. Jump to support (rings at shoulder height) above the rings and then do a forward roll to a pike hang position; do a single leg kip-up and then drop back to a skin the cat and then back to a single leg cut and catch and then a skin-the-cat dismount.

4. On higher rings, muscle up to above the rings into a forward roll to a pike hang and then execute a dislocate into a straddle dismount.

5. With a false grip on the rings, kip up into a support position and then press to a shoulder balance. Roll forward and swing legs backward into an inlocate to a pike hang. Lower the legs to a back lever position and hold momentarily. Bring legs back to a pike hang position and then do a dislocate pike flyaway.

6. Bring legs slowly upward to a straight-body hang and then execute a dislocate to a reverse kip to an L position above the rings. Press to a handstand and then lower the legs down to a support position above the rings and from here lower to a straight-body cross. Hold momentarily, drop below the rings into a pike hang position, and then do a dislocate high straddle dismount.

7. Dislocate to a shoot to a handstand and then lower body to a regular cross. Drop below the rings and do a dislocate to a reverse kip to a backward roll to L position above the rings. Press to a handstand; lower legs, bring the feet forward to forward cast, to an inlocate, to a back uprise, to a backward roll, and then drop below the rings to a dislocate flyaway with a twist.

* For additional routines consider the Age Group Compulsory Exercises for Boys and Girls published by the United States Gymnastic Federation, Box 12713, Tuscon, Arizona 85711.

8

Parallel Bars

Parallel bars were first introduced by Friedrich Jahn in the early 1800s. He hoped through this apparatus and the others that he invented to strengthen the degenerated muscle groups of the body and thus perhaps to liberate man from the shackles of an overcivilized environment that had enfeebled him.

The parallel bars consist of two parallel hand rails made of the finest grained hickory connected to uprights supported by a metal base. All are firmly connected, allowing no undue shaking. The bars are adjustable in width and in height, which allows convenient adjustment for the students of different age groups and sizes. For collegiate competition the bars should be from 5 feet 7 inches to 5 feet 9 inches (1675 to 1725 millimeters) high. The bars are 11 feet 6 inches long with an inside width of 18⅞ inches to 20½ (480 to 520 millimeters). A competitive routine includes a series of swinging, flight, and hold parts that can call for a certain measure of strength, but the swinging and flight parts should predominate.

VALUES

The specific values of working the parallel bars are:

1. The parallel bars develop strength and power in the arms, chest, and back.

2. Balance is essential in parallel bars work and is developed by it.

3. The maneuvers call for great coordination and timing.

4. Confidence is developed on the parallel bars as the fear of falling between the bars is overcome.

ORGANIZATION

Area and Equipment

The parallel bars are easily moved and thus can be set up in any part of the gymnasium. Because the stunts do not require the performer to start or finish far away from the bars, the area needed would be that taken up by the bars themselves plus about 5 feet on all sides. Mats should be under and around the bar. 5' x 10' mats will fit along the sides and ends, but underneath and between the uprights is more of a problem. The same sized mats cannot be placed here without curling up or overlapping, which may cause injuries. The best solution is a special mat to fit the area. These can be obtained from the companies that supply parallel bars.

Teaching Methods

Normally only one person can work the parallel bars at one time, but during the elementary skills period, two performers may work at the same time. When doing dips, one student may work at each end. For a series of straddle seat travels along the length of the bars, a second performer could begin before the first one has finished at the other end. Performers generally proceed rapidly so no undue waiting should result with large squads.

The instructor should carefully supervise the activity at the beginning stages because most students have a fear of falling between the bars. However, this fear is quickly overcome, and with confidence the performer executes the stunts with little danger of injury.

Work on the parallel bars can be evaluated by using a stunt chart. Because of the great variety of stunts possible, it is easier and less time-consuming to make up simple routines for checking purposes. For more advanced classes, regular competitive routines make a good test.

Safety

In order to carry out a successful program of instruction on the parallel bars, a few safety hints should be followed:

1. Check the equipment to see that it is firmly supported on the floor and that the uprights are in a secure position.

2. The area around and under the bars should be safely padded with mats.

3. When students first work with the parallel bars, the bars should be lowered as far as possible. This makes for safe performance and convenient spotting. For balancing stunts, a set of low parallel bars is extremely valuable to use.

4. One or more spotters should be present at all times to assist the performer through the more involved skills.

5. For moves done in the middle of the bars, the spotter should stand to one

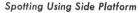

Spotting Using Side Platform

side of the bars. In helping the performer, he should be careful not to allow the arm to be caught across the bars with the weight of the performer on the arm; thus, most of the spotting should be done under the bars, unless using the spotting platform.

PROGRAM OF INSTRUCTION

Instruction on the parallel bars involves three basic steps:

1. *Individual moves.*

2. *Combinations.* As a person learns a new skill, he should be challenged to combine it with another move as smoothly as possible. Because a skill must be learned well in order to combine it with another, the use of combinations in the teaching progression stresses proper execution and increases the safety of performance. In addition, the smaller combinations serve as building blocks for longer routines. Combinations can be suggested by the instructor or coach or can be created by the performer.

3. *Routines.* Ultimately, a pupil should strive to combine moves into a routine. Competition is based on routines, required or optional. The approach to optional routines is one of problem solving. Certain requirements involving the types and number of movements are presented as a problem for the performer to solve creatively within his own capabilities. The instructor or coach and pupil can coordinate their thoughts on the development of a particular routine. For sample routines refer to the end of the chapter.

There are three common starting positions:

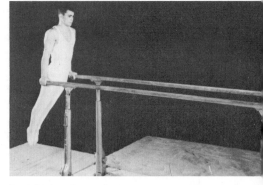

Straight-Arm Support

(a) *Straight-Arm Support.* Jump onto the bars with a hand on each bar. The arms are straight and run along the sides of the body. Keep the head up, chest out, body slightly arched, and the toes pointed.

Jump to Straddle Seat

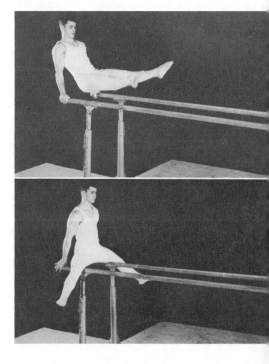

(b) *Straddle Seat.* From a straight-arm support position, swing the legs forward between the bars. As the legs swing slightly above the bars, separate them and place one on each bar, ending in a straddle seat position with the legs and back straight, the head and chest up, and the hands behind the legs.

(c) *Upper-Arm Support.* The body is supported between the bars by the upper arms, which are over the bars. The hands grasp the bars ahead of the shoulders and the elbows are spread out to the side. The body should be able to swing freely from this position.

To become a successful performer on the parallel bars, it is important to progress slowly through the fundamental and strengthening moves. As skill and strength improve, the more advanced stunts may be tried with complete confidence. The following is a description of some of the moves that may be done on the parallel bars, given in recommended order of progression. It is suggested that the bars be lowered for learning the beginning moves.

1. *Dips.* Jump onto the bars in a straight-arm support position facing toward the center of the bars. In this position, flex the arms and drop downward until the elbow joint is at less than a right angle. After reaching the bottom with the arms flexed, push the body upward into the straight-arm position. Do several of these dips at one time to increase arm strength.

2. *Swing.* Jump to a straight-arm support position on the ends of the bars. Bring the legs up slightly and extend the body into an arched position. Swing the legs downward and then backward and forward in a series of swings. Be sure

Upper-Arm Support

to keep the arms straight and make the *shoulders* the fulcrum of the swing. Swing low at first and gradually increase the height of the swing. Control is es-

Dip

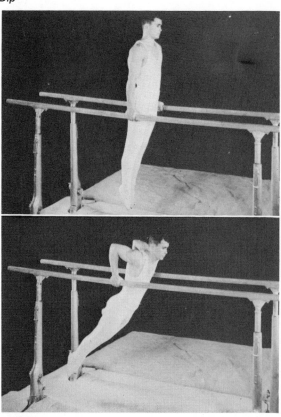

pecially important as the swing becomes larger. Remember to depress the shoulders a little at the bottom of the forward swing. Don't pike the hips; turn the elbow out and extend the shoulders on the backswing as you would swinging into a handstand.

3. *Swinging Dips.* Swing in a straight-arm support position, and when the feet are at the end of the backward swing, flex the arms and drop to a dip position. Remain in this dip position as the legs swing forward. Just as the feet reach the end of the forward swing, push the arms straight and finish in a straight-arm position. This same stunt can be done backward by dropping into the full dip

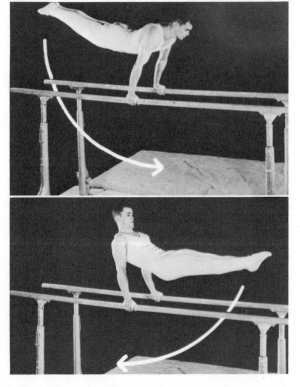

Swing

position at the end of the front swing and pushing up at the back end of the swing. To do this stunt on lowered parallel bars, it may be necessary to bend the knees so that the feet will not hit the mats.

4. *Swinging Dip Travel.* The first half of this stunt is done just like the swinging dips. As the body is swinging forward from the dip position, push vigorously with the arms in an upward and forward direction. The hands leave the bars momentarily, the body travels or hops forward, then the hands regrasp the bars, and the body finishes in a straight-arm support position.

5. *Straight-Arm Walk.* Walk the length of the bars in a straight-arm support position, keeping the arms straight, head up, body arched. As one hand leaves the bar to take a step, shift the weight to the other hand. Be sure to take small steps with the hands.

6. *Front Support Turn.* From a straight-arm support position in the center of the bars, lean to the right and shift the left hand to the right bar, bringing the front of the thighs to rest against the bar. Keep the body straight and back slightly arched. Continue the turn by reaching back with the right hand and grasping the vacated bar, thus ending in a straight-arm support position.

7. *Half Twist Change (Scissors from Straight-Arm Support).* Here is another simple method of turning around. From a straight-arm support position, swing both legs backward, execute a half twist of the body, and bring the right leg over the left bar and the left leg over the right bar. After finishing this scissor action, turn the body into a straddle seat position facing the opposite direction.

Front Support Turn

8. *Front Dismount.* Swing in the center of the bars from a straight-arm support position. As the body reaches the peak of the backward swing and the legs are above the bars, push hard with the left arm and swing the body over the right bar so the front part of the body is closest to the bar. After passing over this bar, drop toward the mat, grasping the bar with the left hand as the right hand releases the grip. Land on the mat with the left hand steadying the landing by holding onto the closest bar.

9. *Rear Dismount.* Swing in the center of the bars in a straight-arm support position. As the body swings forward and the feet reach a point above the bars, push with the left hand and swing the body over the right bar so the rear of the body is closest to the bar. After passing over the right bar, regrasp it with the left hand as the right hand lets go.

10. *Straddle Seat Travel.* From a straddle seat position, lean forward and place the hands on the bars in front of the legs. As the weight is shifted to the

Front Dismount

Rear Dismount

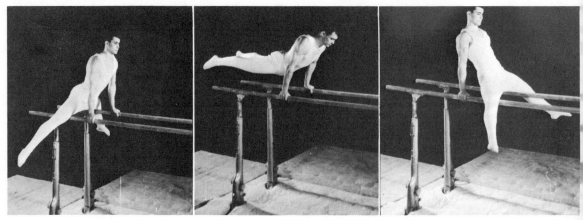

Straddle Seat Travel

straight arms, swing the legs backward above bar level; then bring them together and swing them forward between the bars. At the front of the swing, separate the legs again and place them in a straddle seat position in front of the hands. Travel the length of the bars in this manner.

11. *Side Seat Half Turn to Straddle Seat.* This stunt is a simple method of turning around and is done in the fol-

lowing manner. From a straight-arm support position in the center of the bars, swing both legs forward over the right bar and end up in a side seat position. Release the right hand and place it on the left bar and bring the right leg across from the right bar over to the left bar. Bring the left hand back to the right bar and finish in a straddle seat position facing the opposite direction. This can also be done by swinging to a side seat position on the inside of the right bar.

Side Seat Half Turn to Straddle Seat

Execute the half turn by bringing the right hand to the left bar and turning the body to a straight-arm support position.

12. *Single Leg Cut-Off Forward.* From a straight-arm support position on the end of the bars facing away from the bars, swing the body backward. At the back end of the swing, raise the hips and swing the right leg outside the right bar. On a forward swing, release the right hand and land in a standing position on

Single-Leg Cut-Off Forward

Single-Leg Cut-On

the mat. Remember to keep the shoulders well forward of the hands so there is a definite forward lean into the dismount, which will help to keep the cutting leg from hitting the bar.

13. *Single Leg Cut-On.* Stand on the mats facing the end of the bars and grasp them with the hands. Jump toward a straight-arm support position and as the body moves upward, separate the legs and pass the left leg outside the left hand. The left leg passes over the bar to the inside of the bars while the performer releases the left hand. After the leg has passed over the bar, regrasp the bar and finish in a straight arm position. When first attempting this stunt, cut the leg across the bar; regrasp the bar but land in a standing position on the mat until the proper cutting action is achieved. The spotter may assist by standing behind and lifting at the performer's waist.

14. *Forward Roll to Straddle Seat.* Start from a straddle seat position and grasp the bars in front of the thighs. Lean forward and place the upper arms on the bars with the elbows out to the side. Raise the hips, keeping the body in a pike position. As the hips pass over the head, release the hands, keeping the elbows out to the side, and grasp the hands behind the back. The roll is continued to a straddle seat position.

15. *Backward Straddle Shoulder Roll.* From a straddle seat position, lean backward onto the arms and execute a backward roll. Grasp the bars over the shoulders and continue the roll to a straddle seat.

16. *Back Roll Off Both Bars Dismount.* Start from a sitting position on one bar

Double-Leg Cut-On

Forward Roll to Straddle Seat

with the hands grasping the bar on each side of the hips and the body facing away from the bars. Lean backward so the back rests on the other bar and bring the legs up and over the head. When the feet are as far down toward the mats as possible, release the hands and land on the mats in a standing position.

17. *Lazy Man's Kip.* Grasp the ends of the bars and jump up, placing the feet about halfway up on each of the uprights. Swing the body downward, flex-

Backward Straddle Shoulder Roll

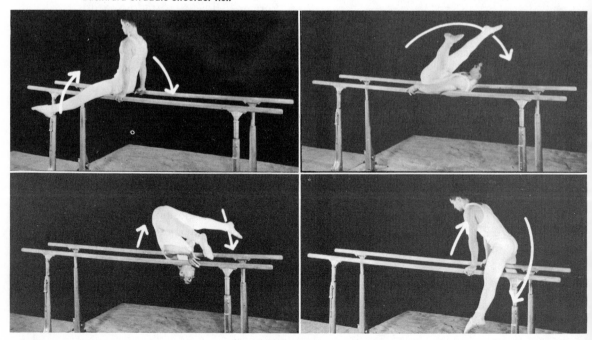

ing the knees, and hang on with the hands. When the swing reaches the point where the knees are fully flexed, start the return swing upward by straightening the legs and pulling forcefully with the arms. Continue this pull and shift the wrists from a hanging position to a support position and finish in a straight-arm support position.

18. *Shoulder Balance (Upper-Arm Balance).* Start from a straddle seat position and grasp the bars in front of the thighs. Lean forward and place the upper arms on the bars, with the elbows out to the side. Raise the hips and extend the legs over the head. Assume the shoulder balance position with the back arched, head up, toes pointed, and the elbows out to the side. Either slowly return the body to the starting position or pike the body and roll to a straddle seat. A spotter is important in first learning this stunt.

19. *Single Leg Circle Forward.* From a straight-arm support position in the middle of the bars, swing the right leg forward over the left bar. Follow with the right hand. Transfer the left hand to the opposite bar and continue swinging the right leg so it ends between the bars. Finish in a straight-arm support position facing the opposite direction. Remember to transfer the body weight to the left bar during the change.

20. *Shoulder Balance—Side Dismount.* From a shoulder balance, lean to the right and push off with the left hand, allowing the body to rotate around the right bar, and land in a standing position on the mat. Hold on with the right hand in order to steady the landing.

Shoulder Balance

21. *Hip Pullover Mount.* Stand at the side of the bars with arms under the near bar and the hands grasping the far bar in a regular grasp. Take a step under the bars and kick upward with the feet, pulling the abdomen into the bar with the legs going on over the top of the bars. Push the body up to a front leaning rest position across the bars. Swing the right leg between the bars and then over the right bar, ending up in a straddle seat position.

22. *Back Uprise.* This skill should be done with the bars at least as high as the performer's shoulders when standing. From an upper-arm support position with the arms extended forward from the shoulders, swing back and forth a couple of times. Then on one of the backswings beat quickly past the vertical line by piking slightly prior to reaching this position and then whip the heels backward and upward, pull hard with the arms, and lift the body upward. Continue the pull and finish in a straight-arm support position. A good, strong swing helps in the accomplishment of

this move. Remember the swing is like a pendulum swing and is initiated from the shoulders. It should feel similar to a back uprise on the horizontal bar.

23. *Front Uprise.* From an upper-arm support position, swing back and forth a couple of times. At the bottom of the forward swing thrust the chest forward, kick the feet upward and forward, and pull hard with the arms. Continue pulling the arms back; the pulling action becomes a push and finishes in a straight-arm support position. If the performer has difficulty, he could finish in a straddle seat position a few times before attempting the regular ending. A spotter can help by pushing under the hips.

24. *Scissors Change from Straddle Seat.* Start in a straddle seat position with both hands behind the legs. Swing the right leg between the bars and transfer the left hand to the right bar. As the right leg swings vigorously backward, put the weight on the hands. Remove the left leg from the left bar and swing it over to the opposite bar, with the right

Back Uprise

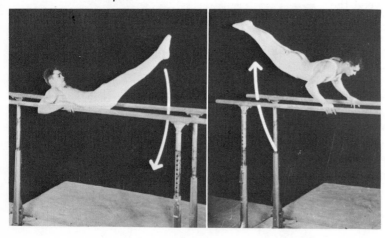

Front Uprise

the back end of the swing, raise the hips and swing the feet outside the bars into a straddle position. Cut the legs forward sharply, releasing both hands, and allow the legs to pass over the ends of the bars. Finish in a standing position on the mat. Remember to maintain a definite forward lean throughout the stunt. The spotter may grab the performer's shoulder or upper arm and help him clear the bars by pulling forward.

26. *Rear Vault Dismount with Half Twist.* From a straight-arm support position between the bars, start the body swinging. On the forward end of the swing, lift the legs up and over one bar as in the rear vault. As the body clears the bar, execute a half twist towards the bar. End in a standing position facing the opposite direction with the near hand on the bar.

27. *Top Kip to Straddle Seat.* From an upper-arm support position in the middle of the bars, raise the legs forward between the bars and over the head so that the body is in a pike position. From

leg moving over to the left bar. Finish in a straddle seat position, facing the opposite direction, with the hands behind the body.

An easier version of this stunt is the straddle circle. Start in a straddle seat position with both hands on the bars behind the legs. Swing the right leg between the bar and transfer the left hand to the right bar. Bring the right leg over the right bar to a position next to the left leg. The body is then in a front support position across the bars. Now swing the left leg up and over the left bar and between the bars and continue on up across the right bar to a straddle seat position facing the opposite direction.

25. *Straddle Forward Dismount.* From a straight-arm support position on the end of the bars facing away from the bars, swing the legs backward. On

Straddle Forward Dismount

this pike position, extend the legs forward and spread them. At the same time pull hard with the arms and finish in a straddle seat position above the bars. Be sure to get the hips high over the bars prior to doing the kip; this will help in the execution of the stunt. A spotter can help by pushing under the hips as the kip is executed.

28. *Top Kip.* This stunt is done the same way as is the top kip to a straddle seat except that the legs are kept together throughout the stunt and thus the finish is into a straight-arm support position.

Straddle Cut-On to Straddle Seat

Top Kip to Straddle Seat

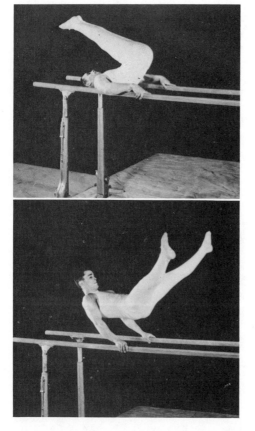

29. *Swing to Shoulder Balance.* Start in a straight-arm support position and swing back and forth a couple of times. At the end of the backswing, flex the arms and slowly drop the shoulders forward toward the bars, keeping the body straight. Place the upper arms on the bars, remembering to keep the body straight and head up. Finish in a shoulder balance position.

30. *Top Kip to Shoulder Balance.* As the top kip is completed, keep the body rotating forward. As the momentum causes a forward lean, flex the arms, drop the shoulders to the bars, and allow the feet to rise over the head to a shoulder balance position.

31. *Straddle Leg Cut-On to Straddle Seat.* As in the single leg cut-on, grasp the ends of the bars and jump upward, straddling both legs over the bars, and land in a straddle seat position on the bars.

32. *Straddle Leg Cut-On to Straight-Arm Support.* Same as the above except

the legs continue over the bars and finish together with the hands grasping the bars in a straight-arm support position. The spotter can grab the back of the performer's waist and give him a boost.

33. *End Kip.* With the hands on the ends of the bars, swing the legs forward and up to a pike position, hanging underneath the bar. As the body swings backward after the forward swing, extend the legs upward, pull with the arms, and finish in a straight-arm support position above the bars. It is similar to a seat rise over the top of a high bar and not like a kip on the high bar. Remember that the lower back and not the buttocks should be at the bottom of the swing.

34. *Glide Kip.* This stunt may be done from the end of the bars or in the middle of the bars. It is very similar to the end kip except for the glide. At the beginning, skim the feet over the mats until the front end of the swing is reached. Then on the backswing bring the legs up to a pike position, and when the body swings past the uprights, kip or shoot upward with the legs and arms pulling

strongly. Finish in a straight-arm support position between the bars. This can be done to a straddle seat position while first being learned.

35. *Double Rear Dismount.* From a straight-arm support position, swing the body. At the end of the backswing, lift the hips and swing both legs forward over the left bar. Continue swinging the legs over the right bar and down toward the mats, where the dismount finishes in a standing position, facing in the same direction as at the start. Remember to keep the weight of the body on the right arm as the dismount is executed to the right. Keep the hips fairly high throughout the dismount. A spotter may assist by grasping the right arm of the performer, pulling slightly while the stunt is being tried.

36. *Backward Giant Roll (Shoulder Roll).* This stunt consists basically of completing a full backward roll of the body in a layout position with the upper arms supporting the weight on the bars. From an upper-arm support position, with the hands grasping the bars in front

End Kip

Backward Giant Roll

of the chest, swing the legs back and forth a few times. Remember that the swing is from the chest and not from the hips. Obtain a forceful swing forward and allow the feet to continue on up and over the head. When the hips reach the height of the bars, push hard with the hands, release the grip, and throw the arms straight out at the sides. With the head back and body arched, allow the legs and feet to continue past the vertical position and down toward the original position between the bars. When the feet are directly overhead and are just starting to continue downward, the hands reach forward and grasp the bars. By grasping the bars, the performer is able to steady the downward flow of the roll. As proficiency increases in this stunt, the backward giant roll may be tried from a shoulder balance position. Two or three of these in a row make for a fine performance.

37. *Cast (Schwabenkippe)*. This move can be done from a straight-arm support position above the bars or from a standing position on the mats between the bars. From a standing position on the mats, grasp the bars with each hand on the inside of the bar, the fingers circling the top side of the bar. Lean backward and jump up slightly off the mat, keeping the arms straight and bringing the legs up so the body is in a pike position. Allow the body to swing downward between the bars, reaching the full bottom of the swing, and start the upward swing. Just before reaching the peak of the forward swing, extend the body forcefully forward by shooting the legs up between the bars and pulling strongly with the arms. Continue this extension of the body with the legs pressing forward until the shoulders move above

Cast

Cast from Support

the height of the bars. At this point, extend the arms to the side and finish in an upper-arm support position. Allow the feet to swing downward and at the back end of the swing execute a back uprise to a straight-arm support position.

To do the cast from a straight-arm support position, raise the legs slightly and drop backward between the bars. This puts the performer in a pike position, swinging beneath the bar, the correct position for completing the cast. This stunt can also be done to a straight-arm support position by swinging and extending strongly so that the performer regrasps with the hands on top of the bars and finishes in a straight arm support position.

Cast to Straight-Arm Support

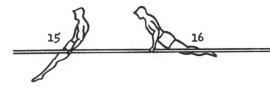

A good practice drill is to do a cast off the end of the bars to a standing position on the mats. Also, try doing the cast from the end in towards the bars but land in a straddle seat position on top of the bars. Another practice move is to hang upside down and commence getting a swing by pumping the body back and forth as you would pump a playground swing.

38. *Dip Half Turn.* Execute a swinging dip movement, and on the upward swing with the body in a slightly piked position, extend an arch in the body, push hard with the hands, and execute a half twist either to the left or right. Hold onto the bar slightly longer with the hand in the direction of the twist. Upon completion of the half turn, regrasp the bars in a straight-arm support position. Try this stunt on the low bars at first.

39. *Swing to a Hand Balance.* After learning a hand balance on the low parallel bars by kicking up from the bar, the performer should try a hand balance from a swing on the higher bars. At first, do this on the end of the bars facing outward, so that you can land safely if you swing beyond the balance position. This can be done by lifting one hand and twisting the body around to face the bars, as in doing a roundoff on the mats. As for doing the hand balance, from a straight-arm support position swing from the shoulders with the arms straight. When ready to swing to the hand balance, extend at the front end of the swing and keep the body stretched throughout the back swing. Allow the feet to swing over the head, keeping the shoulders over the hands. Flex the arms slightly if needed. If going off balance, grip hard with the hands to maintain the balance and do not give up easily. (*Safety precaution:* In coming down from the hand balance, do not allow the body to swing freely back to the straight-arm support position. Slow down the swing with the shoulders and upper back muscles by leaning forward slightly.)

40. *Press to Hand Balance.* This method is similar to the presses in Chapter 5 under "Strength Balance Moves."

41. *One-Arm Balance.* From a hand balance position, shift the weight to one bar and balance on one arm. The free arm may be held along the body or out to the side with the legs in straddle position or held together.

42. *Moore.* Swing in a straight-arm support position. As the body passes the hands on the backswing, lift the hips into the air and pike the body. Reach backward with the left hand toward the right bar and continue to keep the hips high, turning to the left so that the body is facing in towards both bars. Allow the

One-Arm Balance

feet to swing on the outside of the right bar and grasp the right bar with the left hand fairly near the right hand. After the feet reach the midpoint in the circle around the outside of the right bar, release the right hand and reach across and grasp the free bar. Then let the feet pass over the right bar and swing them down between the two bars. This can be spotted effectively with an overhead safety belt rigging. Simply cross the ropes in the proper direction behind the performer's back and follow the Moore through by pulling the rope supporting the performer. This stunt can also be done in a layout manner; the legs are elevated considerably higher, and an effective flying action is simulated in the Moore. This is almost a reverse pirouette movement.

43. *Front Overbar Somersault.* From a straight-arm support position, swing several times. When a maximum swing is obtained on the backward swing, lift the hips upward and forward in a pike

position. Push off hard with the hands and duck the head. Keep the arms spread and land on the upper arms and then regrasp with the hands. This should be tried first from a small swing into a simple forward roll. For more difficulty, this can be done to a straight-arm catch. Remember to keep the shoulders at the same height with a fast action of the arms over to the regrasp. This can be done with the use of a spotting belt overhead or with two spotters at the sides of the bars.

44. *Front Overbar Somersault Dismount.* This stunt is similar to the front overbar within the bars except it is done over one bar in a dismount to the mats. Be sure to look over the dismounting bar just prior to somersaulting. Push with the far hand in order to move the body over the bars toward the mat. Regrasp the bar with the inside hand as quickly as possible in order to steady the landing. While students are first learning this move, it is suggested that

Layout Moore

Front-to-Catch

the bar over which the dismount is attempted be padded. An overhead belt may be used or careful hand spotting applied. For more difficulty, this can be done with half twist.

A good learning progression is to swing and at the bottom of the swing, shrug or dip the shoulders and then execute a simple front vault over one bar to a stand on the mats. Also, you might try swinging back and forth between the bars and on the back end of each swing, release the hands, lift the body upward a little, and then replace the hands on the bars (it becomes a swing and hop and then another swing and hop). Then with a soft elevated landing pad off to the side of one bar,

Front Somersault Dismount with Half Twist

"squaring off" technique so the body will somersault over straight and not crooked. Emphasize a heel drive and also bend the knees a little while first learning the dismount. Do a tuck somersault at first and straighten the legs as skill progresses.

45. *Pirouette.* From a handstand, shift weight slightly to the right hand, change the left hand forward to the right bar, and quickly change the right hand back to the left bar. End up in a handstand, facing the opposite direction. Keep the body stretched out during the change of hands so that the shift in weight will take place without loss of balance. This stunt should be mastered on the low parallel bars before it is attempted on the higher bars. This move can be done in a reverse direction, with the left hand reaching backward behind the right hand, and then from the handstand on the right bar, the right hand moves to the left bar for the completed move (reverse pirouette). On a swinging pirouette, try it first off the end of the bars simply by swinging upward into a sort of pirouette dismount landing on the mats off the end of the bars. Bend the legs a little if desired at first and try dipping the shoulders a little at the bottom of the swing. Then move into the bars a little, place the hand on the pirouetting bar, and then simply drop off. Now try the entire swinging pirouette, but don't push too hard as you swing up into the pirouette action, since you need a little cushion to finish out the move. Make it a count of 1 . . . 2, 3. Push with both hands on the one bar.

46. *Hand Balance—One-Bar Dismounts.*

(a.) SQUAT DISMOUNT. After turning forward to a handstand on one bar, sim-

swing, and on the back end of the swing push the body over the bar and land in a front drop or on all fours onto the landing pad. Next, instead of landing on the front of the body, turn over and land on the back. This will give the gymnast a

Squat Dismount

ply push with the arms and sharply bring the legs down and between the arms in a squat position. Continue downward to a standing position on the mat.

(b.) STOOP DISMOUNT. Similar to squat dismount except that the legs are kept straight while the body pikes through for the dismount.

(c.) STRADDLE DISMOUNT. Again similar to the above two dismounts except that the legs are spread in a straddle position with the feet passing outside the hands during the dismount.

Straddle Dismount

On all three dismounts there should be two spotters, one at each shoulder of the performer, to help him clear the bar. The spotter actually grasps the performer's upper arm during the early stages of learning these dismounts and pulls the body beyond the bar. The spotter must move forward with the performer so as not to interfere with the dismounting action.

47. *Back Uprise to a Cut and Catch.* From a top kip position on the parallel bars, the body is extended upward and forward as far as possible. The purpose of this phase of the stunt is to get a maximum swing. As the body reaches near the bottom of the swing, the hips should lead so the body assumes a small pike position. From this piked position the body swings explosively through the bottom and upward with a hard kick of the legs and a pull of the arms. When the legs are above the bars, they spread quickly and the hands give a strong push before releasing. This enables the legs to pass under the hands and to continue the straddle action to meet in front of the body as the hands regrasp the bars. Try to rotate the hips forward on the straddle phase of the skill. Catch as high as possible as then you have the space and time to settle into the L position.

48. *Stutz.* Swing between the bars, and as the feet rise upward at the forward end of the swing, execute a half turn and then regrasp with the hands and swing downward for the next stunt. Be sure to pike at the bottom of the swing and then extend forcefully prior to turning into the stutz action Initiate the turn with the feet.

For ease of learning and safety, try this stunt with the bars lowered to about

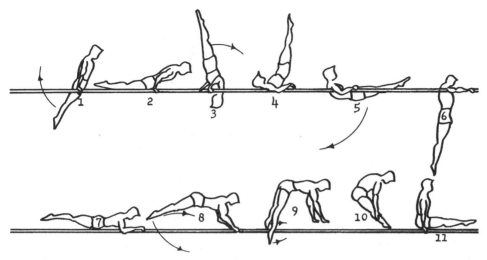

Back Uprise to Cut and Catch

waist height toward the end so that the turn can be executed away from the bars. Later you may want to try this stunt with the bars lowered but in the middle of the bars. The spotter may help by standing on a box alongside the bars and helping to maintain the height of the legs until the turn is executed.

Stutz

Remember as you become proficient at the stutz movement to ride one arm longer than the other as the turn is executed. As this movement is mastered the height may be increased to the point where a handstand can be held after the turn is executed. This then becomes a stutz to a handstand, a very difficult movement.

49. *Reverse Stutz.* From a top kip position extend the legs and body forward to get a good long swing. As you near the bottom of the swing, lead with the hips slightly (small pike of the body) and sink downward a little with the shoulders. Get a feeling of beating past the bottom quickly and thus exploding out of the slightly piked body by leading hard with the heels into a long backward swing. It is a backward swing and not an upward swing. As the body rises above the bar in an extended position, the left hand is quickly shifted to the right where it supports the body while the right hand is brought backward to

Stutz

A good drill is to take a long swing, beating at the bottom and pushing off the bars with the arms and hands, and then dropping to the feet between the bars. When first learning this move it may be advisable to do the reverse stutz to a straddle seat position. A spotter can help by placing his hands under the bars and lifting upward under the performer's hips as the turn is executed.

50. *Underbar Somersault (Peach Basket) to Upper-Arm Support Position.* Start this stunt from a standing position between the bars with the hands grasping the inside of the bars. Jump upward and after reaching the top of your height, fall backward with the arms straight and pike the body. When the body passes the bottom of the downward swing and starts up, extend into an arch and at the same time pull with the hands. As the hips rise above the bars release the hands and swing the arms up in between and over the parallel

the left bar. There should be a moment of weightlessness during this turn. Don't drop the hips as the turn is made but instead try to keep the body stretched.

Stutz to Handstand

Back Uprise to Reverse Stutz

bars, landing on the upper arms and allowing the body to swing forward naturally.

This stunt is actually a preliminary one for the more advanced stunt of an underbar somersault to a straight arm support position. Some pointers are: (1) Keep the hips high throughout the stunt. Do not let them drop too far backward and below the bars; (2) when underneath the bar and executing the last part of the stunt, be sure not to release the hands too soon. An early release of the hands causes the body to travel and prevents a neat-looking finish to the stunt.

51. *Underbar Somersault to Handstand (Felgaufschwung).* This is best learned by executing a cast to the armpits several times, with each attempt landing higher on the back of the arms in the direction of the shoulders. With the aid of a spotter, then do a cast to the back of the arms or even to a shoulder balance position. The spotter assists by placing a hand on the back and one on the chest and lifts the performer upward. When this action is well learned, try to place the hands on the top side of the bar just prior to landing on the shoulder balance position. The legs are extended straight upward above the shoulders, and when the hands regrasp the bar, continue the momentum upward into the handstand position. Do this many times with the help of the spotter

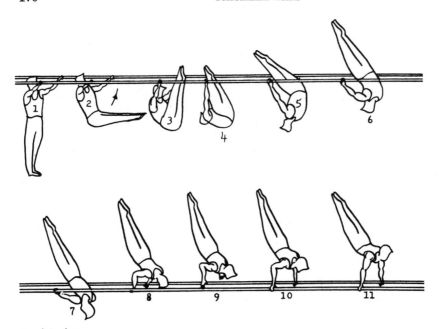

Peach Basket

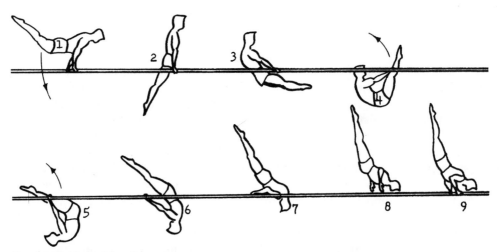

Peach Basket to Bent-Arm Support

and finally the complete move may be executed, with the hands regrasping the top side of the bar and the movement continuing upward into the handstand position. This is one of the finest moves on the parallel bars—good luck with it. When first learning it try it on the end of the bars facing out. Also, think of the felge as being similar to a free hip circle on the high bar. When doing the felge from a support position, it is suggested that the early drop technique be used; it employs a downward scoop of the legs with a backward push of the shoulders as the body falls downward into the action.

52. *Back Overbar Somersault to Catch.* This stunt is executed from a handstand. The body is then allowed to swing downward between the bars in a stretched position. This swing should be free and easy and definitely not tight or tense. The arms should be kept straight and the shoulders should be slightly forward of the hands.

After passing between the arms in a slightly piked position, the body should extend to an arched position, with the head and shoulders extended backward. This is the key spot in the entire stunt. Here we must watch for a few faults, which are as follows: (1) Do not lean forward or backward excessively; (2) Do not bend the arms; (3) Do not release the bars with your hands too soon;

Back Overbar Somersault

rather, allow them to be pulled off by the momentum of the swing.

After the hands are pulled from the bars by the upward and backward momentum of the body, they should reach backward for the catch position. As skill progresses the arms should have a feeling of dislocating with the hands simply rotating a couple of inches above the bar while executing the stunt. As soon as the bars are caught, allow the body to continue its natural swing and finish in the straight-arm support position.

In learning this stunt it is recommended that an overhead safety belt be used. This eliminates many unnecessary bruises and jolts in learning the fundamentals of the stunt. The overhead belt also overcomes fear of the stunt and develops confidence, which is so essential to the successful gymnast. It is also suggested that this stunt be done first on lowered parallel bars with the suggested height being several inches below the performer's armpits when he is standing on the mats.

A back somersault to catch can also be hand spotted with two spotters, one on each side of the performer. Example: The left bar spotter places his right hand on the performer's upper arm with the grip around the bicep (twist the arm so thumb faces downward). The left hand grasps the back of the performer's wrist. To spot, the spotters simply carry the performer over by lifting up on his bicep and turning his wrist over so the hand regrasps the bar. This should be done with the parallel bars low, about waist height.

53. *Back Somersault to Handstand.* This stunt is similar in action to the back somersault to catch except the swing is more forcefully upward and slightly for-

ward with the hips and the arms rotated quickly so that a fast regrasp is executed to this handstand position. It is most advisable to execute this stunt in a belt many times prior to attempting alone.

54. *Back Overbar Somersault Dismount.* This stunt is also similar in action to the back overbar somersault to catch except that the flip is done off to the side and subsequently over one bar to a standing position on the mat. The same upward thrust of the chest and body is necessary, but at this point the left arm pushes the body over the right bar. After

Double Back Somersault Dismount

Back Somersault to Handstand

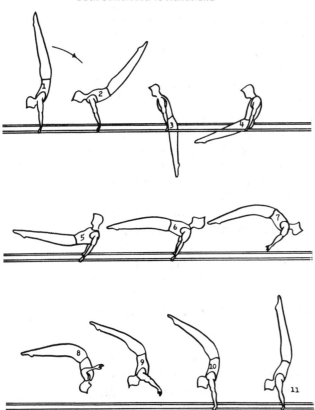

passing over this bar, the left hand quickly regrasps the right bar and steadies the body for the landing. This can be learned in an overhead safety belt with the spotter pulling one rope somewhat more strongly, which in turn assists the performer in passing over the dismount bar. This can also be hand spotted by pulling the performer's sweatshirt at his upper arm as he executes the back somersault.

55. *Streuli.* The basic action of the streuli is a backward roll on the upper arms and then an upward shooting action of the body, finishing in a support position on the hands. As you swing through the bottom, dip the shoulders slightly, and when the legs approach the level of the bars, lift the chest upward, and hold the head back, pushing downward with the arms. Then quickly place the hands on the bars behind the shoulders and push the body upward, taking

advantage of the initial upward surge of the body. Preliminary stages of learning would include doing a simple backward roll to a shoulder balance, on to a straddle seat, then to a shoulder balance, and finally to pushing with the hands into a hand balance position. A good streuli movement passes through a handstand position or even holds it. Be sure to pike the body slightly as it swings upward from below the bar and then arch into the handstand.

56. *Diamidov (Full Twisting Stutz).* On the upward swing of the stutz movement, hold on with the left hand, release the right hand, and turn in the direction of the left arm. Bringing the right arm across the body, under the left arm, and back to the right-hand bar causes the body to execute a full twist. If you miss the stunt slightly, you will generally finish with the right hand on the same bar as the left hand and then drop down to the mats over the right bar. Hand spot-

ting seems to be the most advantageous method of spotting and is done as follows: The spotter stands on the two bars facing the performer and the performer lifts his legs upward toward the spotter's hands. The spotter crosses his arms with the right arm on top of the left arm; the right hand then grasps the performer's right ankle and the left hand grasps the left ankle. From here the spotter simply lifts the performer's legs upward and at the same time commences to uncross his arms, which of course twists the performer. The performer during this time holds on with his left hand, releases his right hand, and follows the twisting action activated and continued by the spotter. With the spotter holding the legs well in the air and the full twist near completion, the performer reaches back with his right hand to the right bar for the finish of the full twisting stutz. After many of these have been done to establish orientation with the stunt, then place two spotters on the outside of the right

Streuli (Back Roll to Handstand)

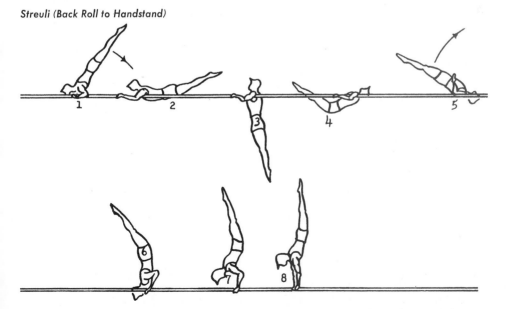

bar and one spotter on the left side on a raised platform at the height of the lowered parallel bars (waist height). Then the performer should try the stunt with the spotter on the raised platform catching his feet and the other two catching the performer in case he falls over the right bar. It can also be spotted using the twisting belt with one rope in front of the arm and the other rope in back of the other arm. It can also be tried on the end of the bars so the performer can land on a landing pad surrounding the uprights. A lead-up move is to do a half Diamidov, finishing in a cross handstand on the support rail.

Full Twisting Stutz

Routines

Creativity, imagination, and resourcefulness can be developed in the sport of gymnastics by the individual's construction and performance of his own sequence of stunts. The following are simply suggestions of combinations that can certainly be enlarged upon within the pupil's ability.*

1. Single leg cut on—swing legs to two straddle seat travels—side seat turn around to straddle seat—forward roll to another straddle seat—lift legs and swing backward to front dismount.

2. Jump to upper-arm hang—elevate legs to a pike position, then do a top kip to straddle seat—shoulder balance and roll forward to another straddle seat—by swinging one leg between the bars, execute a scissors change to straddle seat—forward roll to straddle seat—then swing legs to straddle dismount off the end of the bars.

3. Jump to upper-arm hang—front uprise—swing to shoulder balance—roll out to back uprise—single leg circle forward —shoulder balance—finish with a side dismount.

4. Kip on the end swinging legs backward—do a swinging dip travel in towards the center of the bars—swing legs backward and drop to upper-arm hang—execute a top kip to shoulder balance —roll forward to a back uprise to a rear dismount with half twist.

5. Jump to upper-arm hang—swing to back roll (layout) to straight arm support—continue on to cast below bars to upper-arm hang into a back uprise straddle cut and catch—immediate layback to upper arms again to front uprise to swing to handstand—pirouette into a stutz drop-

---

* For additional routines consider the Age Group Compulsory Exercises for Boys and Girls published by the United States Gymnastic Federation, Box 12713, Tuscon, Arizona 85711.

ping to the upper arms again into a front uprise and then a double rear dismount.

6. Peach basket to L position (hold)—press to handstand—swing down to stutz to cast below the bars to back uprise to straddle cut and catch and on up to a handstand—turn to one bar and execute a squat (stoop or straddle) dismount.

7. Peach basket to support then drop below bar to cast to support—immediate cut and catch to L position—hold—press to handstand—execute a stutz to cast below bar to upper arms to back uprise cut and catch—swing to handstand to back somersault dismount.

9

Horizontal Bar

Friedrich Jahn introduced the horizontal bar in Germany about 1812. In his famous playground he visualized the high bar as being like the branch of a tree. Knowing how children like to play on a strong level branch he thought that they would be keenly interested in working, swinging, and performing on this high bar. His expectations were fulfilled, because soon after its introduction it was well accepted by children and adults alike. Now it is still one of the most popular gymnastic events.

The horizontal bar (often called the high bar) is suspended parallel to the floor by two metal uprights 8 feet apart. Many bars are adjustable so that they can be lowered and raised to heights that best fit the needs. For competition the bar should be at a height of 8 feet 6⅜ inches (2600 millimeters).

In competition a routine is composed of continuous swinging and vaulting movements, including giant swings and grip changes.

VALUES

The specific values of working the horizontal bar are:

1. The high bar develops strength in upper parts of the body, especially the arms, shoulders, chest, and back muscles.

2. A good grip with the hands is essential to working the high bar. Constant work will strengthen the fingers and hands and insure a good grip.

3. Because of the rapid circling of the bar by the performer, a sense of relocation must be developed to reduce any dizziness caused by this action.

4. Courage and confidence in the ability to handle the body is developed from working at a considerable height with the body weight supported only by the strength of the fingers.

5. Rhythm and coordination are developed through constant practice, which in turn reduce the demand for great strength in many stunts.

ORGANIZATION

Area and Equipment

The area required for the horizontal bar is fixed in that it uses fittings in the floor when raised, although some models are completely portable and require no floor plates. Much thought should go into the placing of these fittings when they are put into the floor for the first time. Proper placing will prevent interference with other activities that may be conducted at the same time. Several styles of high bars are available. The wall type, which is supported by cables on one side and the wall on the other side, is easily taken down and stored against the wall. It does have a drawback in that work must be performed close to a wall. Other styles are supported on both sides by cables, which may come from the ceiling or entirely from the floor. These possibly take up more floor space but are clear of building obstructions.

Mats should be used under the high bar and should extend a minimum of 10 feet on either side of the bar. The area should be clear of obstructions for about 20 feet on either side of the bar, and the ceiling should be at least 17 to 20 feet high depending upon the height of the students.

Teaching Methods

Only one person should work the high bar at one time. Thus the mass method of instruction will not work well, as most schools will not have more than two high bars. If missed the first time, many of the beginning stunts can be tried several times without dismounting from the bar, but this could make the class proceed slowly. However, high bar work requires a great deal of energy and wear on the hands, which calls for longer rest periods between stunts. Often it is advisable to teach two stunts at a time to conserve strength. For example, a person may mount by means of a single knee swing-up. While he is in this position, he may as well try a single knee circle backward rather than merely swinging down from the bar. Thus, the squad method of instruction best fits this activity. Probably the high bar will be one teaching station of a gymnastics unit with the squads rotating during the period.

The high bar can be supervised best from underneath the bar along one upright. From this position the instructor is able to see the mistakes as they are made, give manual assistance when needed, and closely spot the performer.

Evaluation of high bar work is easily done by means of a stunt chart. Competitive routines would also be useful in evaluating more advanced classes.

Safety

Great care should be exercised in maintaining safety on the high bar. Because the bar is fairly high off the floor and the activity involves swinging around the bar supported most of the time only by the hands, the danger of falling can be great. This is not to say that the high bar is a dangerous piece of equipment, but it requires close adherence to the safety rules. In many cases the moves do not progress gradually, so each one must be thoroughly learned before you proceed. It is highly important that the skills be tried in an orderly, progressive manner. The instructor should always be at hand to assist the performer through the learning stages of the stunts.

The following is a list of safety rules for working the high bar:

1. Check the cables and make sure they have been attached securely. This should apply also to the nuts and bolts holding the bar in place and the turnbuckles on the cables.

2. Use plenty of mats around the bar for safety and dismounting purposes.

3. Always use high bar chalk (carbonate of magnesium) on the hands.

4. Keep the bar clean of excessive chalk and rust by using emory paper or steel wool to rub the bar.

5. Grasp the bar with the thumbs circling the bar in one direction and the fingers in the other.

6. With a few exceptions, always go around the bar in the direction in which the thumbs point.

7. Always have at least one spotter while learning new stunts to prevent slips or falls. Two spotters are preferred, and one should be the instructor.

8. In working on an adjustable bar, work low at first and gradually increase the height.

9. It is advisable to work the bar for short periods of time because the wear and friction on the hands causes blisters that often tear. When the hands are sore it is suggested that they be soaked in warm water and then rubbed with skin ointment.

10. It is suggested that hand guards be worn to prevent unnecessary blistering and tearing. These hand guards may be of leather, lamp wick material, or gauze.

PROGRAM OF INSTRUCTION

Instruction on the horizontal bar involves three basic steps:

1. *Individual moves.*

2. *Combinations.* As a person learns a new move he should be challenged to combine it with another as smoothly as possible. Because a skill must be learned well in order to combine it with another, the use of combinations in the teaching progression stresses proper execution and increases the safety of performance. In addition, the smaller combinations serve as building blocks for longer routines. Combinations can be suggested by the instructor or coach or can be created by the performer.

3. *Routines.* Ultimately, a pupil should strive to combine moves into a routine. Competition is based on routines, required or optional. The approach to optional routines is one of problem solving. Certain requirements involving the types and number of movements are presented as a problem for the performer to solve creatively within his own capabilities. The instructor, coach, and pupil can coordinate their thoughts on the development of a particular routine. For sample routines refer to the end of the chapter.

Two types of grips are normally used: the overhand, or regular, grip and the underhand, or reverse, grip. On the regular grip the hands circle the bar with the fingers going over the top of the bar and the backs of the hands facing the performer. In the reverse grip the hands circle under the bar with the palms of the hands facing the performer. Less commonly used is a mixed grip, which

Regular Grip

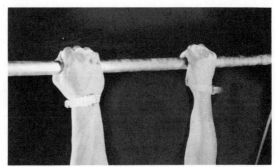

Reverse Grip

consists of one hand in the overhand grip and the other hand in the underhand grip. Normally the bar is grasped with the hands shoulder width apart. However, for a few stunts a wider or narrower grasp may be desirable.

While first working the horizontal bar it is advisable, if possible, to lower the bar to approximately shoulder height. Later, as skill progresses and as the stunts demand, the bar may be elevated to the competitive height.

Low Bar

Skills are listed in recommended order of learning.

1. *Front Support Mount.* Stand in front of the bar at shoulder height and grasp it with a regular grip. Jump upward, pulling with the arms, and finish in a front rest position on the bar, supporting the body with the arms, hips resting on the bar. After jumping up to

Front Support Mount

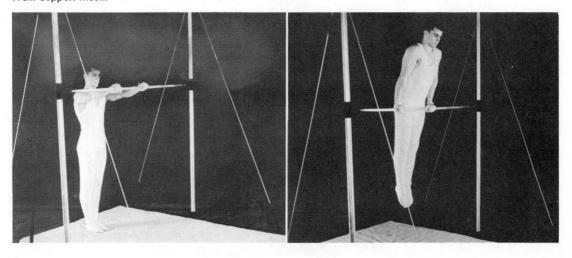

a front support position, the performer may do a half forward hip circle to a position of standing on the mats below the bar.

2. *Back Dismount.* From a front support position swing the legs forward under the bar slightly; then swing them backward, and at the same time push with the hands and release the grip. Keep the body in a vertical position as you drop to the feet, and flex the knees slightly upon landing.

3. *Underswing Dismount.* Grasp the bar at shoulder height in a regular grip, keeping the arms straight away from the

Underswing Dismount

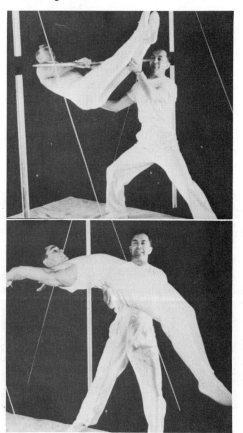

bar. Swing one leg up toward the bar and lean backward with the upper body. Bring the other leg up promptly and shoot both feet beyond and above the bar. Continue the flight of the body into an arched position by pulling up with the arms. Finally push with the hands as you release the bar and finish in a standing position. This stunt may be done from a front support position by swinging the feet forward under the bar while keeping the hips near the bar. When the body is below the bar, shoot the feet upward and forward into the underswing dismount.

4. *Skin the Cat.* Using a regular grip, pull the legs up and between the arms and the bar. Continue pulling the feet between the arms and on over as far as they will go into the skin-the-cat position. Be sure to keep the knees close to the chest for better control of the movement. Return to original position by pulling the legs back up between the arms and under the bar.

5. *Knee Hang.* Hang under the bar with an overhand grip and bring one leg up in between the arms and circle the knee over bar. This can also be done with both knees over the bar, releasing the hands.

6. *Single Knee Swing Up.* Hang under the bar with one knee over the bar in a single knee hang position. The knee may be between the arms or on the outside of the arms. Swing the free leg forward and downward. Pull with the arms and allow the body to swing up to a support position on top of the bar. After this has been learned from the hanging position, it may be attempted from a swing, the knee being placed into position at the front end of the swing.

Single-Knee Swing Up

This move can be attempted from the top of the bar in a single knee support position. From here, drop backward below the bar, allowing the body to swing freely. On the return swing, kick the free leg downward and execute the single knee swing up. If you are having difficulty, try the opposite knee.

7. *Single Knee Circle Backward.* From a single knee support position on top of the bar swing the free leg backward and push the body up slightly away from the bars. Hook the back of the knee to the bar and continue the swing of the leg downward and under the bar. Lean backward with the head and shoulders throughout the circle, and near the finish of the move, pull strongly with the arms to end on top of the bar again.

For greater difficulty, this stunt can be performed with a straight leg instead of hooking the knee to the bar.

Single-Knee Circle Backward

Single-Knee Circle Forward

8. *Single Knee Circle Forward.* Same as the backward circle but in the forward direction. Be sure the hands are in a reverse grip position. Push up and away from the bar at the beginning and lead with the head as the circle is attempted.

For greater difficulty, this stunt can be performed with a straight leg instead of hooking the knee to the bar. Also, try a forward knee circle and after nearly completing it, change the hands to an overgrip and immediately fall backward into a single knee circle backward.

9. *Crotch Circle (Pinwheel).* Sit sideways on the bar with the legs straddling and the hands grasping the bar in front of the body. From this position lean to the right and circle around the bar in a pinwheel manner. Stretch the body out as the circle starts, then pull with the arms and flex the body slightly during the last part of the circle in order to complete the pinwheel to a sitting position again.

10. *Hip Pullover (Belly Grind).* Stand facing the bar and grasp it in a regular grip. Pull the chest into the bar and kick the legs up and over the top of the bar. Continue to pull with the arms and finish in a front support position.

11. *Back Hip Circle.* Start from a front support position. Flex the hips slightly and then extend the legs backward away from the bar slightly. Then allow the legs to swing back toward the bar and as the abdomen strikes the bar, pike the body and continue swinging the legs under and around to the other side. Pull with the arms and complete the circle of the body around the bar, shifting the wrists to finish in a front support position again. For greater difficulty, try to perform with the body free of the bar.

12. *Double Knee Circle Backward.* Start from a sitting position on the bar with the hands close to the hips in a regular grip. Raise the body slightly. Shift the hips backward, catching the bar at the knees, and swing down and under the bar. Hold tightly with the hands, keep the knees flexed, and continue the double knee circle backward. When the hips pass the uprights and

Back Hip Circle

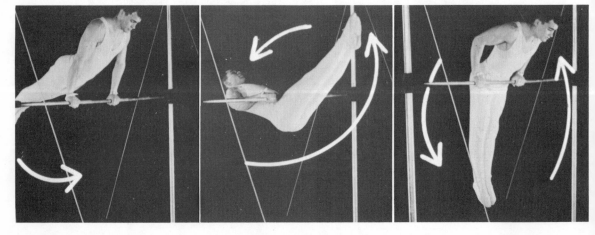

Double-Leg Circle Backward

start the last half of the circle, pull strongly with the arms and try to thrust the hips over the top of the bar. Near the completion of the stunt, shift the wrists so the hands are on top of the bar to give added support. Finish in the starting position of sitting on top of the bar.

13. *Hock Swing Dismount.* Hang by the knees and swing back and forth a couple of times to build up a swing. This swing is obtained by flexing slightly, bringing the arms up toward the thighs, and then reaching out with the arms and arching the upper body. After a couple of swings, the dismount is done after passing the uprights while the body is at the peak of the front end of the swing. Lift the head and arms up, release the knees from the bar, flex the hips, and drop to the feet.

14. *Hock Swing with Half Twist.* As you swing up into the dismount, turn the head and shoulders back into the direction of the bar. The knees are then released, and the feet drop down toward the mat with the hips following the twist-

ing action started by the head and shoulder. The dismount with the half twist is completed by landing on the mat in a standing position facing the bar. The hands may be placed on the bar for added balance.

15. *Front Hip Circle.* Start from a front support position. Straighten the arms and elevate the chest so that the

Start of Front Hip Circle

thighs are resting on the bar. Fall forward, and as the chest passes below the level of the bar, pull hard with the arms and continue the circle around the bar. Shift the wrists at the end so that the front support position is reached again. Try to keep the body in contact with the bar throughout the circle.

High Bar Skills

Because you may want to work on a higher bar, it may be wise to give a few hints about swinging and dismounting. The preceding moves can be performed on the higher bar, and they would be a good introduction to the increased height. Several of the following moves should be learned on the low bar before trying them on the higher bar.

1. *Swing and Dismount.* Learning the proper technique of obtaining a swing and of dismounting at the right moment on the back end of the swing is a valuable skill to learn, especially for beginners for whom it is the safest dismount. To obtain a swing from an ordinary hanging position, pull the body up toward the bar by a chinning action and at the same time lift the legs upward toward the bar. As the legs are lifted up above the level of the bar, extend them outward by pushing with the arms and force an arch in the back. This action should provide a smooth, even swing. The dismount is done at the back end of the swing. As the body swings by the uprights, pull slightly with the arms in an attempt to slow the swing a little and at the same time elevate the shoulders and try to keep the legs down as much as possible. This should have the effect of forcing the body into a vertical position. When the end of the back-

ward swing is reached, the dismount is executed with a slight push of the hands and the subsequent drop to the feet.

2. *Kip.* Swing on the bar, and toward the front end of the swing, arch the body. After reaching the end of the front swing, bring the feet up toward the bar. When the feet reach the bar and the hips are underneath it on the backswing, forcefully extend the legs upward and forward and pull hard with the arms. This kick and pull should bring the body up and forward into a straight-arm support position above the bar. The spotter may assist by pushing under the hips as the performer executes the kick action. An important item to remember is to wait until the body starts its backward movement before bringing the legs up for the kip. Many beginners bring their legs up too early and end up by hitting the bar with the abdomen or forcing the body back away from the bar.

LAND DRILL FOR KIP. A land drill that may be used in teaching the kip is to have the class lie on the floor or on mats with their legs raised and hands up near the ankles. The hands should pretend to be holding an imaginary bar. On a command all should sit up by extending the legs, raising the shoulders up to a sitting position, and at the same time running the hands along the legs toward the hips. This emphasizes the need to keep the legs near the bar throughout the kipping action of the stunt. If wands or broomsticks are available, these may be placed in the hands and drawn toward the hips as the sit-up is completed.

LOW BAR KIP. Another means of learning a kip is to work with the bar lowered to shoulder height. Start facing the bar

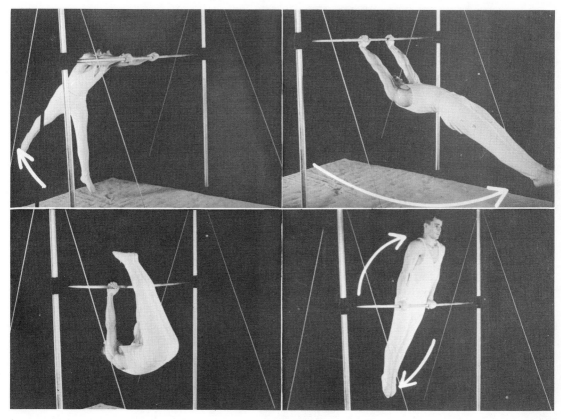

Kip

with the hands in an overhand grip and at straight-arm's distance. Jump up slightly with a pike of the body and then shoot the legs forward along the mats under the bar. At the end of the forward glide, with the body completely extended, drop one foot down to the mat and get a push with this foot while lifting the other foot toward the bar (see first picture). After this, tap with the lower foot then bring it up also, attempting to catch up to the other foot. When both feet reach the bar and the hips are under the bar, kick the legs upward and outward and at the same time pull hard with the arms and execute the kipping action to a straight-arm support position above the bar (see second picture).

A preliminary step to learning the low bar kip is to perform a single-leg kip up, keeping the legs straight and off the bar throughout the stunt. This forces the wrist action and pull, which is essential for the kip.

3. *Circus Kip.* Another variation of a kip is commonly called a "circus kip." This consists in starting with a short swing and at the back end lifting the hips slightly, forcing a small pike in the body. After this pike, swing forward,

Tapping of Foot on Low Bar Kip

One-Two Action of Kip

This extension and pull should snap the body upward into a straight-arm support position above the bar. A spotter can be of great assistance by pushing under the hips.

4. *Drop Kip.* From a straight-arm support position above the bar, swing backward and downward in a pike position, keeping the feet near the bar while swinging. Allow the hips to swing, forward and then backward. As the hips swing back, kick the legs upward and pull with the arms, finishing in a straight-arm support position.

5. *Back Uprise.* Obtain a high swing by lifting the legs up toward the bar and then casting them outward, and at the same time push with the arms and extend the body away from the bar. Swing through the bottom of the swing, and just prior to the end of the backward swing, pike slightly with the hips and pull hard with the arms. This pull and piking action should lift the body up into the bar into a straight-arm support position. A backward hip circle often follows the completion of this stunt.

6. *Seat Rise.* On the forward end of a swing, bring both legs between the arms in either a tuck position or straight-leg position. As the body swings under the bar, pull hard with the arms and shoot the feet up and over the bar, keeping the body in a pike position. Finish in a sitting position on the bar, supporting the body with the hands and the back of the thighs.

7. *Seat Rise Dismount.* This is similar to the seat rise mount, except after reaching the top of the mount continue moving the body over the bar and land in a

extending the legs downward forcefully. This extension or beat should force an arch in the body as it swings forward. As the body swings backward, the legs are lifted up sharply toward the bar and at the same time the arms pull strongly.

Seat Rise

complete circle, holding on with the feet and hands. Keep constant pressure on the bar with the feet while circling the bar. During the latter part of the circle, pull in slightly and even bend the knees if necessary in order to complete the backward sole circle. You can execute this as a dismount by releasing your grip and pushing forward off the bar with your feet just when you have almost completed the full sole circle. As the grip is released, lift your shoulders and chest to achieve an upright position before landing on the mat.

A variation of the sole circle backward is as follows: After doing about half of the circle, release the feet from the bar and extend them outward in front of the bar. Then release the right hand and make a half turn on the left arm. After the half turn is completed, grasp the bar with the right hand in an overgrip. From here you can swing forward, changing the grip to either an over- or undergrip, and then do a kip or some other suitable stunt.

standing position on the mat on the other side of the bar. A stronger shoot of the legs over the top of the bar and a harder pull of the arms are necessary in order to carry the entire body into the dismount.

8. *Sole Circle Backward.* Start from a front straight-arm support position. Flex the body slightly and then whip the legs up and place the feet on the bar outside the hands in a straddle position. From this position fall backward and make a

9. *Sole Circle Forward.* Similar to the backward sole circle except the motion

Sole Circle Backward

Sole Circle Dismount

the feet to ride up part way in the back-swing and then ride downward under the bar with the body remaining in a pike position. Just as the bottom of the swing is reached and the hips start to swing forward, extend the body into an arched position with the head and shoulders pulling back and the legs extended downward. The hands shift as quickly as possible from a hanging position to a support position on top of the bar. Continue the reverse kip action until the body is in a back support position or a sitting position on top of the bar.

11. *Stem Rise.* Grasp the bar in reverse grip and on the backswing pull the body up towards the bar. Bring the legs up and around the bar and then extend them upward into almost a partial handstand and continue to push into a power swing. To prevent the feeling of slipping off, shift the wrists so that the fingers encircle the top of the bar.

12. *Cast Cross Over to Back Uprise.* Start from a straight-arm front support position with the hands in a regular grip. Flex the hips slightly and then extend the body backward and upward; at the same time reach across the left hand with the right hand and grasp the bar on the left side of the hand. With the arms completely extended and the body stretched out, swing the body under the bar. After the body has swung under the bar, then turn naturally to the right in an untwisting action of the arms and at the same time pull with both arms. After the pull, release the left hand first and regrasp the bar in a regular grip and then do the same with the right hand. Continue to pull with the hands and complete the back uprise part of the stunt into a front support position on top

is forward. Start from the straight-arm support position with the hands in a reverse grip. Whip the legs into a straddle position on the bar and from this position fall forward into a forward sole circle. Keep a constant pressure on the bar with the feet and pull strongly with the arms near the finish of the stunt. This stunt fits nicely between two reverse giant swings.

10. *Reverse Kip.* The first part is like the swing into the seat rise mount. Allow

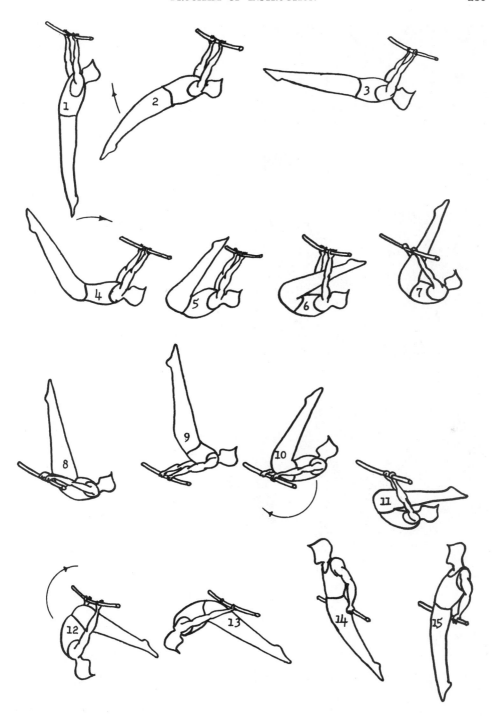

Reverse Kip

Stem Rise

of the bar. Often a back hip circle will follow this move, as in the case of the ordinary back uprise.

13. *Half Giant Swing.* The regular half giant swing is started by grasping the bar with a regular grip and executing a power swing. On the forward part of the swing bring the legs up and over the

top of the bar. At the same time shift the hands from a hanging position to a support position on top of the bar. If this change of the hands is done soon enough, the arms then catch the weight of the body and prevent unnecessary jolting of the abdomen while completing the last part of the half giant.

An excellent practice for learning the shifting of the wrist from a hang to a support is to do free hip circles. This is simply a back hip circle with the body free of the bar while going through the backward circle. The skill is started as an ordinary backward hip circle but the hands follow the stunt quickly and the weight remains constantly on them, thus allowing the performer to hold the thighs away from the bar. This same action once learned is used to do the half giant swing finish. After the under-bar swing into a half giant has been tried a few times, the half giant may be tried from a support position on top of the bar. Cast the legs up and away from the bar and swing the extended body downward into the half giant circle. Shift the wrists early and catch the weight of the body as it completes its half giant action. Do this several times and as skill improves hold a slight arch throughout the half giant and execute a graceful back hip circle in finishing the stunt.

14. *Regular Giant Swing.* After the regular half giant is learned, the complete regular giant swing may be tried. This entails a high cast from the support position and a stronger swing throughout the stunt. A hard pull with the hands and a strong lift of the hips upward after the body circles through the bottom of the swing is essential. Shift the wrists and continue circling the

Half Giant Swing

a lead-up stunt for learning the reverse giant swing. This stunt is simply called the reverse half giant swing. Start from a front support position on top of the bar with the hands in a reverse grip position. Flex the body slightly and then whip the legs over, the head and shoulders dropping slightly so that the entire body swings over parallel to the mats and then into a half giant swing action. The feet and legs stretch out and the arms are extended into a smooth downward swing. The body continues downward and under the bar and back up the other side. The half giant finish is similar to the back uprise finish in that after the body has passed the uprights and has almost reached its peak at the back swing, the hips are flexed a little and the arms pull strongly. This should bring the performer up to a straight-arm support position above the bar as at the beginning.

16. *Reverse Giant Swing.* The reverse giant swing is started from a front support position on top of the bar with the hands in reverse grip as in the reverse half giant swing. Flex the hips slightly and then whip the legs up and over the head, and at the same time extend the arms so that the full swing is started in an almost straight hand balance position. Continue the swing downward and under the bar with the body fully extended. On the back end of the swing, pull with the arms and lift the hips upward slightly. This will force the body upward into another hand balance position and from there on into another reverse giant swing. Remember not to kip or pull with the arms too soon, but instead wait for the moment when the body has almost reached the peak of the backward swing, then pull in toward the bar and allow

body upward through a handstand position. This stunt should be tried in a belt or with the aid of spotters. It is important to cast high in the beginning, swing strong under the bar, and lift the hips forcefully upward over the top of the bar. While learning, bend the arms slightly so that the body can pass over the top of the bar easier. Remember that the finished stunt is done with the arms straight, body extended and straight, toes pointed, and so on.

15. *Reverse Half Giant Swing.* As in learning the regular giant swing, there is

Reverse Giant Swing

the shoulders and head to shift over the bar and the feet to swing upward into the handstand position.

17. *Squat Dismount.* From a reverse giant swing, when the legs are rising

Reverse Giant Swing with Overhead Belt

above the horizontal bar, quickly pull the knees in toward the chest, bending the legs, and pass them through the arms above the bar. Push off with the hands, keeping head and chest up, and continue on downward to a standing position on mats. This also can be done in a straddle position while passing over the bar.

18. *Straddle Dismount from Kip.* Execute a regular kip and then lift the hips up above the bar, at the same time bringing the legs sharply into a straddle position over the bar. Be sure to get a good push with the hands while straddling over the bar and keep the head and shoulders up as much as possible.

19. *Regular Flyaway.* A regular flyaway from the horizontal bar is one of the prettiest and yet one of the more difficult dismounts to master. Perhaps one of the easiest methods of learning this stunt is to use the "skin-the-cat" approach. By this is meant that the first time a performer tries a flyaway he should simply hang on the bar and then pull the legs up and between the arms into a skin-the-cat position and then drop off to the feet. After a few times the stunt is then tried with a small swing but at all times the principle is the same in that a quick skin the cat is performed. The knees are bent and a slight pull of the arms is effected. This principle is continued with the swing slightly increased with each try. Upon gaining confidence and sureness, the flyaway is tried with more swing, later from a cast, and finally from a giant swing. As swing increases, the body is extended to a layout position instead of a tuck. The spotters can assist by grasping the performer's wrists and helping him through the early stages of the dismount.

Straddle Dismount from Kip

the body swings downward, pike slightly, and on passing the uprights thrust the legs and hips into the air. At this time release the hands, duck the head, and turn a reverse somersault in the air, landing on the feet. This may be done with the body in a tuck or pike position. In learning this dismount an overhead safety belt is recommended. Try this stunt at first from a high power swing with the hands in a regular grip. A good spot to look for at the time for releasing

Regular Flyaway

Another method of learning the flyaway is to swing on the bar with an overhead safety belt and then to drop at the forward end of the swing straight downward with the feet. Increase the height at each attempt, thrusting the hips forward and pushing with the hands. After several of these have been tried, then from a cast off the bar, swing outward and upward and attempt simply to sit in the air with the spotter holding the body above the mats. The performer may either tip over backward or extend forward to the feet. This feeling of lofting the body upward into a backdrop or sitting position with the legs above the chest is important in learning the flyaway. Remember on this regular flyaway on the initial downward swing to assume a small pike of the body with the chest hollow and then straighten out prior to swinging past the uprights. Then thrust the chest upward pushing backwards with the hands.

20. *Reverse Flyaway.* This is normally done from a reverse giant swing. After

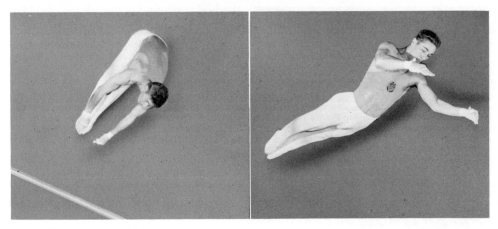

Regular Flyaway, Without Belt

the hands is a chalked line on the mat directly below the high bar. When you see this line, release the bar and the somersault is commenced.

After the technique of dropping and turning over is controlled, you can execute the reverse flyaway first from a cast from the top side of the bar, with the hands in a reverse grip position and yet still in the safety belt. Remember, do not pull in toward the bar upon releasing it and lift the hips and legs upward for maximum height and flight.

This same stunt can be done with a half twist, which is executed after the reverse somersault has been started. Another method, which also includes a half twist, is to execute a barani-type dismount, involving an early twist from the bar and a barani movement to the feet.

21. *Vault*. This stunt consists of a rear vault over the top of the bar with a releasing of the hands and then regrasping with both hands. This may be learned from a power swing, with the performer in an overhead safety belt. Facing the bar, grasp the bar with the right hand in an overgrip and the left

hand in an undergrip. So that the legs may pass conveniently over the length of the bar, the hands should grasp the bar toward the right upright. With the hands fairly close together and the safety belt securely fastened around the waist, execute a high back uprise swing. As the legs swing past the uprights, the body turns and the legs are elevated upward to assume a pike position with the legs parallel to the bar. At the same time, the arms continue to pull and then thrust the body up and over the bar. Remember to kick the feet away from the bar almost partially backward, which then extends the body properly to an open piked position while passing over the bar. As you pass over the bar, release the grip of the hands and turn the body inward (which is left) toward the bar, passing the hands in front of the chest, and quickly regrasp the bar. This stunt once learned is used occasionally as a mount, although the vault may more often be used within a routine with the technique varying as follows:

From a reverse giant swing, when the body flows upward approaching the handstand position and slows to a stalled position, the left hand is at this time changed from a reverse grip to a regular grip and the right hand is passed under the left arm and grasps the bar in a reverse grip. Then the body reverses direction and swings back down under the bar, turning to the left. At this point the performer finds himself in a position similar to a back uprise into a vault, thus the action continues to the regrasping of the bar. This method of doing a vault from a reverse giant swing has been found to be safe and effective.

The vault may also be done from a reverse giant swing with the right hand changing from a reverse grip to a regular grip after the body has passed over the top of the bar. With this mixed grip, one then swings downward and simply executes a back uprise into the vault.

Another method is out of regular giant swings. After the body has passed over the bar, reach under the left hand with the right hand and regrasp the bar in a reverse grip. The body continues downward and turns to the left, and after

Vault

passing the uprights the performer again finds himself in a position similar to a back uprise vault.

22. *Regular Giant Cross-Over to Reverse Giant Swings.* As the performer passes over the bar in a regular giant swing, the right hand crosses over the left arm and grasps the bar in a regular grip near the left hand. The body continues in this crossed-arm position downward and past the uprights. A strong thrust through the bottom is very important. At this time the body turns to the right and swings upward to a reverse giant position, and at the same time the left hand is released and regrasps in a reverse grip position. After this exchange of the hands, the performer continues over the top in a reverse giant swing.

23. *Reverse Giant Swing Pirouette to a Regular Giant.* As you reach a handstand while doing a reverse giant swing, push with the right hand and turn the body to the left. To complete the pirouette, grasp the bar with the right hand in a regular grip and continue downward in a regular giant swing. Do the pirouette as you complete the extension from the pike position. Keep the support arm angle as straight as possible. The pirouette should have a feeling of lifting upward and not forward. This technique can be tried on the floor.

24. *Straddle Cut and Catch.* At the forward end of a swing bring both legs upward between the arms in a pike position. When the body swings upward and reaches its peak, the legs are straddled out to the sides and the hands are released. After the legs have cleared the bar the hands then quickly regrasp the bar and the swing is continued. A good spotting technique is for the coach to stand directly behind the performer and away from the bar slightly so that if the performer misses the bar on the regrasp, the coach can catch him by the hips and place him safely onto the mat.

25. *Immediate Change (Blind Change) from Regular Giant Swing to Reverse Giant Swing.* From a regular giant swing, swing the body through the bottom and with a strong thrust of the legs upward and in the direction of the turn, execute a half turn of the body and finish on top of the bar in a reverse giant position. A good learning progression is to swing easily back and forth under the bar and at each forward end of the swing execute a half turn, changing the grip to a regular grip by changing one hand at a time. After each turn, allow the body to swing down through the bottom again, and on the forward end of the swing make another half turn. This is continued several times. As the technique improves the swing can be increased to the point where on one change the body may swing all the way upward into a handstand position and, with the hands in reverse grip, continue on over into a reverse giant swing.

26. *Dislocate.* On a reverse giant swing as the body swings above the bar toward the handstand position, bring the legs between the arms into a piked position. Keep the arms straight and pike deeply with the legs close to the chest. As the piked body swings downward push away from the bar and commence circling it. On the upward swing extend the legs forcefully overhead and push backward with the arms into a stretched dislocated position with the head back slightly. Continue on over the bar circling with

the hands in an L-grip position and finish at the back end of the swing by changing the hands quickly to a reverse or regular grip. You may also circle completely around the bar with the hands remaining in the L-grip position and thus do a dislocate into an eagle (L-grip) giant.

For learning this stunt an overhead safety belt is recommended, with the performer starting the stunt from a sitting position on top of the bar. With the hands in a reverse grip the performer swings his legs upward and away from the bar. This extends the body outward to approximately a 45° angle. The shoulders are dislocated and the swing continues downward with the hands in the dislocated or L position. The spotter attempts to hold the performer with the belt so that the dislocation of the shoulders will take place above the level of the bar, at which time the body weight is not fully supported by the shoulders and arms. After the dislocation, the spotter gently lowers the performer downward to prevent his grip from slipping.

Another method of doing the dislocation is using a reverse grip to power upward into almost a handstand position. From here, quickly bring the legs downward and between the arms either in a pike or tuck position. In this position the performer circles under the bar and on upward into the dislocate action.

Variations: Shoot into half twist is a variation of the dislocate stunt, and, as pictured, the half twist is done over the top of the bar and a regular giant swing position is assumed.

Another variation of the dislocate maneuver is to stoop in and proceed as if going into a dislocate, only do not

Dislocate

dislocate and continue around in the "undislocated" or inverted giant position. Notice the complete extension of the body at the bottom of the swing and then the tight pike as the performer passes over the top of the bar. Keep the arms at shoulder width. Spot this stunt numerous times using an overhead rigging and also with hand spotting prior to attempting it alone. The hand spotting can effectively be done by standing on a platform placed under the high bar near one upright.

27. *German Giant Swing*. From a rear support position on top of the bar with the hands in a regular grip, swing the legs upward and backward with the shoulders leaning backward slightly but kept as high as possible. The legs continue on over backward beyond the head with the arms pushing downward forcefully; the body, in the German position fully extended, swings downward and beyond the uprights. After passing the uprights, the legs are swung upward strongly into a pike position, and the per-

Eagle Giants

Shoot Into Half Twist

former continues on over to the top of the bar. Be sure to have a strong change of the grip on the latter part of the stunt from a hang to a support position. It is recommended that a safety (overhead) belt be used in learning this stunt. An-

other variation of this stunt is to pass through the first part of the German but on the upward swing, release the hands and execute a half twist. Upon completion of the half twist, regrasp the hands in a regular grip position and

Inverted Giant Swing

continue back downward to a kip. This can also be done to an immediate back hip circle.

28. *Hecht Dismount.* An advanced dismount involving flying over the top of the horizontal bar, which is spectacular and beautiful, is called the hecht dismount. As pictured, this dismount is performed out of a reverse giant swing. Notice the small pike of the body at the bottom of the swing and then the arch followed by still another pike prior to pushing off with the hands. With the proper momentum and beat, the performer should be able to pass over the bar in a complete layout position. It is highly recommended that this stunt be done numerous times in an overhead rigging. To get the feel of the hecht beat, have the gymnast hang on the bar with either grip and from behind push

German Giant Swing

him forward a little by placing your hands on the small of his back. Upon dropping him suddenly, you'll notice that the body swings down into a natural hecht beat.

29. *Veronin (Half Twisting Hecht Vault to Regrasp).* It is essential that a good hecht dismount be learned prior to trying the Veronin. On a reverse giant swing as the body swings over the top of the bar, extended forward as far as possible (stretched position) and near the bottom, pike the body and then whip the legs backward and upward as in the hecht dismount, but do it sooner since it is imperative that the body propel itself up and over rather than up and forward, as in the dismount. After the legs have extended backward and upward,

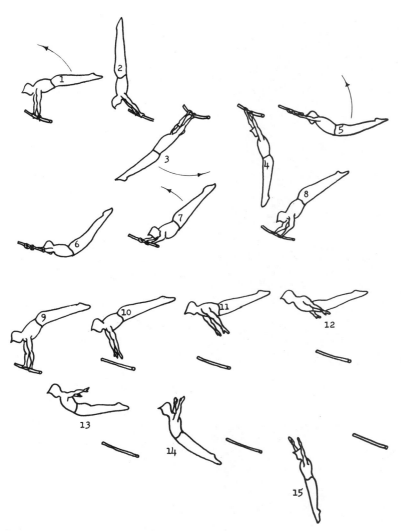

Hecht Dismount

pull down with the hands, release the bar, and assume a piked position with the body in passing over the bar. While passing over in this piked position turn toward the bar and regrasp with the hands. Prior to attempting this move try half turntables on the trampoline in a deep piked position.

30. *Endo Shoot*. As the handstand is approached on a reverse giant swing,

the legs are straddled and brought down on the outside of the arms. Push away from the bar allowing the body to make a full circle in this piked position. Remain in this straddle position all the way around and when the shoulders reach a position above the top of the bar, the legs then lift upward (in a manner similar to a straddle press on the parallel bars) to a reverse giant handstand posi-

Hecht Dismount (Straddle)

Veronin

tion. Good practice for learning this move is to do several straddle seat circles on the low bar.

31. *Stalder Shoot*. From a regular giant swing when the body and legs are almost over the top of the bar, bring the legs in toward the bar as if going into a sole circle, except thrust the feet beyond the bar to assume a straddle piked position. Pushing backward forcefully, swing deeply into a circle under the bar. Upon coming up the other side of the bar and with the hips high, lift the legs outward and upward into a handstand position and continue on into the regular giant swing. Keep the head in (chin towards the chest) and pike from the chest rather than from the hips. On the low bar a spotter can assist by lifting upward under the shoulders on the last phase of the circle. It is also helpful to practice many backward straddle seat circles on the low bar.

32. *Double Flyaway*. On the double flyaway, as the legs are thrust past the uprights the knees are brought forcefully upward into a tucked position in prepa-

Endo Shoot

Stalder

overhead belt and also try many double backs on the trampoline in an overhead belt. Another technique as a lead-up to the double flyaway is to do many one-and-a-quarter flyaways, landing in a back drop position on a high stack of soft cushions or landing pads. After complete orientation and confidence are gained through repeated tries, do the complete double flyaway with spotters and ample landing pads.

Routines

Creativity, imagination, and resourcefulness can be developed in the sport of gymnastics by the individual's construction and performance of his own se-

Kriskehre Into Stalder Shoot

Double Flyaway—Tucked

ration for the double somersault. The hips also are rotated under and around into the somersaulting action. After releasing the bar, keep the knees in a tucked position with the head back, grasp the shins with the hands, and continue the dismount toward the mats. In learning, try this stunt many times in an

Double Flyaway—Piked

circle—underswing dismount forward.

2. (Low Bar). Jump into single leg swing up—single leg circle backward—continuing swing under bar—single leg swing up—bring leg that is over bar back to a front support position—swing legs to back dismount.

3. Single leg swing up—bring other leg over to sitting position into a back double knee circle—drop below bar into a hock swing dismount.

4. Kip into a back hip circle—into under bar swing—execute half turn at front end of swing into a single leg swing up into a front leg circle—place backs of both knees on bar and execute a hock swing dismount with half twist.

5. Back uprise to back hip circle—underbar swing with half turn at front end of swing into kip—forward hip circle—cast to three-quarter regular giant swing—drop kip to sole circle dismount.

6. Reverse kip—drop back and bring legs between arms to drop kip—forward hip circle—cast back to a cross-over into a back uprise—back hip circle into underswing—dismount forward with a half turn.

Full Twisting Hecht Dismount

quence of stunts. The following are suggestions for combinations that can be enlarged upon within the pupil's ability.*

1. (Low Bar). Hip pullover—back hip

* For additional routines consider the Age Group Compulsory Exercises for Boys and Girls published by the United States Gymnastic Federation, Box 12713, Tuscon, Arizona 85711.

7. Back uprise to back hip circle—underbar swing to kip—cast into regular giant swings (2)—cross over to reverse giant swings (2)—jump change to back hip circle to drop kip—cast into a fly-away.

8. Jump to reverse grip—execute power swing and then reverse giant swing. After one reverse giant swing, stoop the legs between the arms and execute a dislocate—hop to reverse giant swing again—after one reverse giant swing execute a vault (either by turning one hand over as the body passes over the bar or by changing the hands on this side of the bar and then swinging back and under the bar for the vault—see vault description in text). After the vault do a reverse kip into a half German giant, executing a half twist to a regrasp of the bar (on the upward swing of the half German giant swing). From here do a kip into an immediate straddle dismount.

10

Women's Vaulting

In women's vaulting the vaults are performed over the horse from the side. After a running approach the performer takes off from a beat board, placing the hands on the middle of the horse, and vaults over the horse. For competition, each vault has a predetermined difficulty rating, and the performer is allowed two trials with the better one counting as her score. In judging, two phases of the vault are considered: (1) the flight, which includes arriving on the horse, and (2) the pushing off and afterflight of the vault, including the landing.

The approximate measurements of the horse are 5 feet 3 inches long and 14 inches wide, and the height of the horse from the mat to the top of the horse during the vaulting competition is 47 inches (1200 millimeters).

VALUES

The specific values of vaulting are:

1. Vaulting develops coordination, timing and agility.

2. It develops strength and power in the large muscle groups of the entire body.

3. It develops courage and confidence.

ORGANIZATION

To avoid repetition here it is suggested that reference be made to the lengthy discussion on vaulting in chapter 6. The same general principles apply for women in learning the correct techniques of springing from the beat board and over the horse.

It is suggested that the horse be set at a comfortable height for beginners. It is further suggested that a considerable amount of time be spent on practicing the correct fundamentals of taking off from the beat board. Be sure to post a spotter on the far side of the horse while practicing the vaults and, if available, have two spotters, one in the front and the other in the back of the horse.

Approach for Take-Off

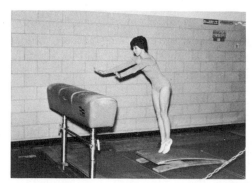

Take-Off

A good fundamental activity in learning proper vaulting technique is to have the gymnasts try layout dive-and-rolls from the beat board to a soft landing mat. Also have them do dive-and-rolls from the board over the horse to the landing mat. You may want to have them try vaulting off the trampoline into a layer of soft landing mats, as explained in the men's vaulting chapter.

Prevaulting Practice

Some fundamental vaulting skills that can be performed on the mats by a large group and serve as a lead-up to vaulting over the horse follow (for drawings of these skills see chapter 6 on men's vaulting).

1. From a front support position, spring to a tuck position and then stretch jump to a stand.

2. From a front support position, spring to a kneeling position and then jump to a stand.

3. From a front support position spring to a straddle stand then stretch jump to a stand.

4. From a front support position, spring to a wolf stand (half squat and half straddle), then stretch jump to a stand.

5. From a front support position, spring and swing the legs to the side, landing in a sitting position facing left or right side (rear vault lead-up).

6. Repeat skill 5, but land sitting in opposite direction.

7. From a front support position, spring and swing the legs to the side and under one arm. Land in sitting position facing forward (lead-up to side or flank vault).

8. Repeat skill 7, but swing legs to opposite side.

9. From a front support position, spring to a pike stand and then stretch jump to a stand.

10. From a front support position, spring to tuck position, rock forward to squat head balance, arch over to a bridge position, then straighten arms. Keep the body low during the arch-over.

PROGRAM OF INSTRUCTION

It is suggested that the following series of vaults be learned in the order given.

Squat Stand

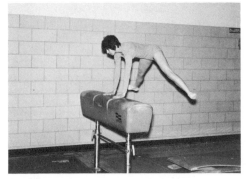

Straddle Vault

Squat Vault

1. *Squat Stand—Jump Off Dismount.* After the approach and take-off, place the hands on the horse and bring the legs up between the arms and stop in a squat stand position. From this position leap forward to the mat.

2. *Squat Vault.* Take off from the beat board, place hands on the horse, lift the hips and then bring the knees up between the arms. Push hard and fast with the arms, pass over the horse in a squat position, and land on the mat on the other side.

3. *Straddle Stand—Forward Jump Off.* Jump to a straddle stand on the horse, with the legs outside the arms. From this position, straighten up and jump forward to the mat.

Straddle Stand

Please keep in mind that many of these basic vaults are not used in competitive vaulting but serve their purpose as basic learning skills.

4. *Straddle Vault.* After the approach place the hands on the horse with the body in a slightly piked position, the hips higher than the shoulders, and the legs together and straight. After a quick hard push off the hands, the legs then straddle and the body straightens out for the landing. Keep the head and chest up and try to sail over the horse in a neat, straight position rather than in a low, forward-leaning position.

5. *Flank Vault.* This skill consists of passing over the horse with the side (flank) of the body closest to the horse. After the take-off, place both hands on the horse and lift the hips so the body is in a slightly piked position. Then shift the weight to one arm and lift the other arm. As the legs lift upward and over the horse extend the body forcefully so it assumes a straight line upward from the supporting arm. The supporting arm then pushes off the horse so the body lifts into the air and drops to the mat with the back toward the horse.

6. *Front Vault.* This is done somewhat like the flank vault only the front part of the body is turned toward the top of the horse while it is passing over it. Allow the feet and legs to lift into the air so that a graceful stretched position of the body is obtained. After obtaining a good push with the hands into the short afterflight, land on the mat with the side of the body facing the horse.

7. *Rear Vault.* This vault entails passing over the horse in a sitting position with the seat of the performer closest to the horse. Upon taking off, initiate a slight twist off the board, lift the legs to the side and pass them over the horse in a piked position. One arm contacts the horse slightly sooner than the other, with the hands placed on the horse parallel to its length. At the height of the vault the weight of the body rests on both arms. The toes should be higher than the head with the shoulders leaning slightly backward. As the legs drop toward the mat, push forcefully with the hands and extend the hips; the body will then straighten and land crosswise on the mat.

8. *Thief Vault.* This consists of taking off from one foot, lifting the other leg upward toward the take-off foot, and sailing over the horse in a sitting position. It is important to have the take-off board a comfortable distance away from the horse to allow the lead leg to swing upward without bending. The hands drop to the horse and push quickly downward and backward as the body continues on over to the mat. The feet are elevated as the hands touch the horse and a neat shoot forward is executed with the body straightening toward the landing.

9. *Stoop Vault, Bent Hips Ascent.* This vault is similar to the squat vault only the legs are kept straight instead of bent as they are brought through the arms. Also, the ascent to the vault itself is done with the body in pike position.

10. *Layout Stoop Vault.* This is similar to the stoop vault, bent hips ascent except the emphasis is on thrusting the body upward into a stretched position at a 45-degree angle prior to landing on the horse. When the hands touch the horse the stoop action is initiated. With a shrug of the shoulders keeping the arms straight the vaulter gets propelled off the horse into a final pike through and then extension of the body prior to landing.

11. *Handspring.* This consists of springing from the board and reaching forward with a stretched body towards the horse. The body should be at approximately a 45° angle when the hands contact the horse. With the center of gravity still moving upward the hands should push quickly and with a shrug of the shoulders the body should propel itself in a layout stretched position upward and over into the handspring. Keep the head between the arms and in line with the body until you drop toward the mats, and then bring the

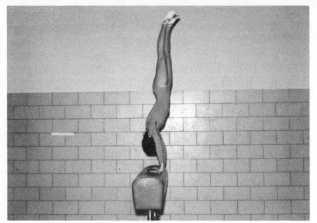

Handspring

hind the balls of the feet and the shoulders over the hips. The arms should be overhead diagonally and head in line with the body. Good landings take considerable practice, so spend adequate time on it.

COMPETITIVE VAULTING

The following series of figure drawings from the United States Gymnastic Federation Code of Points illustrates the competitive vaults along with their degrees of difficulty. Appreciation is extended to the USGF for their use.

head forward slightly in preparation for the landing. Upon landing bend the knees only slightly, with the hips be-

Table of Vaults and Their Values

Group I (Straight Vaults)

1 Hecht   10.00 points

2 Hecht with full turn or more   10.00 points

Group II (Handsprings, Yamashita)

3   Handspring   9.20 points

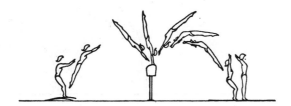

4   Yamashita   9.40 points

Group III (Turns Around Longitudinal Axis)

5   Cartwheel   9.00 points

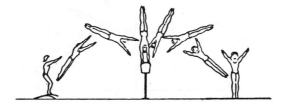

6   Cartwheel—¼ turn outward   9.40 points

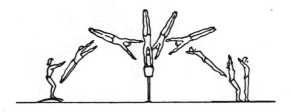

7 Cartwheel—½ turn outward   10.00 points

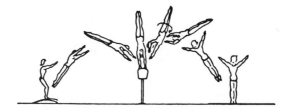

8 Cartwheel—¾ turn out (in same direction)   10.00 points

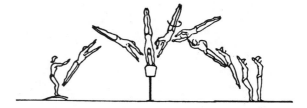

9 Cartwheel—full turn outward   10.00 points

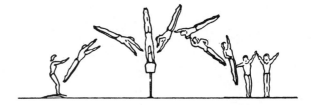

10 Handspring—full turn out   10.00 points

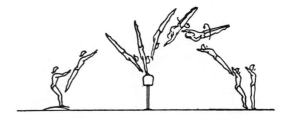

11   Handspring—1½ turn or more out   10.00 points

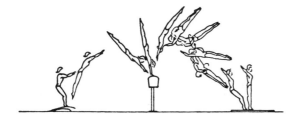

12   ½ turn into handspring—½ turn out   10.00 points

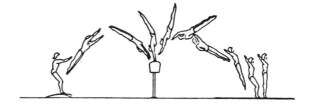

13   ½ turn into handspring—full turn out   10.00 points

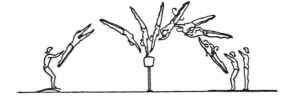

14   Full turn into handspring—handspring or Yamashita out   10.00 points

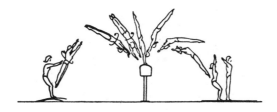

15   Full turn into handspring—full turn out   10.00 points

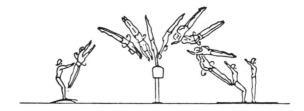

16   Yamashita—½ turn out   10.00 points

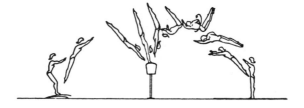

17   Yamashita—full turn out   10.00 points

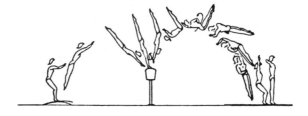

18   Yamashita—1½ or more turns out   10.00 points

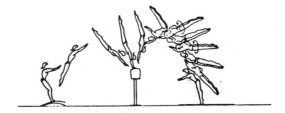

Group IV (Turns Around the Horizontal Axis)

19 Handspring—1½ forward tucked somersault out   10,00 points

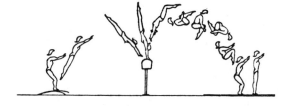

20 1½ forward tucked somersault to handspring—handspring out   10.00 points

21 1½ forward tucked somersault to handspring—1½ forward tucked somersault out 10.00 points

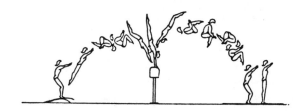

Group V (Combination of Turns Around More Than One Body Axis)

22   Cartwheel—1½ backward tucked somersault out (Tsukahara)   10.00 points

23   Cartwheel—1½ backward piked somersault out (Tsukahara)   10.00 points

24   ½ turn into handspring—1½ backward tucked somersault out   10.00 points

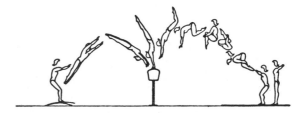

25 ½ turn into handspring—1½ backward piked somersault out   10.00 points

26 Cartwheel—1½ backward tucked somersault with ½ or full turn out   10.00 points

27 ½ turn into handspring—1½ backward tucked somersault with ½ or full turn out   10.00 points

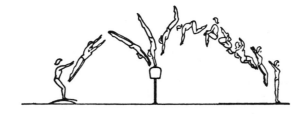

28   Cartwheel—1½ sideward tucked somersault out   10.00 points

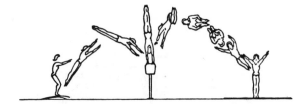

29   1½ forward tucked somersault—handspring with ½ or full turn out   10.00 points

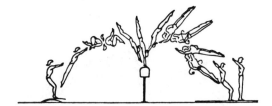

11

Uneven (Asymmetrical) Parallel Bars

The even parallel bars was an event in the women's gymnastic field for many years. The uneven (asymmetrical) bars were first introduced to the competitive world in 1936 and have been used continuously since the Olympic games in 1952. It was realized that the even bars involved a preponderance of support work and that the uneven bars offered greater possibilities for performing more varied moves and combinations. Since the change was made, the development of the event has been phenomenal, until now it is the most spectacular of the women's events.

The measurements of the uneven bars are:

Height of low bar: $59\frac{1}{16}''$ (1500 mm)
Height of high bar: $90\frac{9}{16}''$ (2300 mm)
Width between bars: $21\frac{1}{4}$–$30\frac{23}{32}''$ (540–780 mm)

A competitive routine on the uneven parallel bars should consist predominantly of kipping, swinging, and circling moves and releasing and regrasping moves, with support moves used only for momentary positions. A gymnast should work in both directions, above and below the bars, and use twisting movements.

VALUES

The uneven bars help develop

1. Strength and endurance in the arms and the upper body.

2. Confidence in one's ability to control the body while maneuvering through moves of moderate difficulty at substantial height.

3. A sense of balance and timing as the gymnast works from one bar to the other.

4. An ability to create a fine artistic exercise.

ORGANIZATION

Because some of the skills on the uneven parallel bars are similar to horizontal bar moves, a low horizontal bar may be helpful to supplement instruction. Having the horizontal bar lowered to about chest or shoulder height will provide for easier learning and safer spotting. The spotter should spot moves done on the higher bar from a position underneath that bar, as is done for the horizontal bar. It is preferable, while gymnasts are learning routines, that two spotters be used in order to cover safely the variety of moves. Be sure students progress slowly and surely so that the fundamental movements are mastered.

PROGRAM OF INSTRUCTION

Instruction on the uneven parallel bars involves three basic steps:

1. *Individual moves.*

2. *Combinations.* As a person learns a new move, she should be challenged to combine it with another stunt as smoothly as possible. Because a skill must be learned well in order to combine it with another, the use of combinations in the teaching progression stresses proper execution and increases the safety of performance. In addition, the smaller combinations serve as building blocks for longer routines. Combinations can be suggested by the instructor or coach or can be created by the performer.

3. *Routines.* Ultimately, a pupil should strive to combine skills into a routine. Competition is based on routines, required or optional. The approach to optional routines is one of problem solving. Certain requirements involving the types of movements are presented as a problem for the performer to solve creatively within her own capabilities. The instruc-

tor or coach and pupil can coordinate their thoughts on the development of a particular routine. For sample routines refer to the end of the chapter. Skills will be presented here for the uneven parallel bars.

The skills that can be done on the uneven parallel bars will be grouped into the following four divisions:

1. Mounts.

2. Moves on and around one bar.

3. Moves between bars.

4. Dismounts.

Mounts

1. *Jump to Straight-Arm Support.* Stand facing the low bar with the hands grasping the bar in a regular grip, hip distance apart. Jump upward toward the bar, finishing in a straight-arm support with the thighs resting on the bar, buttocks squeezed, arms straight, chest and head held high, legs straight, and toes pointed.

2. *Jump to Hang on High Bar—Shoot Over Low Bar.* Start from behind the high bar facing the low bar. Jump to a

Straight-Arm Support

regular grip on high bar and swing the legs forward into a slight pike position. Swing them quickly backward into a slight arch, and at the top of the backswing push down on the bar, lift the hips into the air, and bring the legs into a tucked position to shoot over the low bar. Finish in an extended position with the back of the thighs resting on the low bar. This mount can also be performed in the piked or in the straddle position. An additional variation is to raise only one leg over the bar, finishing in a stride support.

3. *Back Hip Pullover.* Start facing the low bar with the hands in a overgrip (regular), hip distance apart. Step under the bar, pulling the hips toward the bar, and lift one leg as the other leg pushes against the ground. Continue pulling the hips toward the bar as both legs come together in the air and continue to circle the bar. Finish in a straight-arm support.

4. *Jump to Hang on High Bar—Single Leg Stem Rise to High Bar.* Stand behind the high bar facing the low bar and jump up to grasp the high bar. Bring both legs up over the low bar and bend one leg, placing that foot on the bar with

Back Hip Pullover

the other leg extended forward. Bring the extended leg upward toward the high bar and execute a kip action, pushing with the foot on the bar, and pull with the arms to finish in a front support position facing the low bar.

5. *Jump to Hang on High Bar—Double Leg Stem Rise to High Bar.* Stand behind the high bar facing the low bar

Single-Leg Stem Rise

and jump up to grasp the high bar. Bring both legs up, placing the balls of the feet on the low bar, with knees flexed. Push with both feet and pull with straight arms to finish in a front support position on the high bar, facing the low bar.

6. *Jump to Squat Stand.* Start a few feet in front of the low bar. After an approach run and a 2-foot take-off (from the ground or a beat board), place both hands on top of the low bar, shoulder distance apart. Push down on the bar, drive the hips up into the air, and bend the knees up toward the chest so as to finish in a squat stand on top of the low bar. From here, the gymnast

Squat Stand Mount

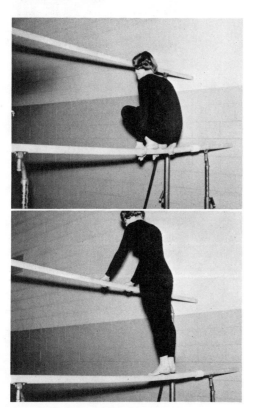

may rise to a straight standing position and grasp the high bar with both hands.

7. *Squat Vault Over Low Bar to Long Hang on High Bar.* This is very similar to the jump to squat stand mount except that upon contacting the low bar, the gymnast pushes down slightly and backwards, moving her body over the low bar and immediately catching the high bar with both hands. This mount can be performed in the straddle or piked position as well. A long hang kip can be executed following this mount, or if the high bar is caught in a mixed grip, a half turn into a drop kip may follow.

8. *Front Hip Circle Mount.* Start by facing the low bar. After an approach run and a 2-foot take-off from the beat board, jump to a high front support position, buttocks tight, chest held high, and thighs in contact with the bar. Arms may be extended above the head or may immediately assume contact with the bar. As the body begins to circle the bar, hold it in an extended position until the upper body passes below the horizontal. At this point pike deeply to speed up rotation and place the hands around the bar in a regular grip. Push down on the bar with straight arms, hollowing the chest. Finish in a straight-arm support.

9. *Glide Kip Mount.* Stand facing the low bar a few feet away with the arms held down by the sides. Bend the knees and push, driving the hips up into the air and slightly backward. At the same time reach toward the low bar in a regular grip, fully extending through the shoulders. The head should be held between the arms. From this pike position the body moves forward and under the bar, extending smoothly so as to finish in an extended position with the feet

Front Hip Circle Mount

13. *Glide Kip to Straddle Cut.* Similar to the glide kip into double-leg shoot-through except that as the body rises

Glide Kip

a few inches above the mat to the end of the forward swing. Bring the ankles quickly toward the bar and ride the legs up the bar until the bar reaches the hips. While the legs are riding up the bar, push down on the bar and round the back so as to get on top of the bar. Continue moving the legs backward until you finish in a front support position. The kip may also be performed in the straddle position. The legs are brought together at the end of the forward swing.

10. *Glide Kip—Catch High Bar.* This is performed in the same manner as the glide kip except that just as the hips come into contact with the bar the hands are released and reach for the high bar.

11. *Glide Kip Into Single-Leg Shoot-Through.* Same as the glide kip except as the ankles come toward the bar, one leg shoots between the hands so that the gymnast finishes in a stride support.

12. *Glide Kip Into Double-Leg Shoot-Through.* Similar to the single-leg shoot-through except that both legs shoot through the arms.

Straddle Glide Kip

Glide Kip Into Double-Leg Shoot-Through

Glide Kip—Catch High Bar

above the bar on the finish of the kipping action, the gymnast straddles the legs to the sides, releases the bar, and catches the bar again in a straddle glide kip position.

14. *Reverse Kip.* Similar to the glide kip into double-leg shoot-through except that instead of riding up immediately into a sitting position on top of the bar, the movement begins to repeat itself in reverse. Move the body downward in a

Single-Leg Circle

Glide Kip to Straddle Cut

Cast

piked position, but hold the buttocks close to the bar so that the body will rotate in this position upward to a sitting position on top of the bar. As the upper body reaches the vertical on the downward and forward swing, push down on the bar with the arms and lift the chest upward away from the legs. This move is fully described in chapter 9 in the section on high bar skills under "Reverse Kip."

Moves On and Around One Bar

1. *Cast.* Start from front support position on low bar, hands shoulder width apart in a regular grip. Keeping the shoulders in front of the bar, bend the hips slightly so that the legs will swing forward and under the bar. The elbows will bend slightly at this point. From here, drive the legs backward and upward while pushing down on the bar

Thigh Roll

Back Hip Circle

with the arms. Continue the movement upward with the legs, squeezing the buttocks and driving the entire body above the bar. The shoulders must be kept in front of the bar so that as the body rises upward, the center of gravity remains directly over the bar. After the body reaches the height of the cast, allow the legs to return to the bar while maintaining a fully extended position.

2. *Thigh Roll.* Begin in a rear lying position on low bar, hanging onto high bar in an undergrip. Keeping the body fully extended, reach the right hand across the body, and grasp the low bar in an overgrip next to the left thigh. At the same time turn the entire body to the left so as to finish in a front support position, right hand on the low bar, left hand on the high bar in an undergrip.

3. *Back Hip Circle.* Begin from a cast. As the legs renew contact with the bar, drive the shoulders backward, keeping the arms straight and the thighs in contact with the bar, and driving the legs forward in a circling motion around the

bar. When the body reaches the horizontal, stabilize the legs by squeezing the buttocks and pull the shoulders backward to arrive in a front support.

4. *Mill Circle (Stride Circle).* From a stride position on the low or high bar, hands in a reverse grip on top of the bar and hips facing squarely forward, lift the weight off the bar by pushing down on the bar with the arms. At the same time lift the forward leg up and out and press the rear leg against the bar to begin the forward rotation. Keep the chest high and the legs in a wide stride throughout the circle. Finish on top of the bar in a stride support.

Variation: Mill Circle—Regrasp. Perform a mill circle, and when you see the high bar about three-quarters of the way around in the circle, release the low bar and grasp the high bar.

5. *Front Hip Circle.* Begin in a high front support position. Lean forward with the body extended, and as the body begins to circle the bar, hold it in an

Mill Circle

Front Hip Circle

zontal, hands next to hips in a reverse grip. Press down on the bar, putting your weight on the hands and lifting the hips above the bar so as to arrive in a deep pike position with feet slightly in front of bar. At this point drive the hips forward so as to begin the forward rotation. At the bottom of the swing try to maintain the deep pike position with a slight rounding of the back. Ride the pike position until you have nearly reached the top of the bar; then open up the angle between the chest and the legs, but only to 90°, to stop the forward rotation. It may also be helpful to move the thumbs around to the front of the bar to stop the forward action.

7. *Back Seat Circle.* Begin in a sitting position on top of bar, legs horizontal to the ground, hands next to hips in a regular grip. Take the weight on the hands and lift the legs so that the body is in a tight pike above the bar. Lean

Front Seat Circle

extended position until the upper body passes below the horizontal. At this point, pike deeply to speed up rotation and shift the hands around toward the top of the bar. Push down on the bar, straightening the arms and hollowing the chest to finish in a straight-arm support.

6. *Front Seat Circle.* Begin in a sitting position on top of bar, legs hori-

back and maintain this tight pike position while circling the bar backward. At the end of the circle pull the body back into a sitting position on top of the bar by rotating the wrists around the bar until the hands are on top and pulling the shoulders back to a position above the hands.

8. *Single-Leg Cut.* Begin in a front support and perform a cast. At the height of the cast lift one leg to the side so as to pass over the bar. At the same time release the grasp on that side of the bar so that the weight is momentarily taken on one hand. As soon as the leg passes over the bar, regrasp in the original position. Finish in a stride support.

9. *Single-Leg Shoot-Through.* Begin from a cast, in a manner similar to the single-leg cut. At the height of the cast drive the hips upward while bending one knee toward the chest. As the leg passes over the bar in the bent-knee position, push down and slightly forward on the bar, bringing the shoulders to an upright position by the time the leg has extended in front of the bar to finish in a stride support. This may also be performed with a straight-leg shoot.

10. *Double-Leg Shoot-Through.* This is performed similarly to the single-leg shoot-through except that both legs are brought over the bar in a bent-knee or straight-leg position to finish in a seat support. As the legs arrive in the horizontal forward position, press the arms tightly against the sides of the body so as to stop the forward movement of the body.

11. *Sole Circle Backward.* Begin in a front support position and move into

Single-Leg Shoot-Through

a cast. At the top of the cast, drive the hips upward and bring the feet to the bar in a straddle position to the outside of the hands. As the hips begin their descent, push against the bar with the balls of the feet, at the same time exerting a pulling action on the bar with the arms. This pull-push action aids in keeping the feet in contact with the bar until the desirable point of release. This move may be used as a mount, a dismount, a move from low bar to high bar, from high bar with one-half twist to low bar, and from either one of the bars with one-half twist back to that bar. It may also be performed in the stoop position.

12. *Sole Circle Forward.* Begin in a front support and move into a cast. At the top of the cast drive the hips upward and forward so as to arrive in a straddle stand on top of the bar. During a momentary pause, prior to the movement of the hips forward, release the bar and regrasp in a reverse grip. From this position drive the hips forward, and exert a pull-push action as described above in the backward sole circle, finish-

Straddle Sole Circle Backward

Sole Circle Forward

ing in the straddle position on top of the bar, from which another move can be executed. The sole circle forward may also be performed in the stoop position.

Moves Between the Bars

1. *Back Hip Pullover from Low Bar to High Bar.* Start from a rear lying position with one knee bent and the ball of that foot on the low bar. Pull the hips

toward the bar as the bent leg pushes against the low bar and the other leg begins the lift upward. Continue pulling the hips toward the bar as both legs come together in the air and continue to circle the bar. Finish in a straight-arm support.

2. *Skin-the-Cat-Basket.* Sit on the low bar facing the high bar, grasping the high bar in an overgrip. Drop off the low

Back Hip Pullover

bar into a long hang position from the high bar. Bring the legs up between the hands in a tuck or pike position. Continue to bring them through the arms until they are resting on the thighs on the low bar. Release the right hand, letting the body pivot three-quarters to the left until you finish in a riding seat position, facing the length of the bar.

3. *Underswing from High Bar to Low Bar.* Begin in a front support position on the high bar. Lean back with the shoulders, keeping the body fully extended, arms straight, and hips in contact with the bar as the body begins to circle around the bar. At the point at which the hips can no longer be held in contact with the bar, pike deeply, allowing the hips to drop away from the bar while lifting the toes toward the bar and extending the arms overhead. Keep the toes in close proximity to the bar, allowing the hips to move in a slight upward arc. Extend upward and outward with the legs, finishing in a rear support position on the low bar.

4. *Kip Between the Bars.* From a rear lying position on the low bar, grasping the high bar, extend the body. Bring the ankles quickly to the high bar and pull into the kip action. While the legs are riding up the bar, push down on the bar and round the back so as to get on top of the bar. Continue moving the legs backward until you finish in a front support position on high bar.

5. *Drop Kip.* Begin from a long hang position on high bar facing low bar. Swing the legs backward, and at the top of the swing drive the hips into the air while pushing down on the high bar. Remain in this position and swing slightly forward. Release the high bar

and reach forward to grasp the low bar. Perform a glide kip from here.

6. *Backward Sole Circle—Catch High Bar.* (Refer to "Moves On and Around One Bar.") When approximately two-thirds of the sole circle has been completed, release the feet from the bar and extend the hips and legs upward and outward toward the high bar. Release the grasp on the low bar and regrasp in an overgrip on high bar.

7. *Cast from High Bar to a Back Hip Circle on Low Bar.* From a front support position on high bar facing low bar, perform a casting movement in which a full extension occurs through the shoulders. At the top of the cast the body will be in a horizontal position extended backward from the high bar, the head held in a neutral position between the arms, the chest slightly hollowed, and the hips tucked under. From this position the body swings downward toward the low bar. As the body reaches the vertical hang, allow the hips to lead slightly, trailing with the legs. As the hips make contact with the low bar, the legs should come forward under the low bar, moving the body into a pike position to circle the bar. As the circling begins, release the high bar and grasp the low bar. When the legs reach the horizontal position after circling the bar, squeeze the buttocks in an attempt to stabilize the legs. Open up out of the pike by lifting the chest upward and pulling the shoulders back. Finish in a straight-arm support.

8. *Underswing One-Half Turn (Sole Circle One-Half Turn) Into Back Hip Circle on Low Bar.* In a front support position on the high bar with the back toward the low bar, start an underswing,

and at the end of the hip extension lower the left hip and release the grasp of the high bar with the right hand pulling the right arm across the face toward the left. As the half turn is near completion, regrasp the high bar with the right hand in a regular grip. This will result in the hands being in a mixed grip as the body swings downward toward the low bar for the hip circle. The turn may also be performed to the right.

9. *Flying Hip Circle to Eagle Catch.* Move into a back hip circle on low bar from any one of the previously mentioned moves without grasping the low bar. When the legs have rotated around and slightly past the horizontal position, pop upward and backward by very rapidly extending through the hips and squeezing the buttocks. Simultaneously, thrust the arms from the overhead position, backward, lifting the chest and grasping the bar behind the head in an overgrip with the thumbs turned outward.

10. *Flying Hip Circle—Full Turn—Catch High Bar.* Perform similarly to the eagle catch. As the extension through the hips begins, reach back with the left hand to grab the high bar in an overgrip. At the same time reach the right arm across the face to the left, and as the left hand grasps the high bar, continue to pivot until the body has made one full turn, grasping with the right hand in an overgrip facing the low bar.

11. *Back Straddle Jump Over High Bar to Back Hip Circle on Low Bar.* Stand on low bar, back toward the high bar, one hand touching high bar for momentary support. Flex the knees and jump upward and backward into a straddle position over the bar. As the

Flying Hip Circle—Eagle Catch

hips and legs pass over the bar, catch the bar between the legs in an overgrip. As the body swings down, bring the legs together and execute a back hip circle on low bar.

12. *Belly Whip to Stand on Low Bar.* Start from a stand on the low bar facing the high bar, hands in a regular grasp on high bar, shoulder width apart. Flex the knees slightly, push down on the bar, and jump the body into an extended position above the low bar. As the body descends toward the low bar, extend fully through the shoulders and squeeze the buttocks. As the body comes into contact with the low bar, allow the legs to swing forward underneath the bar into a deep pike. Then extend backward through the hips by squeezing the buttocks. As the body reaches the extended

position, ride the rebound of the bar by staying straight and pushing down on the high bar with fully extended arms. At the height of the flight drive the hips up and pull the legs in underneath the body so as to arrive in a stand on the low bar. Several moves may be performed prior to the belly whip to put you in the proper position. For example: (1) sole circle or underswing on high bar facing the low bar, one-half turn into belly whip position; (2) from front support on high bar facing away from the low bar, cast back and out over low bar into belly whip. A variation within the move is to add a full twist.

Half Seat Circle Backward to Drop Glide Kip Low Bar

13. *Half Seat Circle Backward on High Bar—Drop to Glide Kip on Low Bar.* From a sitting position on high bar facing low bar, legs horizontal and hands in a regular grasp, move into the start of a back seat circle. As the body moves around the bar to the point at which the low bar can be seen, release the grasp of the high bar and reach forward for the low bar. Catch the low bar with the hips lifted up and to the rear. Perform a glide kip from this position.

14. *Backward Sole Circle on Low Bar Regrasp High Bar.* This move is performed on the low bar facing the high bar. As the low bar is released, reach up and forward in order to catch the high bar. Finish in a long hang from high bar. A variation of this move consists of catching the high bar in a mixed group so that upon grasping the bar a half turn may immediately be executed.

15. *Handstand Pirouette to Back Hip Circle on Low Bar.* Begin by standing on low bar facing high bar, hands in a mixed grip on high bar, shoulder distance apart. Flex the knees and jump, pulling the hips up and over the shoulders into a straddle or pike position. From here, lift the legs upward so as to arrive in a handstand on top of the high bar. Shift your weight over your left hand, keeping your body tight, hips tucked under, buttocks squeezed. As the weight is transferred onto the left hand, the body will pirouette a half turn and end up so that the right hand may grasp the bar to the right of the left hand. At this point the body should still be in an erect handstand position on top of the bar. From here, allow the body to swing down and toward the low bar. Perform a flying hip circle on a low bar.

Dismounts

1. *Cast Off Low Bar with Quarter Turn to the Right.* Starting from a straight-arm support on low bar, begin to perform a cast. As the legs are driven up behind, push down and forward on the bar, moving the body backward behind the bar. At the same time turn the body to the right, and toward the end of the push release the bar with the

right hand. The gymnast should finish in a standing position with the left side toward the bar, the left arm extended straight out to the side with the hand grasping the bar, and the right arm extended out to the side. This dismount may also be performed turning to the left.

2. *Forward Roll Off High Bar.* Begin in a high front support position, thighs resting on top of the high bar, facing away from the low bar. Lean forward, tuck the chin to the chest, and rotate the hands around the bar so that they finish in an overgrip. Pike at the hips as the body moves around the bar. Finish in a long hang, allowing the legs to swing slightly to the rear, then forward, and release. On the forward swing a one-half turn may be added.

3. *Hock Swing Dismount.* Begin by hanging from the high bar in a regular grip, facing the low bar. Both legs are resting on the low bar with the backs of the knees in contact with the bar and the hips below the bar. Pull downward on the high bar with straight arms, lift the hips upward, and raise the chest and head slightly. From this position of extension to the knees, release the high bar and bend the knees sharply so as to keep the bar in contact with the legs as the body drops downward. The arms may be left in an overhead position or dropped down to the sides of the body. Just before reaching the top of the upward swing, extend at the knees, continue to drive the chest upward and forward, and bring the feet underneath the body to arrive in a bent-knee stand in front of the bar.

4. *Straddle Sole Circle Dismount from Low Bar.* Cast up into a straddle sole

Hock Swing Dismount

circle position. Push down on the bar with the balls of the feet and pull the bar toward you with the hands. Keep the feet on the bar until just before reaching the height of the forward swing. At this point release the feet from the bar, extend the hips and legs upward and outward, and pull the bar backward behind your head just before releasing it with your hands. Continue the extended flight upward and outward until arriving onto the feet. This dismount may also be performed from the high bar. In this case the feet will be released slightly sooner than on low bar.

Underswing Dismount from High Bar

5. *Underswing Dismount from Low Bar.* Begin in a front support position. Lean back with the shoulders, keeping the body fully extended, the arms straight, and the hips in contact with the bar as the body begins to circle around the bar. At the point at which the hips can no longer be held in contact with the bar, extend upward and outward with the legs and pull the bar backward behind your head before releasing the hands. Continue the extended flight upward and outward until arriving onto your feet. This dismount may also be performed from the high bar. In the latter case the feet will be released slightly sooner than on low bar. A variation of this move is to add a one-half or full twist.

6. *Handstand to One-Quarter Turn from Low Bar.* Start in a front support position on high bar, facing the low bar. Lean forward, reaching the arms out so as to grasp the low bar in a mixed grip (left hand in an undergrip, right hand in an overgrip). From this extended position, pike slightly at the hips, then drive the legs upward and over the low bar, arriving in a handstand position on the low bar. Hold the handstand momentarily. Execute a quarter turn by releasing the right hand and leaning the body toward the left so that all of the weight is centered over the left hand. Drop the feet toward the ground while the body maintains an extended position. Finish in a standing position with the left side toward the low bar, the left arm extended straight out to the side grasping the low bar, and the right arm extended straight out to the side.

7. *Squat Vault Dismount.* Start from a straight-arm support on the low bar, facing away from the high bar. Perform a cast into a double-leg shoot-through. As the legs pass over the bar, push down and backward with the arms and then release. Drive the chest forward and upward and land in a standing position in front of the bar.

8. *Handstand–Squat Through Dismount.* This is very similar to the squat vault dismount except that the starting position is a handstand on the low or the

high bar. Allow the shoulders to move slightly in front of the hands, following a stretched handstand position. Execute a strong push down and back, driving the chest forward and upward and bending at the hips and the knees. After the body passes over the bar and is nearly in the vertical position, extend through the knees and hips so that the finish of the flight will be in the extended position. Land on the feet with the chest and head erect. This dismount can also be performed in a straddle, piked, or flanked position.

9. *Straddle Cut Dismount.* Start in a rear support on the high bar facing the low bar. Lean backward and move into a deep piked position with the back held as flat as possible. In this position swing down and then back up by pushing downward on the bar with the arms. As the body rises above the bar, straddle the legs to the sides and release the bar. Finish in an upright position standing behind the high bar and facing the low bar.

10. *Hecht from Low Bar.* Begin from a cast on high bar, facing the low bar. Move into a flying hip circle on the low bar. When the body has completed approximately three-quarters of the hip circle, pop upward and forward away from the bar by very rapidly extending through the hips so that the shoulders and legs are lifted. Remain in the stretched position until just before making contact with the ground. At that point, pike slightly at the hips, bringing the feet underneath so as to arrive in an erect stand. The hecht can also be performed out of a back hip circle from the high bar.

Back Hip Circle (Hecht) Dismount

11. *Back Somersault Dismount from Seat Bounce on High Bar.* From a front support position on high bar facing the low bar, cast upward. At the height of the cast, drive the hips into the air as the legs are brought forward into a straddle position over the bar. Release the hands as the legs come together, contacting the bar on the middle of the thighs. As the legs bounce from the bar, reach upward and backward with the arms to perform a back somersault to the mats below.

12. *Cast Out Into a Front Somersault Dismount.* From a front support position on the high bar, facing the low bar, cast upward and backward away from the bar. At the height of the cast drive the hips into the air and push the bar away, releasing the hands. Continue to drive the hips upward and forward as the head is tucked and the knees bent. Grasp the shins and pull into a front somersault. As the somersault reaches completion, move into an extended position for the finish.

For additional routines consider the Age Group Compulsory Exercises for Boys and Girls published by the United States Gymnastic Federation, Box 12713, Tuscon, Arizona 85711.

12

Women's Balance Beam

Balance beam work consists in performing on a beam 4 inches wide (100 millimeters) and 16 feet 4 inches long (5000 millimeters) and held off the floor by supports at each end. Competitive rules requires the beam to be at a height of 47 inches (1000 to 1200 millimeters). A beat board, or take-off board, may be used in mounting. On the beam, gymnasts perform basic locomotor movements including steps, runs, jumps, and turns, along with rolls and balances plus flexibility and tumbling moves. This activity presents an exciting challenge to the performer because it requires much control, balance, courage, and concentration to maneuver the body through the intricacies of a routine.

Each competitive routine consists of a mount, combinations of moves on the beam, and a dismount—done within a time limit of 1 minute 15 seconds to 1 minute 35 seconds. Within the time limit mentioned, approximately 5 to 7 passes are performed using the entire length of the beam. The exercise must be lively and continuous, avoiding monotony of rhythm, having a minimum of held positions showing different levels of height, including sitting and lying positions. The routine should present a picture of confidence and control as well as of elegance and grace.

VALUES

The specific values of working the balance beam are the development of

1. An accurate sense of balance.
2. A feeling of confidence at heights and in a narrow and restricted area.
3. Control and coordination of bodily movements.
4. Strength throughout the entire body.
5. An ability to create a fine artistic exercise.

AREA AND EQUIPMENT

As can be seen from the dimensions of the balance beam, a long and narrow area is required. Several feet on both sides of the beam should be cleared for dismounts and possible falls. However, the full length of the beam is not needed for individual moves.

For teaching purposes, one need not have an official beam at the regulation height. A line on the floor may be used to introduce many movements; or a piece of wood about ½-inch thick and 4 inches wide placed on the floor can be used. A beam 5 to 6 inches wide can also be used for learning some of the skills. Also, beams of different heights are excellent for learning. Although commercially made beams are superior, inexpensive training models can be constructed by someone with a little skill in carpentry.

TEACHING METHODS

It is advisable to practice all the skills on a straight line on the gymnasium floor first. The line can be painted on the floor or put on temporarily with tape. Not only is this a good practice method for individuals, but it lends itself readily to the mass method of instruction. This can be handled much like mass calisthenics.

The next step in learning moves on the balance beam is to try them on a low beam just a few inches high. Some schools find it feasible to construct several of these low beams and thus enable more students to work at one time. When confidence has been established, students can then try the stunts on the high balance beam with an assist from the instructor. Because of the equipment needed, instruction here is best suited to squads or individuals. Perhaps a system of rotating squads from the line on the floor to the low beam would provide a good way to utilize class time.

SAFETY

A few safety rules to be followed in working the balance beam are:

1. Mats should be used on the floor under and at the sides of the high beam to provide a soft landing place.

2. The finish on the top of the beam should be a natural lacquer so that it is smooth but not slippery. The latest beams have a covering of synthetic leather material.

3. Progression in the use of equipment should be followed as mentioned above.

4. Learn the moves in a progressive order so that the proper lead-up activities will be included.

5. Use spotters, particularly on the high beam. One spotter on each side of the beam is preferable.

PROGRAM OF INSTRUCTION

Instruction on the balance beam involves three basic steps:

1. *Individual moves.*

2. *Combinations.* As a person learns a new skill, she should be challenged to combine it with another stunt as smoothly as possible. Because a move must be learned well in order to combine it with another, the use of com-

binations in the teaching progression
stresses proper execution and increases
the safety of performance. In addition,
the smaller combinations serve as building blocks for longer routines. Combinations can be suggested by the instructor
or coach or can be created by the performer.

3. *Routines.* Ultimately, a pupil should
strive to combine moves into a routine.
Competition is based on routines, required or optional. The approach to optional routines is one of problem solving.
Certain requirements involving the types
of movements and the time limit are presented as a problem for the performer
to solve creatively within her own capabilities. The instructor or coach and pupil
can coordinate their thoughts on the development of a particular routine.

Straight-Arm Support Mount

Mounts

1. *Straight-Arm Support Mount.* Start
from a stand or take two or three running steps forward, and after a take-off
from both feet, place the hands on the
top of the beam, shoulder width apart,
and jump up to a straight-arm support
position with the arms straight and the
thighs resting on the beam. Hold the
head up and arch the body slightly,
pointing the toes.

2. *Straddle Seat Mount.* Jump to a
straight-arm support position and then
swing the left leg over the beam with a
quarter turn to the right of the body.
The right leg remains on the approach
side of the beam and the left leg then
swings down. The performer assumes a
straddle seat position with the hands on
the beam in front of the crotch.

3. *Step-Up Mount.* Either from the
end or the side, run and take off from

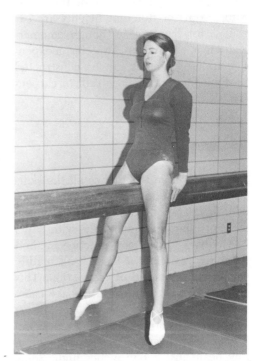

Straddle Seat Mount

the beat board with one foot. Lift the
other leg into the air and step, landing
on the ball of the foot. It is important
not to sit back as the foot is placed on

Step-Up Mount

4. *Squat Mount.* From a stand facing the beam or a run with a take-off from both feet, jump into a straight-arm support and immediately lift the hips, bringing both legs into a squat position between the hands on top of the beam. Keep the back flat and the chest held high.

5. *Wolf Mount.* This mount is similar to the squat mount except that one leg is brought into a squat position between the arms, while the other leg is lifted with a straight knee to an extended position on the beam outside of the arms.

the beam, but rather lean slightly forward with a straight back, putting the center of gravity over the supporting leg. The gymnast must be careful to control her free or back leg throughout the mount. This mount can also be done by taking off the board with one foot and jumping to a two-foot landing on the beam or by bouncing off both feet from the board to a two-foot landing on the beam.

Wolf Mount

Squat Mount

6. *Straddle Mount.* Jump to a straight-arm support position, moving the shoulders forward and slightly to the other side of the beam. At the same time lift the hips and spread the extended legs so as to place the feet on the beam outside of the hands. Finish in a straddle support position. Be sure to have a spotter on the opposite side of the beam while trying this skill for the first few times.

7. *Scissor Mount to a Stag Sit.* Approach from a slightly oblique angle, taking off from the board with the foot furthest from the beam. Place the near-

Straddle Mount

place the hands on top of the beam, lift the hips, duck the head, and perform a piked forward roll to a lying position with the legs pointing straight up.

9. *Press to a Handstand Mount.* From either the end or the side of the beam, run and take off with both feet from the beat board. Place the hands on the beam, and move the shoulders forward in front of the hands as the hips lift. As the legs lift higher, extend through the shoulders to finish in a vertical alignment. From the handstand position the gymnast can move into a pivot, a forward roll, a front walkover, or numerous other moves. This mount can be performed in the tuck, pike, straddle, or wolf position.

Some additional superior difficulty mounts include the following:

est hand on top of the beam and lift the near leg up and over the beam, followed by the take-off leg. The first leg is extended downward by the side of the beam and slightly to the rear. The second leg finishes with the thigh forward, the knee bent, and the foot pointing toward the opposite leg.

8. *Diving Forward Roll Mount.* Facing the end of the beam, run a few steps and execute a take-off with both feet off the beat board. Reach slightly forward,

10. From the end of the beam, roll to the shoulders and then kip to a stand on one leg.

11. From the side of the beam, take off beat board with one leg and execute a forward somersault with the legs in a

Scissor Mount to Stag Sit

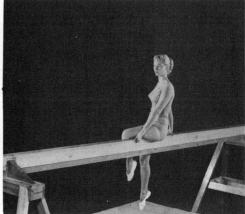

Diving Forward Roll

split position and finish in a side seat (Amazon Seat) support position. The run at the beam is from an angle.

12. Leap to the end of the beam to a handstand in cross support (one hand on each side of the beam), make a half turn on the hands, and land on one leg.

13. Leap to the end of the beam to a handstand in cross support, make a quarter turn, splitting the legs, and land on one leg in a stand facing sideways.

Locomotor Movements, Leaps, and Turns on the Beam

One of the basic requirements of a routine is the use of locomotor movements. They are used to combine skills in a fluid manner and to give grace and elegance to the routine. This section will deal with the various steps, jumps, and turns that are used on the beam.

Basic Walk

Walking on the balance beam should be practiced until it becomes almost as natural as walking on the floor. The body should be extended, maintaining good posture at all times. The shoulders should be held down as the arms move gracefully. The legs should be rotated out slightly and the buttocks held firm. The foot should be placed on the beam with a slight turn-out, contacting the ball of the foot first. The little toe can grasp the edge of the beam to help maintain balance. Begin by walking forward and backward and then add variations such as the following:

1. *Side Step.* This is moving sideways along the beam by sliding one foot to the side and then bringing the other foot beside it. A variation is to cross one foot in front of the other in the sliding action.

2. *Chasse.* Move forward along the length of the beam with a step—together —step—hold.

3. *Step—Tap—Hop.* Stepping forward on the left foot, bend the right knee and touch the right foot to the left knee. Then hop on the left foot while extending the right leg forward. Land on the left foot, followed immediately by a step onto the right foot.

4. *Cat Walk.* Walking forward, jump off the left leg, bringing both knees up toward the chest. Then extend the legs, landing on the right leg, closely followed by the left leg. The landing should be soft, like a cat's.

5. *Run.* This is the same as walking, except at a faster pace. Start by using small steps and as skill improves lengthen the steps.

6. *Scissors Leap.* Step forward on the left foot and lift the right leg forward and up to approximately hip level. Then lift the left leg up in the same way, as

the right leg drops down for a right-foot landing on the beam. The legs pass each other in a scissors action.

7. *Cat Leap.* Similar to the scissors leap except the legs are lifted with nearly a 90° bend of the knees and a slight turnout from the hips.

8. *Cabriole.* (Refer to chapter 13 for description.)

9. *Tour Jeté.* (See chapter 13 for description.)

Turns

The following variety of turns may be done on the beam:

1. *Pivot.* With one foot ahead of the other and the feet close together, raise up on the balls of the feet and turn the body 180°. Squeeze the buttocks and maintain good body alignment throughout the turn. On the completion of the turn lower the heels to the beam.

2. *Squat Turn.* While in a squat position, execute a pivot turn. Lift the weight off the feet during the turn by raising the hips slightly while on the balls of the feet.

3. *Pirouette.* (Refer to chapter 13 for description.)

4. *Kick Turn.* Facing the length of the beam, step forward on the left foot, lifting the straight right leg forward and upward. When the right leg is at the top of the lift, execute a quick push with the left foot, accompanied by a one-half turn to the left. Upon completing the turn, step forward onto the right foot and on to the next move.

5. *Pivot in Wolf Position.* Begin in wolf position with the left leg bent and directly underneath the body and the right leg extended sideways on the beam. One arm is brought forward of the center of the body. A strong push-off is made with the right foot as the left arm opens to the side and the left shoulder

Pivot Turn

Squat Turn

point at the completion of the turn. The back should be held very straight and upright. A one-half, full, or one-and-one-half turn can be completed in this position. The turn is stopped by placing the foot down on the beam.

6. *Tuck Jump.* From a bent-knee position leap upward bringing the knees toward the chest and assume an open tuck position momentarily and then extend the legs to a firm landing on the beam.

moves in the direction of the turn. As the body turns the right leg is held outward and slightly above the beam in an extended position. During the turn the center of gravity must remain over the supporting leg. The head should be held high with concentration on the focus

7. *Tuck Jump with One-Half Turn.* This is the same as the tuck jump except a half turn is executed while in the air. Finish facing in the opposite direction with the opposite foot forward.

After reaching the top side of the beam by a mount, a routine consists in combinations of skills and movements. Many of these skills are described in the following sections.

Kick Turn

then moves gracefully on to the next movement or position. Here are a few such poses:

1. *V Sit.* This position is the same as that found in the floor exercises in chapter 13 except that while the gymnast is sitting on the beam her hands should remain on the top of the beam with her fingers grasping the sides behind her body. Start into this position by pulling the knees into the chest and then extend the legs upward.

Pivot in Wolf Position

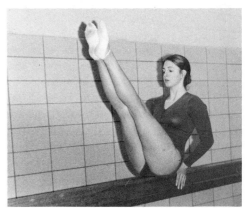

V Sit

Poses

A pose is a momentary hold of a position and may take many forms. For example, it may consist of the performer's holding a slightly flexed leg in front or in back while she is supported on one foot with the hands held gracefully out to the sides. The same thing might also be done while in a kneeling, sitting, or lying position. A great variety of poses can be developed by the gymnast. It must be remembered, however, that poses are no longer used as static positions. Instead, the gymnast moves into the desired position and pauses only long enough to "mark the position." She

Attitude Pose (Front Scale)

2. *Attitude Pose (Front Scale)*. This move consists of standing on one leg with the other leg elevated to a position at least parallel to the beam and the upper body bent forward, parallel to the beam. The body should have an elegant arch and the raised leg should be straight with the toes pointed. The arms should be extended from the side in a graceful manner, with the head up and the eyes looking toward the end of the beam.

5. *Splits*. Forward or side splits can be done on the balance beam. Be sure these can be done on the floor before attempting them on the balance beam.

Needle Scale

Swan Scale

3. *Swan Scale*. Place the right shin along the beam with both hands forward on the beam. Slide the left leg on the beam behind the right foot until the leg is straight. Lift the hands and straighten the upper body until the head and shoulders are directly above the hips. Place the arms gracefully out to the sides.

4. *Needle Scale*. Start by leaning into a front scale and continue the lean until the forehead touches the shin of the supporting leg, and the other leg is elevated directly overhead. The performer may grasp the bottom of the beam to aid in the balance.

Split

Combinations and Agility Moves

1. *One-Leg Squat*. From a standing position, lower into a full squat position on one leg with the other leg held parallel to the beam. Lean forward slightly over the support leg, keeping a straight back. Arms may be held to the side or forward for balance. This move may start in the squat position and move up to a stand.

2. *Swedish Fall*. This is similar to a move done in floor exercise. From a standing position, fall forward, landing on the hands. Flex the arms as the fall continues toward the chest and lift one leg gracefully until it is pointing upward.

3. *Straddle Hold*. From a straddle stand, shift the weight of the body to the hands and lift your feet off the beam, moving them forward while supporting yourself solely with straight arms. For greater difficulty, try lowering to this position from a handstand and then execute a quarter turn on the hands and do a pressroll or whip of the legs into a forward roll.

Other Skills

1. *Body Wave*. (Refer to the floor exercises in chapter 13 for a detailed description.)

2. *Forward Roll*. Start from a squat position with the arms reaching forward, thumbs on top of the beam, and fingers grasping the sides. Lift the hips by extending the knees. At the same time duck the head through the arms so as to contact the beam with the back of the head. At this point the thumbs should still be on top of the beam where the slight hollow of the neck is. The legs extend fully, the elbows are squeezed tightly toward the face for greater control, and the hips are lowered to the beam. The finish of the roll can be to roll up to a V-sit; or roll up to a one-leg stand, with the free leg pointing down toward the floor or extended along the top of the beam. Once the basic forward roll is mastered, many variations can be used, such as: a forward roll from a lunge position; a forward roll from a pike stand; a forward roll from a handstand; or a free forward roll (without

One-Leg Squat

Straddle Hold

Forward Roll

ach for initial support. As the gymnast lifts the legs overhead, use the free hand to grab the hip furthest away and with the other hand move to a position on the near hip. From here, continue to lift and guide the hips.

4. *Shoulder Balance (Candlestick).* Start this from a kneeling position. Place the back of the shoulders on the beam by ducking the head under as if going into a forward roll. With the fingers gripping the sides of the beam, slowly lift the hips over into an extended balance position.

use of hands). For spotting, stand at the side of the beam, slightly in front of the gymnast, and assist in lifting the hips and controlling them down to the beam.

3. *Backward Roll.* Begin by lying on the back on the beam with arms positioned so that the thumbs lie on top of the beam in the hollow of the neck and the fingers reach behind the thumbs grasping the sides of the beam. From this position the hips are rapidly flexed and the straight legs are brought overhead. Just prior to contacting the beam with the knees or feet, extend the elbows and push with the thumbs, thus allowing the head to lift off the beam and finish in an upright position. The backward roll is a difficult maneuver for the gymnast who is tight through the neck, back, and hamstrings. Prior to attempting it, have the gymnast practice the plough position on the floor (lying on the back, lift straight legs overhead until the feet are touching the floor behind the head). Once this position can be easily assumed, the backward roll will come very quickly. For spotting, stand beside the beam with the hand nearest the gymnast's head placed on her stom-

5. *Cartwheel.* To receive credit in competition, the gymnast should face sideways to the beam at all times during this move. Therefore, start with the arms overhead facing sideways, not looking down at the beam. Bend the forward leg and lift the back leg overhead. As the first hand comes into contact with the beam, the ball of the hand should be placed on the top with the thumbs and the fingers on the same side. Give a strong push with the flexed leg. The second hand should reach down the length of the beam so as to make a long cartwheel. The head should remain in a neutral position throughout this movement. On the finish, the body lifts sideways up to a stand. It is very helpful to squeeze the buttocks for balance upon completion.

6. *Cartwheel to a Hand Balance.* Begin this the same as a cartwheel. When the lead leg gets nearly to the vertical, stop its movement and bring the second leg up next to it. The second hand should be placed closer to the first hand than in a full cartwheel, since the hands should be under the shoulders for balance in the handstand.

Cartwheel to Hand Balance

7. *English Hand Balance*. This is a hand balance facing the length of the beam with the hands close together on each side of the beam. Start from a standing position, bend the forward leg and place the hands on the beam with the fingers down the sides and the thumbs on top, almost touching each other. From this position kick into the English hand balance. Remember to strive for good vertical alignment by pushing down on the beam to show full shoulder extension, by keeping the head neutral, and by squeezing the buttocks and pulling the hips slightly under. A variation would be to execute a scissors action of the legs as they are lifted upward and then returned to the beam after the momentary hand balance. The landing is on the opposite foot from which the take-off is executed.

8. *Back Walkover*. This should be performed very much like the same move in floor exercise. In the beginning stance, with the weight over the support leg and the other leg pointed forward onto the beam, make sure that the hips and shoulders are squarely in line with the beam as well as at even levels to the beam. The hand position should be with the thumbs and palms of the hands on top of the beam and the fingers grasping the sides. On the completion of the move, bring the trailing leg down quickly to a point directly behind the lead leg, while at the same time squeezing the buttocks and lifting the chest and arms to an erect stand.

For spotting, the spotter should stand by the side of the beam with her back toward the gymnast's legs. As the gymnast begins the move, the spotter reaches up with both arms, placing one hand on each hip. The spotter helps to lift and guide the gymnast's hips over her head. As the first foot is placed on the beam, the hips can be released and the hands can grasp the gymnast's arms to aid in coming to a stand. Prior to performing this move on the high beam, perfect it on the ground and on the low beam. A mat draped over the beam or a special beam covering may be used during the first attempts. Another safety method is to have mats piled on the sides so they are flush with the top of the beam.

9. *Front Walkover.* (Refer to the floor exercises in chapter 13 for a complete description.) In performing this move place both hands on the beam with thumbs and palms on top and fingers grasping the sides. Maintain a full stretch through the shoulders at all times. It is not necessary to see the first foot contact the beam as long as the shoulders and hips stay in good alignment. Once the body is nearing the vertical, draw the second leg tightly to the first while squeezing the buttocks, tightening the stomach, and hollowing the chest. This will assist finishing in a stable, vertical stand.

Spotting is the same as that for the floor exercise. The support is under the back and the shoulder. Again it is suggested that this move be tried first on the floor and then on a low beam before moving to the high beam. A mat draped over the beam or a special beam covering should be used when this move is first attempted. Or, as has been suggested, pile mats on each side so they are flush with the top of the beam.

10. *Far-Arm Cartwheel.* This move is similar to the two-arm cartwheel except that only one arm, the far arm, is placed on the beam. As the forward leg is bent and the back leg is thrust into the air, the first arm (near arm) is brought down and past the hip to a position slightly behind the back. A very forceful push is given with the support leg as the far hand is placed on the beam, palm on top, fingers and thumb grasping the side. As the lead foot contacts the beam and the body rises to the vertical, the free arm may move to a sideways position or lift forward and upward to join the other arm overhead.

11. *Valdez.* (Refer to the floor exercises in chapter 13 for additional description.) The move is executed the same as in floor exercise. The performer starts by sitting on the beam with one leg flexed and the other leg extended straight

Far-Arm Cartwheel

ahead. The arm is rotated laterally with the fingers on one side of the beam and the thumb on the other. The gymnast lifts the straight leg up and over and throws the forward arm over toward the beam, and at the same time the foot on the beam provides a push into the valdez. action. The action continues to a handstand on the beam. This move can be used as a dismount by dropping the body to the side of the beam following the one-arm vertical balance. It can also be used as a mount by stepping onto the beam in a bent-knee position and lifting the trail leg forward and upward over the head, completing the valdez movement.

12. *Back Handspring.* From a lunge position step back onto both feet and execute a back handspring. The placement of the hands on the beam will depend upon the individual gymnast and what feels most comfortable to her. Some typical hand positions are: thumbs and palms on the top of the beam with the fingers grasping each side; the same basic position but one hand in front of the other; one hand on top of the other on top of the beam; and both palms on top of the beam with the thumbs and fingers of both hands grasping the same side of the beam. The handspring finishes in a walkout fashion.

13. *Front Handspring Walkout.* This is performed in the same way as on the floor and should be perfected on a line on the floor prior to being attempted on a balance beam.

14. *Aerial Cartwheel.* This, too, is similar to one on the floor and should be practiced on a line on the floor. A good block with the front leg and a solid lift are essential elements of this skill.

15. *Aerial Walkover.* This action is very similar to the aerial cartwheel, except the beam is momentarily lost to sight. Once again it should be perfected on a line on the floor prior to being attempted on the beam.

Dismounts

The are several methods of dismounting to the mat at the end of the routine.

1. *Half Pirouette.* From a stand facing one end of the beam, swing the arms above the head and jump off the left side. Execute a half turn to the left and land on the mats facing the opposite end, with the left hand on the beam.

2. *Straddle Touch.* From a stand on the beam, jump into the air away from the beam and straddle the legs, touching the feet with the hands. Then bring the legs together for a landing on the feet on the mats. The performer may try touching only the knees or shins at first while learning the dismount. As skill progresses, the hands may reach to the feet or toes.

3. *Front Vault Dismount.* From a front leaning position, resting on the toes of the feet and straight arms, swing one leg down by the side of the beam and then lift it upward. As the lift is taking place, push off the foot that is in contact with the beam and lift it up to meet the other leg. At the same time move the body slightly to the side so as to finish in a stand next to the beam facing lengthwise.

4. *English Hand Balance Dismount.* From a standing position, move into an English hand balance. From this position, tilt the body slightly to the side

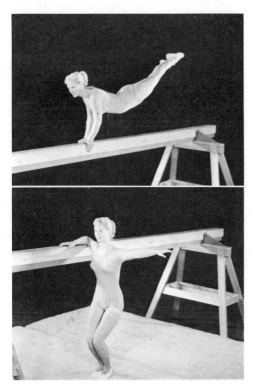

Front Vault Dismount

8. *Cartwheel.* Execute a cartwheel on the end of the beam and continue off the end onto the mat. Be sure to lengthen the cartwheel so the landing is done squarely to the feet and not too far over to the side of the body. It is also suggested that the performer execute a quarter turn in or out prior to landing to avoid knee injuries.

9. *Roundoff.* Place the hands on the end of the beam as in a roundoff action and land on the mats below, facing the end of the beam. Be sure to try it on the low beam prior to attempting it off the high beam. For spotting, the spotter stands on the mat facing the beam and catches the gymnast around the waist as she drops to the mats.

Roundoff Dismount

and drop down through a front vault dismount to the feet.

5. *Wendy Dismount.* From a handstand on the middle of the beam, execute a one-arm pirouette and continue moving the body to a stand on the mats on the other side of the beam.

6. *Hand Balance Squat-Through.* From a hand balance in the middle of the beam, execute a squat-through to the mats. As skill progresses, try doing a straight-leg stoop-through or a straight-leg straddle dismount.

7. *Valdez Dismount.* (Refer to the discussion of the valdez earlier in this chapter.)

10. *Front Handspring Off the End.* From a position a few steps from the end of the beam, take a step or two and lean forward toward the end of the beam, placing the hands on the end, and execute a front handspring dismount. Be sure to strive for an upward afterflight on the front handspring, since otherwise you may overspin.

11. *Barani.* This is similar to the skill executed on the floor exercise mat. Place one foot near the end of the beam and then thrust the other leg upward and over into the barani action. Quickly follow with the other leg and continue over to a landing on the mat. A spotter is essential during early learning stages and should stand on the side of the performer with a hand under her hips, assisting her throughout the move. Adequate landing mats are highly recommended during the early stages.

12. *Front Aerial Dismount.* This, too, is executed in a manner similar to an aerial walkover on the floor. With the

Barani Dismount

Handspring Dismount

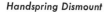

additional height, not as much arch is required of the performer. Two spotters should assist during early learning stages by grasping the arms of the performer. A mat draped on the end of the beam will provide for safe learning of this dismount.

13. *Somersault (Front, Back, or Reverse) Dismount.* The somersault action is described in detail in chapter 2. The forward somersault can be performed at the end of the beam or at the middle of the beam. If it is performed at the middle, the gymnast can begin by facing sideways and performing it or she can face lengthwise to the beam, moving slightly to the side of the beam in the air and finishing facing lengthwise with the nearest hand on top of the beam for support.

Front Aerial Dismount

Front Somersault Dismount

The back somersault can also be performed at the end of the beam as well as at the center. If it is performed at the center, the gymnast can face sideways to perform it, or she can face lengthwise to the beam. If facing lengthwise, the gymnast will often take one or two steps into the move, kicking up one leg and joining it with the other. This is called a gainer somersault and can also be performed at the end of the beam.

For additional routines consider the Age Group Compulsory Exercises for Boys and Girls published by the United States Gymnastic Federation, Box 12713, Tuscon, Arizona 85711.

13

Women's Floor Exercise

Floor exercise for women is performed to music on a resilient pad within a square area measuring 12 meters by 12 meters (39 feet 4 inches). A routine has a time limit of 1 minute minimum and 1 minute and 30 seconds maximum. The total area of the square should be used in the routine. Exercises should make use of the entire body and contain artistic movements, leaps, poses, balances, flexibility moves, and tumbling skills. These are done with a change of pace and with individual expression and amplitude. The composition should have a minimum of three tumbling passes performed on different parts of the floor exercise mat. A strong routine should have front, back, and twisting or mixed tumbling. The connecting moves and dance combinations should have a difficulty value corresponding to that of the rest of the routine. These connecting moves should make use of several levels of height. The gymnast should constantly try to change level and direction, never spending too much time in one area or at a given level. The

routine must be performed with musical accompaniment of a single instrument, and the types of movements being done should conform to the nature of the music. The advanced gymnast will try to select music that will fit her body type as well as her particular style. A great amount of inventiveness and artistic thinking can be displayed throughout the floor exercise routine. It is one of the most creative events in women's gymnastics.

VALUES

The specific values of performing floor exercise are the development of:

1. A sense of and appreciation for rhythm and timing.

2. Coordination and balance to a high degree.

3. The ability to create a fine artistic exercise.

4. Strength and endurance through the

hard workouts necessary for the accomplishment of the final routine.

ORGANIZATION

Many floor exercise moves for women should be tried first on tumbling pads placed on the floor exercise mat. Later, as skill improves, the mats may be removed and the moves performed on the floor exercise pad alone. It is highly recommended that a spotter be used while students are learning some of the more difficult moves such as walkovers, valdez, back handsprings, somersaults, and so forth.

In composing a routine, it is suggested that individual moves be learned thoroughly first, and then added to other moves to form combinations which can become parts of the larger routine. This may be seen as a problem to be solved by the performer, using creativity within the limits set by the instructor and the performer's own ability. This will give the performer a feeling for the event, and later, as more difficult moves are learned, they may be inserted at the performer's discretion. Routines should make use of the entire body and include movements and jumps that are full of expression, elegance, individuality, and originality. Remember that an effort should be made to make the connecting moves harmonious when there is a change in rhythm, style, or pace.

PROGRAM OF INSTRUCTION

Instruction in floor exercise involves three basic steps:

1. *Individual moves.*

2. *Combinations.* As a person learns a new skill, she should be challenged to combine it with another stunt as smoothly as possible. Because a move must be learned well in order to combine it with another, the use of combinations in the teaching progression stresses proper execution and increases the safety of performance. In addition, the smaller combinations serve as building blocks for longer routines. Combinations can be suggested by the instructor or coach or can be created by the performer.

3. *Routines.* Ultimately, a pupil should strive to combine moves into a routine. Competition is based on routines, required or optional. The approach to optional routines is one of problem solving. Certain requirements involving the types of movements and the time limit are presented as a problem for the performer to solve creatively within her own capabilities. The instructor or coach and pupil can coordinate their thoughts on the development of a particular routine.

The specific skills or movements that can be done in this women's event come under the following groups: ballet, balance, agility, and flexibility. The movements that appear within these groups are in a recommended order for learning.

Ballet Movements

1. *Toe Stand.* Start from a standing position and raise up on the toes, extending the arms to the side, palms down. Then, return to a full standing position with the arms at the sides. This can also be done with the arms extending overhead and then dropping down to the sides.

2. *Ballet Touch.* In a standing position, with one foot ahead of the other, lean

Toe Stand

Body Sweep

forward gracefully to touch the forward foot with one hand. This is often used as a transition from one movement to another.

3. *Body Sweep.* As pictured, execute a graceful sweep of the body by swinging one arm forward, with the weight on the other arm and knee, keeping the other leg

Ballet Touch

extended backward. The arm can continue overhead and backward so you end in a fully arched position and then into a fall to the mat and into another connecting move.

4. *Body Wave.* From a standing position with the hands at the sides, the performer executes four movements at once: slight flexion of the knees; contraction through the stomach; contraction through the chest; and dropping of the head. From this position extend the body, starting at the knees and hips and moving upward to finish in an upright position with the arms overhead and the back slightly arched. From here the downward motion begins with flexion of the knees, contraction of the stomach and chest, and dropping of the head. The movement finishes in a contracted position with the arms down by the sides. The body wave should be executed in a smooth, continuous manner.

Variations of Body Waves: (1) Same, but circle the arms to the rear; (2) begin

Body Wave

in the extended, upright position, move into contracted phase, and then finish in extension; (3) same as original move but performed on knees.

5. *Stride Leap.* On the last step into the leap bend the take-off leg so as to start in a plié position, ready for a strong push from the ground. Move into approximately a 90° split while suspended in the air. Land on the forward leg in a plié position with the back leg extended behind.

6. *Split Leap.* Same as the stride leap except the performer moves into a full 180° split position in the air. Continue to lift the forward leg in particular throughout the leap.

7. *Stag Leap.* Similar to the split leap except the performer moves from the extended, split position into the stag position by bending the lead leg and bringing the lead foot backward quickly to the knee of the rear leg. Land on the

lead leg in a slight plié position, with rear leg behind.

8. *Cabriole.* Push off of one leg into the air while lifting the opposite leg forward and upward. Bring the extended push-off leg quickly up to meet the other

Body Wave

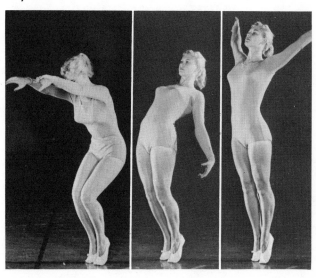

Stride Leap

Split Leap

leg and tap the feet together. Then drop the push-off leg down to the floor while keeping the other leg slightly lifted. Finish in a plié on the push-off leg.

9. *Tour Jeté.* Step forward on the left foot, swing the right leg forward and upward, and, *while in the air,* turn the body a half turn and land on the right foot with the left leg extended straight behind.

10. *Soada Bas.* Like the tour jeté except a full turn is executed, with the performer landing on the foot that is kicked upward, and during the turn, the other leg is flexed with the foot placed near the shin of the straight leg.

11. *Fouetté.* This is like the tour jeté except that the leg kicked into the air is held aloft, and landing is done on the same foot from which the performer leaps.

12. *Pirouette.* The pirouette consists of a turn on one foot. Force for the turn is

Stag Leap

Cabriole

generated through the arms, legs, and head. It begins with a demi-plié of both legs, at which time one arm is brought forward of the center of the body. The next step is a strong push-off, finishing in a firm balance on the supporting leg. The free leg should move to a position somewhere between the ankle and the knee of the supporting leg. At the same time the other arm is brought forward to center body so that both arms are in front of the body, slightly below the chest during the turn. The arms open sideways at the completion of the turn.

A factor of importance in performing a turn is the head. The head remains stationary, focusing on a point straight in front of the body as the turn begins. The head then turns quickly in the direction of the turn, until it arrives on the focal point again. This should be done quickly so that the head arrives there before the rest of the body. This quick snap of the head aids in the speed of the turn, as well as decreasing dizziness.

Variations: (1) The direction of the spin can vary; the pirouette can turn outward in the direction of the raised leg or inward in the direction of the supporting leg; or (2) the pirouette can be performed from nearly any pose.

Balance Movements

This division describes the floor exercise moves mainly requiring a balancing technique. Many of the balancing skills described in chapter 3 may be used. Additional ones are included here. The balance positions in floor exercise are mainly transitional moves rather than held positions. A momentary holding position is called a pose and may take many forms.

Front Scale

1. *Arabesque.* This is a one-leg balance in which the rear leg is extended behind at any level from the floor up to 90°. The upper torso is allowed to lean only slightly forward. The arms are extended so as to create a line of symmetry from fingertips to toes.

2. *Front Scale.* Similar to the arabesque except the rear leg is held above 90° and the upper torso is allowed to lean farther forward.

3. *Attitude.* Attitude is a pose on one leg in which the free leg is lifted behind, turned out at the hip, and bent at the knee. The arms may be held in a variety of positions.

4. *One-Leg Balance.* In this balance the leg is raised to the side, slightly forward, and as high as possible. The hand of the same side grasps the instep of the raised foot. The opposite arm may be held to the side to assist in balancing.

5. *Needle Scale.* From a high front scale the gymnast moves her chest and head downward toward the supporting

Attitude

One-Leg Balance

like balance with the chest and head flush against the supporting leg and the other leg held vertically. This movement is more often performed on the balance beam than it is in floor exercise.

Needle Scale

6. *V-Sit.* The move consists simply of sitting on the floor with the legs together, elevated to make a V with the body. The hands may be either on the floor behind the performer or raised outward from the shoulders. This move is most often used on the balance beam and as a transitional move in floor exercise rather than as a held position.

7. *Hand Balance.* The techniques of a hand balance are thoroughly covered in chapter 3. Many different methods of moving into the hand balance position are possible. A straight kick up, straddle press, back bend, or cartwheel into a hand balance are some suggested meth-

leg while continuing to move the back leg upward until it is in a vertical position. The gymnast finishes in a needle-

V Seat

Yogi Hand Balance

Straddle Press to Handstand

Hand Balance, Split Legs

ods. A variation of holding a hand balance can be achieved by moving from a legs-together position to split legs.

8. *Yogi Hand Balance.* As pictured, this hand balance calls for an unusual position of the body. The hips are forward, the legs back, and the head lifted so that the entire move looks fascinating and challenging. One of the easiest methods of moving into the yogi position is to jump into it with the hands on the floor; push off both feet and immediately execute the yogi hand balance.

Agility Moves

Many tumbling moves such as those described in chapter 2 may be used to demonstrate agility in floor exercise. Additional moves requiring agility are included here.

1. *Swedish Fall.* From a standing position, fall forward and land on the hands with the arms straight, then flex the arms, continuing the fall downward to the chest. Lift one leg as the fall is executed so that in the finished position one leg is lifted gracefully and one leg remains on the floor. The upper part of the body should almost rest on the floor with the weight supported by the arms. Prior to having students do this move, make sure they can perform push-ups easily.

2. *Knee Turn.* From a kneeling position on the left knee with the right leg

Swedish Fall

extended to the side, bring the right knee alongside the left knee, turning the body to the left, with the right arm coming across the chest and the left arm behind the left shoulder. After completing a full turn on the knees several moves may be executed, such as: a fall to the floor, a slide into a split, a front walkover from the knees, and so on.

3. *Leg Circles.* This move may begin in a split or in a hurdle position. If a split is performed with the right leg forward, the next movement is to lean slightly backward and to the right. At this time the weight is taken off the left leg and the leg is circled in an extended position forward and to the right. The gymnast is now lying on her back and the left leg continues to make a full circle with the leg circling close to the chest and overhead. At this point the right leg is still on the ground, and a wide split position is demonstrated. The right leg now begins a circling action upward and over the head toward the left. The circling of this leg assists the performer in rolling over onto the stomach, completing the movement. From here the gymnast can perform any

number of moves, for example, a log roll onto the back or pulling the body into a forward roll or headstand.

4. *Aerial Cartwheel.* After taking a couple of running steps, place the take-off foot forward, have the knee partially bent to facilitate a good blocking action, and lean slightly forward with the upper body. Then whip the back leg up and over and at the same time lift the arms and push forcefully with the take-off leg. This will thrust the body upward so you feel suspended momentarily in midair. Continue pulling the lead leg over toward the mat and finish in a stand. Don't lean too far forward with the upper body on the take-off; try to keep the chest horizontal to the mat and be sure to get a good block with the take-off leg by bending it slightly and then forcefully pushing as the aerial is started. Lift hard with the arms. Keep the center of gravity behind the take-off foot for maximum upward push. A good lead-up is to do cartwheels with as much elevation as possible and touching the hands minimally.

Flexibility Movements

It is suggested that the gymnast include flexibility and stretching exercises as part of her warm-up and conditioning to improve the performance of the following moves.

1. *Splits.* From a standing position the performer moves downward extending one leg out in front while extending the other leg backward with the top of that foot flat against the floor. The performer should be facing toward her forward leg with her shoulders and hips squarely in line with the leg.

Aerial Cartwheel

taining a strong forward and upward lift through the chest, hips, and second leg, the body continues to an upright position. A spotter is essential while gymnasts are first learning this stunt. Support should be given under the shoulders and hips while the gymnast transfers weight from the hands to the lead leg and continues up to the standing position.

Variations: (1) Perform a front walkover from a kneeling position. (2) *Switch-leg front walkover:* As the vertical position is reached with the legs in a full split, switch the legs so that the opposite leg becomes the lead leg. The walkover continues as before from here.

Straddle Lean

2. *Straddle Lean.* The move begins in a straddle stand. The gymnast stretches downward into a wide forward split position, then leans forward to touch the chest to the floor.

3. *Front Walkover.* Begin in a standing position with arms stretched overhead. Lean forward, flexing one knee, so as to place both hands on the mat while kicking other leg up behind. Continue to drive the leg overhead. When the vertical position is reached the head should be neutral, the shoulders should be directly in line with the hands, and the hips should be squarely over the shoulders, demonstrating a full stretch through shoulders, stomach, and back. At this point the legs should be in a full 180-degree split position. From here the lead leg continues over until it contacts the floor, at which time the hands release from the mat. Keeping the head back in line with the arms and main-

Front Walkover

4. *Front Tinsica.* This movement is a combination of a cartwheel and a front walkover. It begins with a sideways cartwheel, and as the gymnast reaches the vertical position, she shifts the hips so as to finish in a manner similar to a walkover. The body should maintain the cartwheel position, like the spokes of a wheel, throughout the movement. The head should remain neutral and be prevented from coming forward as the first hand is released from the mat.

5. *Valdez.* Sit on the floor with the right leg extended forward and the left knee bent so that the left heel is close to the buttocks. One of two arm positions can be assumed: Either the right arm can be extended forward with the left hand behind the back, or the left hand can be extended with the right hand behind the back. The hand behind the back (hips) should be at a comfortable distance from the hips. The wrist should also be turned as far as possible, as the arm must rotate around that base of support. From this position the extended leg and arm lift up and backward toward the mat behind. At the same time, the bent leg pushes forcefully against the mat. When the vertical position is reached, the body should be in an alignment similar to that of the back walkover, except for the rotation of the arm. The movement is carried over to the feet and finishes like a back walkover.

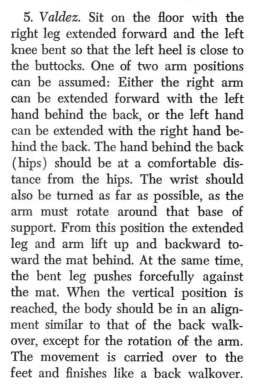

Valdez

6. *Back Walkover.* Start from a stand with one leg slightly in front of the other, the hips squarely aligned and at an even level, the arms stretched overhead. Leading with the arms not the shoulders, reach backward toward the mat. As the body leans backward, the leg directly under the hips bends slightly to achieve a pushing action. The leg held in front drives upward and backward overhead. As the vertical position is reached, the head should be held neutral between the arms, the shoulders should be directly in the vertical alignment showing a full stretch, and the hips should be squarely over the shoulders, at an equal level. The legs demonstrate a full 180-

Back Walkover

degree split position. The lead leg continues to drive backward until it contacts the floor. Upon contact the knee may bend as the hands are lifted off the floor and the upper torso is brought up to an erect stand. At the same time the second leg is brought down to the mat in a stretched position behind the first leg.

Support by a spotter under the back and lead leg is necessary when gymnasts first learn this movement.

Variations: (1) *Switch-leg:* Similar to the switch-leg front walkover. When the vertical position is reached, the legs are switched so that the original trailing leg now becomes the lead leg. (2) *Back walkover to kneeling:* Rather than arriving onto the bottom of the foot of the lead leg, the gymnast slowly swings down to the top of the foot, eventually rolling onto the knee and extending the second leg behind to finish in a swan position.

For additional routines consider the Age Group Compulsory Exercises for Boys and Girls published by the United States Gymnastic Federation, Box 12713, Tuscon, Arizona 85711.

14

Springboard Trampoline

The springboard trampoline is a recently invented piece of gymnastic equipment that is meeting with unanimous approval throughout the country. Commercially manufactured under such names as "Trampolet," "Mini-Tramp," "Gym-Tramp," and "Takeoff-Tramp," its purpose is that of a springboard.

Mechanically speaking, it consists of a rigid steel tubular ring about 3 feet in diameter or a square frame about 3 feet wide supported by legs and cushioned with rubber traction shoes, which will grip smooth gym floors. The legs are adjustable so that the angle of the woven web bed may be changed to suit the performer. The woven web bed is suspended by rubber cables or springs. This provides a maximum bounce for the performer.

VALUES

The specific values of working on the springboard trampoline are:

1. The springboard trampoline supplements or assists instruction in such activities as tumbling, diving, trampolining, cheerleading, and vaulting.

2. It fulfills the natural desire to jump into the air and to execute various other expressive movements.

3. It develops agility, coordination, and balance as the performer learns to maneuver his or her body while in the air.

4. Because of its compactness and easy maneuverability, it is an excellent device in staging exhibitions.

ORGANIZATION

Before elaborating on the many stunts that can be done on the springboard "tramp," a few basic safety hints should be mentioned:

1. Progress slowly in learning the use of the apparatus. The first few attempts should merely consist of bouncing off to the feet. Practice the art of leaning

forward or backward, depending on the stunt in mind.

2. The springboard tramp may be padded with mats for safety. This is especially effective when students are first trying stunts with it. As skill is developed, the mats may be eliminated.

3. Use the safety belt when attempting somersaults for the first time.

4. Be sure the mechanical phases of the device are always in readiness, all shock cords securely fastened, rubber pads on the legs secure, adjusting screws tightened, and so on.

5. In spotting the activity, have two spotters standing one on each side of the tramp to assist the performer through the first few attempts of the particular stunt.

6. When used to assist in tumbling or as an activity by itself, the springboard tramp may be placed on mats so that landings can be made on mats.

PROGRAM OF INSTRUCTION

The springboard trampoline may be employed in many ways: for tumbling, diving, cheerleading, vaulting, and so on. Before elaborating on these, a detailed program of instruction will be presented for activity with the device itself.

The art of simply bouncing off the springboard tramp is learned in much the same way as the approach and take-off on a diving board. The performer merely trots toward the apparatus and just prior to reaching it, lifts one leg up, follows immediately with the other, and leaps onto the bed of the tramp. This acts as the hurdle. Upon landing on the bed, the performer sinks downward, and the recoil of the tramp bed sends him or her into the air for the execution of the stunt.

At the time of the bounce, the arms are lifted into the air and the head and

Tuck Leap and Landing

chest are also raised. Diligent practice is needed to master the basic technique of bouncing off the springboard tramp, for only then can the many fine and enjoyable stunts be performed.

1. *Ball-Up.* This stunt is a slight variation of simply bouncing forward off the tramp. Upon taking off, bring the knees up to the chest and momentarily grasp the shins. This ball-up or tuck position is assumed for a split second, then released, and the legs are extended downward in preparation for the landing on the mat.

2. *Straddle Touch.* The performer, upon leaving the tramp, leaps into the air and extends the legs forward and to the sides in a straddle position. The toes are touched lightly with the hands and then the legs are snapped downward to the mat. This takes practice, so it is suggested that the performer try touching the knees first, then the shins, and finally the ankles or toes. This also can be done with the arms down between the straddled legs.

3. *Half Twist.* Take off from the tramp in a forward bounce. While taking off, start a half turn to the right by pulling the right shoulder back. Look in the direction of the turn and execute the half twist. Land on the feet facing the tramp.

4. *Full Twist.* This is similar to the half twisting jump except that a com-

Straddle Touch Leap

Arms Between Straddle Legs

Pike Leap

Full Twist

plete turn is executed before the performer lands on the mat. Be sure to keep the body straight while twisting. Also, do not twist too hard off the tramp, as this will cause the body to tilt and an improper landing will result.

5. *Stag Leap.* This stunt consists of bouncing forward off the tramp and assuming a stag leap position while in the air. See "Women's Floor Exercise" for the stag leap.

6. *Half Turn on Tramp.* This stunt involves bouncing straight up off the tramp, executing a quick half twist, landing back on the bed, and then bouncing off to the feet in the direction of the original run.

7. *Backward Bounce Stunts.* For the most part, many of the stunts such as the straight forward leap, tuck bounce, straddle touch, half twist, clap hands, and so on, may also be tried going backward from the tramp. Be sure to get the proper lean backward so that the feet clear the frame upon landing.

8. *Leap to Feet into Forward Roll.* Leap forward from the tramp, land on the feet, and then go into a neat forward roll. Be sure to emphasize to the students that they must land squarely on the mat with their feet before starting the forward roll.

9. *Leap Backward to Feet into Backward Roll.* Bounce backward from the

tramp, land on the feet, and then go into a quick backward roll.

10. *Bounce Twice on Tramp into a Backward Leap.* Bounce straight up on the first rebound, then hit the bed again with the feet, and lean back slightly to a backward bounce to the feet. Try this stunt first from an extremely low bounce. On second bounce, be sure to anticipate the backward leap so that the feet will clear the frame upon landing on the mat.

After the fundamentals of bouncing have been taught and the performer feels at home on the springboard tramp, it may be used effectively to assist in instruction in other areas or as a technique for a performance in itself. Some of these areas are as follows:

Tumbling

This apparatus is a fine device with which to assist the tumbler in executing somersaults, twisters, and so on. Some suggested stunts are:

Over the low or back end:

1. Back somersault—tuck, pike, or layout position.
2. Hand balance on high end, kickdown, back somersault.
3. Back somersault with half twist.
4. Back somersault with full twist.

Over the high or front end:

1. Front somersault—tuck, pike, and layout.

A method of hand spotting the front somersault is as follows:

The performer stands between two spotters all facing the springboard tramp. The inside hands of the two spotters grasp the wrists of the per-

former. Have the other hand ready to grasp the upper arm of the performer as the front somersault is commenced. All three run toward the small tramp, and just as the performer leaps to the bed, the spotters turn in and grasp his or her upper arm. With a hold on the wrist with the inside hand and on the upper arm with their outside hand, the spotters then assist the performer through the forward somersault movement. The spotters should retain the grip on the wrist and upper arm upon completion of the forward somersault, as this allows for a safe and softer landing by the performer.

2. Barani.
3. Gainer.
4. Front somersault with full twist.
5. Front somersault with one-and-a-half twist.

Although these tumbling stunts are generally executed in a gym onto mats, they are also fun on a sandy beach. This type of apparatus has been used a great deal at the famous Santa Monica Beach in California.

Cheerleading

This apparatus has become widely used by cheerleading squads throughout the country. It is beneficial to the squad in practicing their leaps, endings, and so on. It has become a clever means of counting the score, by having each cheerleader jump off for a count of the team's running score. Somersaults may also be executed by the advanced tumbling cheer squad to count the score. Be sure to have a spotter next to the tramp while the girls and/or boys are performing their somersaults, and so on, because

Front Somersault

Back Somersault with Spotter

Barani with Spotter

Half Turn Into Front Somersault

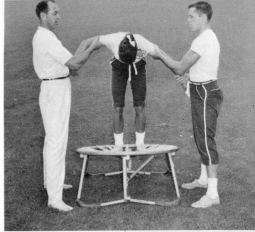

the grass can become slippery and thus somewhat hazardous. Because of its compactness, the springboard trampoline can easily be transported from game to game.

Diving

The springboard tramp can be used effectively for diving practice. By using the overhead safety belt, many "dryland" dives can be tried with comparative ease. It can also be used as a substitute for a diving board alongside a swimming pool or on a pier.

Trampoline Mounting

Trampoline performers can use the device as a means of mounting onto the

trampoline. In exhibition, this method of mounting is particularly effective.

Some of these mounts are:

1. Swan dive to a front drop.
2. Swan dive over a back drop.
3. High bounce to a feet bouncing position—with half, full twist.
4. High bounce to a seat drop.
5. High bounce with a half twist to a back drop.
6. Back pullover out of above stunt.
7. Front somersault.
8. Barani.
9. Front one-and-a-quarter somersault to a front drop.
10. Front one-and-a-quarter somersault with a half twist to back drop into back pullover.
11. Front one-and-three-quarters somersault to a back drop.

Stunts for Two Performers

Two people can use the apparatus effectively in staging exhibitions of tum-

Mounting to the Shoulders

273

bling and balancing skills. Some of these stunts are:

1. Bounce to a swan position overhead.
2. Bounce to shoulder mounts.
3. Bounce to high arm-to-arm balance.
4. Bounce to hand-to-hand balances.

Vaulting

The device can be used for vaults over apparatus such as long horse, buck, side horse, and parallel bars (covered with mats). A few of the vaults that can be done are flank vaults, front vault, rear vault, squat vault, straddle vault, headspring, and handspring.

Double Mini-Trampoline

A recently invented piece of gymnastic equipment called a double mini-trampoline has been received with enthusiasm by the trampoline and tumbling athletes throughout the United States and the

Somersault off Double Mini-Tramp

Half Turn Into Back Somersault

world. It evolved from competition in performing somersaults off the single springboard (or mini-tramp) onto a soft landing pad. The presently-used double mini-tramp has a slanted portion merging into a horizontal area completely supported within the frame by springs. The entire apparatus is 11 feet long, 5 feet wide, and 2 feet high. A thick pad covers the top of the frame, and a 12- to 15-inch landing mat approximately 15 feet long and 8 feet wide is adjacent to the dismounting end of the apparatus.

The performer approaches from the slanted end, takes a hurdle step onto this part, and bounces toward the horizontal area. He or she can bounce to this level area in a straight body, tuck, straddle,

Barani

Rudolph Off Double Mini-Tramp

Spotting Back Somersault

Barani

Fliffis off Double Mini-Tramp

or pike position, or may execute some type of somersault, such as a forward somersault, gainer, barani, rudolph, full-twisting gainer, and so on. Upon landing on the level part of the double mini-tramp, the performer casts forward toward the landing pad and executes a straddle leap, pike jump, tuck jump, or a somersault with or without twists. He or she may choose to do a spotting somersault, landing back on the level area again and then bounce forward into a dismount.

Rules for competition have been established and may be obtained from the United States Tumbling and Trampoline Association at 930 27th St. S. W., Cedar Rapids, Iowa 52406, or the National AAU, 3400 W. 86th St., Indianapolis, Indiana 46268.

The photos of double mini-tramp stunts are identified and the techniques of performing each are covered in the earlier part of this chapter or in the trampoline chapter.

15

Rope Activities

Rope activities include rope skipping, jumping, and climbing. Rope skipping employs a single light leap to each swing of the rope, which is swung by the individual doing the skipping. Rope jumping refers to the more erratic, jolting movement over a longer rope swung by two helpers. The term may also refer to jumping over a static rope at various levels or as it wiggles on the ground. Rope climbing refers to the actual climbing of a suspended rope or the stunts done while on such a rope.

VALUES

1. Children of all ages can have a great deal of fun in skipping and jumping because it is such a natural play activity. One can witness this enjoyment among a group of children indulging in normal play on a summer afternoon. It definitely serves as a release for pent-up muscular energy.

2. Rope skipping is fundamentally simple, but it can be advanced to a high degree of skill and achievement and is interesting enough to carry over into postschool life. Because one can skip rope in a small space and during any free time, it promotes self-enjoyment, thus providing a good medium for recreation and sport expression, regardless of age or sex.

3. The physical benefits derived from rope activities are numerous as witnessed by their heavy use in conditioning programs of boxers and other athletes. Rope skipping exercises, such as those boxers perform, develop agility, motor coordination, and a sense of rhythm and balance. Rope activities also build endurance and stamina and strengthen the skeletal muscles. Rope climbing is especially good for building up the arm, shoulder, and chest muscles, and for developing explosive power. For this reason it is of particular value in training pole vaulters, wrestlers, and gymnasts.

ORGANIZATION

The rope activities of skipping, jumping, and climbing can be easily added to the physical education program. First, they are very inexpensive to incorporate into existing facilities. Only the climbing ropes require a structure, and any substantial beam or ceiling can be used as a point of suspension. The ropes seldom need replacing because of their durability. Rope activities are also economical in space requirements in that a small storage space is required for the skipping or jumping ropes, and the climbing ropes may be pulled out of the way easily.

PROGRAM OF INSTRUCTION

Rope Skipping

Sneakers or moccasins are recommended for skipping rope. Shoes may be used, but the rope is apt to catch on the heel. If allowance is made for the heel, the jump is too high for good skipping form. For exhibition skipping, pliable dress shoes with the heels removed and a patch of rubber sole to prevent slipping are recommended. These shoes are light and flexible yet give good support.

A number 8 or number 9 sash cord is recommended for use in rope skipping, although any rope can be used with varying degrees of success. It should be long enough to extend from armpit to armpit as the skipper stands on the center of the rope, or from hip to hip as the skipper stands in a stride position on the rope. For speed skipping, one or two knots in each end will shorten the rope enough for maximum performance. Some skipping ropes are adjustable through a device within the handles.

Any available space with sufficient headroom can be adapted for skipping rope. However, some surfaces have preference over others:

1. A smooth, hard-packed dirt surface is fair. The people at the rear of the skipper should be cautioned about the stones and dirt picked up and thrown by the rope. Dust will be stirred up and inhaled if the earth is too dry.

2. A hard wooden surface is good if not too slippery and hazardous. Care should be taken to see that the skippers do not overdo so that the muscle attachments become irritated in the legs.

3. A semihard wooden surface is good because of the "give" it has. It helps performance and reduces fatigue.

4. Cement, asphalt tile, or marble floors can be used and are more efficient for speed skipping, but they are fatiguing and may be injurious to the metatarsal arch and may cause shin-splints. If the surface is rough, it retards performance and causes undue wear on the rope.

All surfaces should be free of loose dirt and dust. Rope skipping lends itself to mass instruction. A comfortable distance must be provided between jumpers. The instructor may find it advisable to teach from a small platform, 2 or 3 feet high. It is also imperative that the instruction start from the simple and progress to the more difficult. The following are some suggestions for handling the entire class:

1. A demonstration of rope skipping can be given by the instructor or by other students during the class period.

2. The class may be divided into squad leaders.

3. Rope skipping competition in the fundamental skills can be held with emphasis on quality rather than on quantity.

4. The use of films on rope skipping will help the teacher instruct students in the fundamental and advanced skills.

5. Current articles on rope activities should be made available for added motivation.

The following suggestions may be used to introduce and teach the activity of rope skipping:

1. *Mimetic games.* These involve jumping, hopping, and skipping. This serves as a warm-up for the activity of skipping rope.

2. *Jumping in response to commands.* The instructor asks the class to hop to a cadence that is called out; it should be varied by the instructor to maintain alertness.

3. *Jumping in response to music.* To develop a sense of timing, the instructor may play several records of different rhythms, or a piano may be played and the students asked to hop to the beat of the music.

4. *Jumping with an imaginary rope.* Using no rope but allowing the hands to respond as if a rope were present, try skipping this imaginary rope and keeping the following techniques in mind:

a. Feet, ankles, and knees should be together.

b. Head erect, back straight, chest out, and eyes up.

c. Jump off the floor about one inch.

d. Each landing must be on the balls of the feet, with the knees bent slightly to break the shock of the landing.

e. The upper arms should be close to the sides, with the hands 8 to 10 inches from the thighs.

f. The hands should describe a circle of about 5 inches in diameter while skipping.

5. *Introduce the rope to the students.* Have all of them try skipping the rope independently of each other. Allow the students a sufficient amount of free time to practice on their own.

6. *Mass skipping.* Have all the students start with the rope behind them and do 5 to 10 forward consecutive skips. They should start on a given command, and a cadence should be kept while the entire class executes the specified number of skips. Progress to series of 20 skips or more.

7. *Skip rope backward.* Have the entire class first try skipping backward with an imaginary rope and after the students have gotten a feel for it have them attempt 2 or 3 skips with the rope. They should start with the rope in front and lift it over the head into the backward spin. Have them start this on a given command and execute a specified number of backward skips.

8. *Skip forward or backward at a faster pace.* This improves confidence and results in skilled performers.

9. *Skip the rope forward while hopping on one leg.* Try alternating the foot after so many hops on one foot with the same number on the other foot.

10. *Alternating spreads.* The legs are spread apart on one jump and brought together on the second.

Rope Skipping Class

11. *Consecutive spreads.* This is done as above except the legs are brought together on each downward swing of the rope and spread apart to land.

12. *Leg flings.* One leg is flung sideways or forward alternately as the rope passes under the feet, and the legs are brought together as it descends for the next jump.

13. *Sideward and forward jumps.* Both legs are lifted sideward or forward as the rope passes under the feet.

14. *Alternate to the sides.* Jump rope forward, and on every other circle of the rope, allow it to pass by the side of the body instead of under the feet. Thus it will pass first under the feet, then to the right side of the body, then under the feet, then to the left side of the body, and so on.

15. *Crisscross—forward and backward.* As the rope descends, the arms are crossed at the elbows, forming a loop with the rope large enough for the performer to skip through. The arms are uncrossed on the second skip.

16. *Double jump—forward and backward.* As the rope descends, an extra snap of the wrist gives the rope more speed, and it passes under the feet twice with one jump.

17. *Partner skipping.* Two students skipping in the same rope, with one of them turning the rope.

18. *Combinations.* Any of the above suggested stunts in rope skipping can be combined into clever and stimulating routines. It is important to start with the simple routines and progress to the more difficult.

Competition

Rope skipping competition may be held to determine the champion of each room, grade, sex, or school. Some suggested items to be used for testing or competition are as follows:

1. A set number of consecutive forward skips.

2. A set number of consecutive backward skips.

3. A set number of consecutive forward alternate to the sides (front, left side, front, right side, etc.).

4. Same as above but backward.

5. A set number of consecutive forward skips on one foot.

6. A set number of consecutive backward skips on one foot.

7. A set number of consecutive forward crisscrosses.

8. Same as above but backward.

9. A set number of consecutive forward double jumps.

10. Same as above but backward.

11. Highest number of consecutive skips in 30 seconds (may use any of the above mentioned stunts for this).

12. Time required for 50 skips.

13. Relay contests may be used with individuals running in a skipping rope.

Rope Jumping

For variety and additional stimulation, the class may divide into small groups and attempt some rope jumping. Rope jumping consists of two persons swinging the rope while a third person jumps it. The rope should be approximately 10 feet long and heavy enough to describe the circle without losing its tautness. The rope should be swung at a clean, brisk pace. Some suggested rope jumping skills include:

1. *Entering a turning rope.* The student should place himself/herself near one of the twirlers and on the side where the rope circles downward toward the floor.

As soon as the rope passes him/her and strikes the floor, the student jumps into the area of the skipping. The rope in the meantime continues on up and over into another circle, and on the downswing, the student proceeds to jump and continues thereon.

2. *Exit from turning rope.* The exit is done from the opposite side from which the entrance is made. After the rope passes across the floor and proceeds to lift up into the arch, the student leaps out with the flow of the rope and "exits" to the side.

3. *The twirlers swing the rope back and forth across the floor* without describing an arch and the jumper jumps over the rope each time that it passes under his or her feet.

4. Same as the preceding but after a couple of half swings the twirlers should send the rope into a complete circle and the jumper jumps it.

5. In the two preceding exercises the jumper should face one of the twirlers, but now he or she should face outward, side to the twirlers, and execute the jumps with the rope describing complete circles.

6. *One leg jump combinations.* The jumper may try jumping the rope by hopping on both feet, then on one foot, and then alternating from one foot to the other. The jumper may also try spreading his legs, and so on.

7. *Doubles jumping.* Two students jump the rope at the same time.

8. *Complicated maneuvers.* Many complicated maneuvers may be attempted, such as having a doubles team enter and exit a turning rope, or having

a student simply run through the rope with a fast entrance and exit or doing a jump or two prior to exiting. A doubles team can work in tandem fashion; the first person enters the rope, executes a skip or two, and then exits, and the second person enters just as the first person exits. Two persons may try entering, jumping, and exiting at the same time.

9. *Skipping along with jumping.* The student may try to skip an individual rope while jumping in the larger jumping rope. All the variations suggested for both single skipping and long rope jumping may be tried together in this phase of the activity.

10. *Circling rope.* One person in the center swings the rope along the floor in a wide circle. Any number of persons standing within the range of this circling rope must jump over the rope as it approaches them.

Rope Climbing

The activity of rope climbing can be interesting and challenging in a modern physical education program. It is basically the activity of climbing up and down a vertical rope suspended from a support overhead. The rope should be 1½-inch manila; secure it safely from beams overhead and place a mat under it.

When climbing for the first few times it is suggested not to climb too high. Just a few feet at a time will accustom the climber to the rope and the techniques involved. Be sure to learn to climb downward as well as upward. Never slide down the rope as this will burn the hands and legs severely.

Because of the tiring effect of this activity, it is advisable to limit the amount

of time devoted to it. When first introducing the activity to the students, a full period may be devoted to it for demonstration and presentation of safety hints. Thereafter it is best undertaken at the end of the period. Rope climbing at this time can serve to bring the group together and to motivate them to an all-out effort. Contests of various sorts can also be planned, which will keep interest and enjoyment high.

The following list represents a progressive order for learning the art of rope climbing, finishing with the intricate skill of climbing the rope with the hands alone for speed. This latter method is specified for official competition.

1. *The activity of chinning,* with legs either vertical or horizontal to floor.

Rope Climbing

2. *Start from a standing* position, climb two pulls (strokes) upward, and lower slowly to a standing position. Increase the number of strokes upward with each try.

3. *From standing position,* hold onto rope and lower down to the mat to a supine position.

4. *From supine position,* pull up to a standing position.

5. *From supine position,* grasp the rope and do chin-ups by pulling with the arms.

6. *From standing position,* lower hand over hand to a sitting position, pull back up to a standing position (legs receive no support from floor although touching it).

7. *From standing position,* grasp the rope, flex the arms, and raise the legs to L position (parallel to floor) and hold for two or three seconds. Increase holding time with each try.

8. *From standing position,* grasp the rope and raise the legs to an inverted hang position, then lower slowly to a standing position.

9. *Grasp the rope and climb upward 3 to 4 strokes* and raise the body to an inverted hang position.

10. *Climb upward, using the foot and leg lock method.* In this method the rope passes between the legs and around the back of the right leg and across the instep of the right foot. Step on the rope with the left foot. Pull with the arms, allowing the rope to slide through until making it fast with foot at the end of the pull. From this clamp or lock position straighten the legs and reach upward with the arms for new grip. Climb and descend with this lock.

11. *Climb upward, using the stirrup method.* In this method, allow the rope to pass along the side of the body, down along the leg, under the near foot, and over the other foot. Grasp the rope and pull the knees up, with the rope passing through this position. Clamp the feet together, hold the body in position, and straighten the legs while the hands reach upward for new grip.

12. *Climb upward, using the cross leg method.* In this method, allow the rope to pass down between the legs, over the instep of one foot, and against the back of the other foot; clamp the two feet together while reaching upward for a new grip.

13. *Using feet and hands, climb upward for speed* 10 to 20 feet (start from a standing position).

14. *Using hands only, climb upward for speed* 10 to 20 feet (start from a standing position).

15. *Using hands and feet, climb upward from sitting position* 10 to 20 feet.

16. *Using hands only, climb upward from sitting position* 10 to 20 feet.

At times it may be desirable to hold a position on the rope in order to rest a few moments. Three hold or rest positions will be described here.

1. *Foot and Leg Lock Rest Position.* Climb rope, using foot and leg lock method. At rest position, hold the foot and leg lock on rope and pass the right arm in front of the rope so it is along the right side of body and in back of the right armpit. Circle both arms in back of body and grasp wrists. This position is held by applying foot and leg lock and squeezing right arm against rope.

2. *Inverted Hang Rest Position.* Climb upward to the rest position, spot, and swing legs upward to an inverted hang position. Place one leg in front of the rope and one in back. Reach behind the head with the right hand, grasp the rope, and pull it across the back and in front of chest, passing under left armpit. Squeeze with the legs and arms and the position is accomplished.

3. *Single- or Double-Leg Seat Position.* Climb upward a few feet and then stop and reach down with either hand and pull the rope below the thighs up to the rope above. Grasp both ropes and hold seat rest position. The rope may pass between legs to make a single leg seat or may pass under both legs and make a double-leg seat.

Two ropes close to each other can also be used in the climbing program.

Competitive Rope Climbing

Competitive Rope Climbing

Competitive rope climbing is truly an art and skill by itself. It does not involve all the intricacies and maneuvers of apparatus work, yet the art of climbing can be detailed and exacting in nature. A great deal of practice is involved to produce a champion rope climber. Because the record for climbing a rope 20 feet high with the hands alone is under 3 seconds, it is easily understood why considerable practice is necessary for top performance. With this in mind, the following paragraphs explain in detail the techniques of climbing the rope for speed.

Start standing on the floor with the rope in front of the body about arms' length away. Grasp the rope with the arms straight out from the shoulders. The hands should grip the rope so the backs of the hands face the climber. Lower the body to a sitting position on the floor so just the back side of the thighs touch the floor. The rope should continue to be in a vertical position with the body leaning slightly backward and the elbows bent a little. The take-off is the most difficult part of the climb, so the two-hand pull should be very forceful and strong. After this initial pull of both arms, continue to lean back with your upper body and look up toward the tambourine during the climb. Pull one hand down on the rope and continue the pull until that hand is near the hips, and at the same time reach straight up with the other hand for the next pull. Try to avoid sweeping across the chest to grasp the rope and always keep your palms away from your body. Avoid a straight L position of the body during the climb but instead strive for an open L or almost-open horizontal position of the body.

The legs add power and speed by kicking down just before the pull with the hand. The leg action should not be wild or exaggerated but should instead be smooth and controlled.

The number of strokes taken by the best climbers for the 20 feet is usually seven or eight plus the reach. The reach should be made with a straight up motion. When practicing, the reach should always be made with the same hand so strength and general timing is perfected to the finest detail. A good reach should be more than three feet and closer to four. Only the fingertips need to touch, and to pull beyond that height will add to the climber's time.

The best exercise for rope climbers is climbing itself. Each time climbers work out, they should be timed several times for speed.

Tug of War

Another rope activity that involves some of the same action as rope climbing is a tug of war. Such contests are usually greeted with enthusiasm and interest by both participants and spectators. Teams may be composed of almost any number of members, and each one gets an equal amount of exercise. The only equipment that is needed is a rope the size of a climbing rope or larger and some marks on the floor or ground, past which the front person must be pulled for the victory. A little teamwork in pulling will make up for the lack of individual strength.

16

Gymnastic Exhibitions

A gymnastic exhibition is a display of the imagination and the productivity of the students and teachers, limited somewhat by what is available at the particular school in terms of equipment, talent, space, time, and various other determining factors. Some schools with unlimited facilities can stage large productions, while others with limited facilities must be content with smaller productions calling for greater ingenuity. It is the plan of this chapter to present some general ideas that may be helpful in planning any exhibition.

VALUES

Some of the values of gymnastic exhibitions are:

1. They offer the opportunity to demonstrate to the community some of the activities that are included within the physical education program.

2. They provide recognition for the boys and girls who are not participating in varsity sports.

3. They provide a school project in which many students are involved. This may bring greater unity to the school in that several departments and teachers of the school can cooperate in the staging of the entire production.

4. They provide a fine means of gaining some money for worthwhile school projects.

5. The exhibitions provide an entertaining show for the community to witness.

Gymnastic exhibitions can be of several types, depending on their purposes. They may simply provide a short period of entertainment for the half-time at a basketball game. Occasionally entertainment is requested for a social engagement, and a limited performance of gymnastics skills could serve this purpose. Often gymnastics performances will occupy a large portion of physical education demonstrations or community recreation programs. In many cases, gymnastics will provide the entire program of entertainment in itself. Following are some suggestions for preparing a full-length show.

Planning

Planning is definitely the key to a successful gymnastic exhibition. Extensive planning must be done early and involves considerable thought and di-

Outdoor Show for the Community

Gymnastic Exhibition in Progress

rection by the teacher-director and his or her committee.

Committee Assignments

The initial work on any production is to divide the staff, class leaders, and students into various committees. People placed on these committees should be those who have indicated a keen interest in the show and are willing to work diligently on it. The director should appoint an assistant as this will save him/ her the burdensome task of making all the decisions. To avoid further confusion, it is suggested that each committee chairman be given a copy of the tentative program with a detailed list of instructions to be followed. The successful show depends on each committee's fulfilling its obligations on time. A series of time deadlines for each committee should be worked out in order to keep things moving at a regulated pace.

Theme

One of the first decisions to be made is the theme. Pick out a particular theme for each show and build the entire production around it. Some themes that have been used successfully by schools include: Physical Panorama; Sight-Seeing Tour to Foreign Lands; Daze in Tulip Land; Fantasy Land; Toyland Capers; Playland, USA; and Out of This World.

Poster Advertising Forthcoming Exhibition

Length of Show

The duration of the show should be approximately 1½ hours; it should not exceed 2 hours. It may be wise for the production committee to consider including a 15 minute intermission to break up the program.

Publicity

With the publicity committee rests the major responsibility of stimulating interest in attending the big show. Some means of creating this interest and enthusiasm are as follows:

1. Mimeographed flyers may be made, and distributed to all the students and to members of the community.

2. Posters advertising the show may be made and placed in convenient or strategic places.

3. News articles covering all the details of the show along with photographs of some of the acts may be distributed to the local newspapers.

4. Spot announcements on radio and television are possible in some areas.

Tickets

The ticket committee has a very important position in the production of the show. Through consultation with the director, this committee proceeds to set the price of the tickets and arranges for the printing and distribution of them at the various purchasing sites. This should all be done two or three weeks prior to the show.

Costumes

The costume committee has a very difficult task to perform in that each costume should be attractive and in theme and yet kept to a minimum of expense. Whenever regular physical education activities are demonstrated, it is suggested that the regular gym outfit be used. The specialty numbers generally call for a different outfit. These may be made by the student involved, his or her parents, or perhaps by the home economics department of the school. All costumes should be approved by the committee chairman and the director of the show. None should be designed or cut so as to receive criticism from the parents or patrons.

Decorations

Decorations create the atmosphere for any type of performance and are an essential factor in a successful production. Gymnasiums are rather difficult to decorate, but any change of scenery will be an added attraction for the audience.

Property

Because numerous pieces of equipment and props must be moved about throughout the show, it is imperative that a good property manager and crew be obtained. Many times this committee can make or break a show.

Concessions

Another source of revenue in addition to tickets is the concession stand. Items such as popcorn, candy, soft drinks, and so on can be sold by the refreshment committee. Small extra revenue can also be obtained by posting a clown or two in the lobby of the building to sell canes, flags, pennants, or other souvenirs. It is suggested that balloons or other noise-making items not be sold.

Printed Program

When the schedule of acts has been decided on, a committee should begin working on a well-designed printed pro-

The Stage Is Set

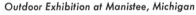

Outdoor Exhibition at Manistee, Michigan

gram. This program may or may not carry advertisements, depending on the policies of the school. The program should list the entire agenda along with the names of the participants and committee members. For public relations purposes, some of the administrative staff of the school and outstanding townspeople may be given special invitations and then listed as honored guests.

Program Schedule

Although the program is variable and flexible, some principles to follow in planning and arranging acts are presented here:

1. A parade, which should include all participants, is effective to use as the opening event.

2. Use the smaller children early in the program.

3. Acts involving beginners should be at the early part of the program so that a climax of advanced skills may be reached at the end of the show.

4. For variety, acts involving groups of performers should be mixed with acts involving individuals or small groups of two or three.

5. For variety, mix up the types of numbers. For example, a fast, snappy mass tumbling act would be good following a slow, precise doubles balancing routine. Also, if the program includes more than gymnastic acts, these activities should be intertwined with each other.

6. Short comedy skits can be included, interspersed throughout the program. These may be simple clown acts or comedy gymnastic routines.

7. Any lengthy delay between acts should be avoided. If a delay is neces-

sary for reasons such as moving equipment, comedy skits could be used to fill in the time.

8. An intermission of about 15 minutes is advisable if the program is of considerable length. This allows for the moving of heavy equipment and props as well as concession-stand sales.

9. An act including the entire cast should be used as the finale.

PROGRAM OF INSTRUCTION

Most of the gymnastic acts will involve stunts learned as part of the regular classroom instruction as described in the other chapters of this book. Because it is important that comedy be included in some of the gymnastic acts, the following routines and stunts are suggested for the various pieces of apparatus. They represent those that have been either used or seen by the authors. Perhaps they will stimulate ideas in the development of more stunts of this type.

Not everyone is suited to be a comedian, so be careful in casting these roles. Although it is essential that clowns wear uniforms that are different and funny, they must also have a personality that is suited to clowning. The comedians should also be good performers because many of the funny stunts require special skill.

Tiger Leaping

This involves long horse vaulting with the use of a springboard. The group should be comprised of 6 to 10 vaulters including the comedian. The general pattern is for the vaulters to follow one another in close order, with the comedian bringing up the rear. The vaulters should start with the easier stunts, such as straddle vaults or squat vaults, and gradually work up to the more difficult vaults such as cartwheels, headsprings, and handsprings. The comedian's routines might be as follows, keeping in mind that he or she is last in each series of vaults:

1. Hesitate as if bewildered and afraid to do the stunt but finally be persuaded to start the run. Immediately prior to reaching the springboard, veer off to one side and run past the equipment and circle back to the starting position.

2. Run toward the springboard, take a high hurdle but miss the end of the board, and land between the board and the horse with the end of the horse touching the abdomen.

3. Run up the springboard onto the horse and off the front end.

4. Follow the last two vaulters, attempting to imitate their headspring off the neck. Instead, do a forward roll into a lying position on the neck with the arms and legs circling the horse. As soon as this position is reached, the other vaulters should straddle vault over the clown. When the last vaulter has completed his or her vault, slide off the horse and run back to the starting place.

5. A proficient tumbler may do a complete front somersault over the long horse. Emphasize poor form and clutch hat to head while sailing through the air.

6. Finish the tiger-leaping act by stacking several people on the neck of the horse. Build this up gradually, one at a time, and when four or five or more

Doubles Balancing Act

people are piled up, do a straddle vault over all of them.

Tumbling and Balancing Stunts

This group could comprise 6 to 10 tumblers including the comedian. The general pattern of action on the tumbling mats is for the tumblers to follow one another down the mat. They should start with easier stunts such as forward rolls and cartwheels and gradually work up to more difficult stunts such as handsprings, somersaults, and twisters.

1. *Routine.* In this, as in tiger leaping, the comedian should be the last one for each trip down the mat. The routines for the comedian might be as follows:

a. Follow the last tumbler by simply running straight down the mat as if a difficult stunt is to be done, but never do it.

b. Do a series of cartwheels and tinsicas and then walk off the mat as if extremely dizzy.

c. After all the tumblers have executed successful dives and rolls over each other in a kneeling position, prepare to dive over the entire group. Audience participation may be obtained by asking for volunteers to kneel in between the tumblers. This is especially successful if children are in the crowd. After much preparation run up to first person but instead of diving over, run across the buttocks of all the kneeling persons.

d. Follow a tumbler who does a forward roll into a somersault or some such forward stunt and do a similar routine, but instead of completing the somersault out of the forward roll go only three-fourths of the way and land squarely on the buttocks, with the legs extended straight ahead. Jump up and run off holding the "injured" portion.

e. Have two tumblers and comedian straddle-jump over and forward roll under each other (see triple rolls in tumbling chapter). The comedian jumps higher and faster than the other two.

f. Log rolls (see tumbling chapter).

g. If comedian is a proficient tumbler, finish your performance with a good "straight" series of back handsprings, somersaults, twisters, and so on.

2. *Newspaper Dive and Roll.* A person is sitting on a low stool reading a newspaper. Another person does a high dive over the first person, grabbing the newspaper as he goes over, and then executes a roll with the paper in his hands. He or she may either end up sitting on the mat or continue rolling to a standing position. In either case he or she ends up reading the paper nonchalantly.

3. *Broom Swing Flip.* During an argument between two people, the one person swings a broom at the other one. The broom should be swung low at the legs. As the broom approaches the legs, the nonswinger does a back flip, thus allowing the broom to pass under him/her without touching.

4. *Wobbly Low Hand-to-Hand.* Comedy can be worked into a doubles hand balancing stunt, such as a low hand-to-hand. It involves the bottom person's presenting a shaky support as the top person attempts to kick up into a balance position. The bottom performer should be very relaxed and loose when the top one attempts to get into position. After some maneuvering to get the bottom

person's arms solid, perform the stunt in the regular manner.

5. *Hand-Clap Routine.* One person is lying in a supine position with the other standing near his or her head as if to proceed into a low hand-to-hand balance. The top person claps his or her hands as if to motion "Well, here we go" and promptly after this is done, the bottom person claps his/her hands with the same type of rubbing motion that would indicate "Okay, here we go." Then the top person claps again followed by the bottom person. This is repeated several times and each time the two performers' handclaps occur closer together until they both are clapping at the same time, which they continue to do briskly at the same time turning to the audience as if applauding for themselves.

6. *Stiff Arm, Stiff Leg.* One person is in a supine position with the other standing near his/her head as if about to proceed into a low hand-to-hand balance. Suddenly, one leg of the bottom person lifts up straight. The top person walks over to the leg and pushes it down and immediately one of the bottom person's arms is elevated stiffly. The top person then walks around and pushes this arm down, at which time the other arm is lifted stiffly into an elevated position. The top person walks around to this arm and pushes it down, and the other leg of the bottom person is lifted upward. The top person walks over to this leg and pushes it down and immediately the bottom person sits upright to a straight-back sitting position. The top person then walks over the bottom person to a position straddling his/ her waist facing the bottom person's shoulders and face. He/she then pushes

the shoulders back as if to get the performer into the original supine position and then promptly the bottom person's legs are elevated swiftly, and they strike the top person in the buttocks. The blow is supposedly hard enough to cause the top person to topple over the bottom person's head into a dive and roll.

Horizontal Bar Stunts

Not many stunts of the comedy nature can be done on the horizontal bar. A few will be described here. In addition to these, synchronized work done in opposite directions by two performers can be entertaining. Simple routines, not involving stunts causing the performer to move along the bar, will be suitable. One such routine is back uprise, back hip circle, underbar swing, single knee swing up, single knee circle backward, kip, underbar swing, hock dismount.

1. *Barber Pole.* Jump up and grasp one of the vertical standards with one hand. The jump should be with a slight forward motion so that the performer will rotate around the bar in a circular direction. By slowly releasing the grip, the performer will gradually descend as he rotates. One or two complete revolutions is usually sufficient to produce laughs.

2. *Double Hip Circles.* This stunt requires two performers. The first person does a belly grind mount. The second one grasps the bar inside of his partner's hands and pulls his legs up as if doing the same stunt. However, he spreads his legs and hooks them behind his partner's back. The second man is now upside down. After a little rocking motion, they start into a backward hip circle. Halfway through the hip circle, the second

man is upright and on top while the first man is underneath and upside down. The performers may pause here and then continue the action for a few more circles or do several circles in rapid succession. One person may hit the other's seat while he is in the top position.

3. *Straddle Stoop Gag.* While one man swings on the high bar, another man walks beneath the bar and stoops as if picking up a piece of chalk or some such object. Timing should be such that the man stoops as the high bar performer swings through, straddling his legs to avoid hitting him. This provides for a quick and exciting comedy gag.

Parallel Bar Stunts

Many comedy stunts are possible on the parallel bars. Several involve falling, which requires careful attention and much practice to avoid injuries.

1. *Scratching Leg.* When holding a hand balance (or shoulder balance) casually scratch the calf of one leg with the toes of the other. It is best to scratch with the leg nearest the audience.

2. *Lazy Man's Kip.* This stunt is described in the parallel bar chapter as a lead-up stunt to the ordinary kip on the end of the bars. However, it can be used as a comedy stunt if the clown does it immediately following a performance of an ordinary kip by a fellow gymnast.

3. *Walking into the Bars.* This stunt may be used by the clown in pretending that he does not see the bars while walking along. Just before he supposedly hits his chin or head on the bar, he kicks one foot up in front of him, and places his hands by the buttocks to brace himself

when he falls on his back beneath the bars. Sound effects would be effective if carefully timed.

4. *Hock Swing Fall.* A hock swing dismount may be done from the parallel bars by lifting the legs between the bars and hooking them over one bar. From this position, perform the stunt as on the horizontal bar. The comedy part occurs in releasing the legs too soon and landing on the stomach between the bars. Most of the weight of the body is absorbed by the hands and arms as they hit the mats first. This may be more effective if preceded by a straight performer actually completing the stunt.

5. *Collapse.* From a straddle seat position relax completely and fall backward, releasing the grasp as you fall. The legs remain hooked over the bars as long as possible in order to lessen the force of the fall. If the body is kept straight, it will swing as in the hock swing dismount, and the ending can be a fall on the chest.

6. *Stoop-Kick.* This stunt involves two performers. One has just finished a stunt at the end of the bars and is slow leaving, because he stoops to pick up an object or to look at the mat closely. The second performer may either jump to an upper-arm support or do a backward giant roll. With proper spacing and timing, the second performer's feet swing forward and kick the buttocks of the stooping first performer, thus causing him to lunge forward and fall.

7. *Arm Slide.* This is done by a performer wearing a long-sleeved shirt. The performer either takes a running jump to an upper arm support or does a fast backward giant roll. In either case he

releases his grasp and allows the momentum to slide him on his arms along the bars. The slide may even continue to the end and off from the bars, where the performer could land on his buttocks on the mats.

8. *Tickle Gag.* A gymnast maneuvers himself into a bird's nest position below the bars, holding on to the rails with his feet and hands. Maintaining that he is stuck, he calls for help from his fellow gymnasts. One or two proceed to push, pull, and shove him off the bars. Nothing seems to work, though, until one person holds up his hand as if to say "Ah, I've got the solution." Then he moves in close to the gymnast and "tickles" his stomach with his fingers, which causes him to drop to a prone position on the mats below.

Trampoline Stunts

The trampoline is suited to comedy stunts. A little imagination can produce many funny routines because of the various ways a person may fall and bounce without getting injured. No attempt will be made to present all of the known comedy stunts, but a few will be described as representative of the various types possible.

1. *Step Through Springs.* When attempting to mount the trampoline, the performer steps through the springs. This is best done by running toward one corner where the most clear area for stepping is available. A good gag to accompany this is to pretend to mash the face against the tramp bed after stepping through. By carrying a few beans in the mouth, one can spit them out as if they were teeth that had been knocked out.

2. *Rope Pull from End.* From a position of sitting on the end frame bar with the legs braced under the springs and tramp bed, the comedian falls backward so that his or her body is parallel to the tramp bed. He or she pretends that someone from the other end has thrown a rope and is pulling him/her up. The performer raises his/her body slowly by applying pressure on the tramp bed with the feet and occasionally slips back before coming to an upright position and mounting the trampoline.

3. *Suicide Dive.* From a high bounce, straighten the body and dive head first for the bed. Duck the head before landing and land on your shoulders and back. A screaming noise will add to the excitement of this stunt.

4. *One-Leg Dive.* At the top of the bounce, the performer bends over and grabs one leg, allowing the other leg to swing backward, parallel to the tramp bed. As the performer nears the bed, he/she releases the grasp and straightens out the body, landing in a front drop.

5. *Waving Turntables.* While doing a series of turntables, look and wave at the audience each time around.

6. *Low Back Drops.* Do a series of back drops and get lower on each one. Then you can pretend you are pulling on a rope and gradually raise the height of each back drop until you end in a standing position.

7. *Back Walk Over.* Do a backward three-quarters somersault to a front drop. As you are doing the flip, move your feet as though walking.

8. *Highest Back Flip.* Start bouncing and work up to as high a bounce as you

Trampoline Exhibition for Stadium Crowd

can. Then kill the bounce and immediately do a low back flip. Prepare for this stunt by announcing that you are going to do the highest back flip in the world. While bouncing, encourage the audience to shout "Higher!" with each bounce. Then the very low flip comes as a complete surprise.

9. *Basketball Bounce.* This stunt is done by two performers. The first performer does a back drop in a tuck position and remains in that position after the bounce. The second performer pushes the first performer into another back drop as though bouncing a basketball. Repeat the stunt several times.

10. *Straddle Over.* This stunt is done by two performers. The first performer bounces high with the legs in a straddle position. The second performer walks underneath while the last performer bounces. When walking underneath, he looks at the audience and waves at someone. Repeat this sequence a second time. On the third time, the person walking underneath only walks through halfway, pretending to be interested in something in the audience, then suddenly looks up and sees his partner coming down on top of him. He lets out a shriek and does a back drop while the bouncer straddles him. The audience thinks the bouncer has landed on him.

11. *Wild Bouncing Routine.* An instructor or performer asks for a volunteer from the audience, and with the boy or girl on the tramp, the instructor suggests that the first thing to try to do is to learn the art of bouncing. The instructor then grasps the upper arm of the volunteer and tells him/her to bounce up and down. When the volunteer bounces, the instructor pulls the arm forward and backward with each ensuing bounce, which causes the person to bounce forward and then backward. From the audience's viewpoint it looks as though the volunteer is bouncing wildly and the instructor is just staying with him/her—hanging on to the arm.

12. *Girl's Seat Drop Routine.* Demonstrate the seat drop to the audience and at first show them a straight sit-down landing and then up to the feet. This, the performer states, is the way a man will do a seat drop. Now demonstrate the way a girl will do a seat drop. After a few bounces the performer lifts his feet into the air and on the way down the performer wiggles his seat back and forth a few times prior to landing on the seat.

13. *Chewing Gum Routine.* If a volunteer from the audience is chewing gum, suggest to him or her that perhaps one should not chew gum while bouncing and so should find a place for it. The performer then takes the gum from the volunteer and looks about and finally places the gum on a spring. This is good for a small laugh, but the climax is that when the volunteer is through, the performer retrieves the gum and gives it back to the volunteer, who inadvertently will place it back in his or her mouth and commence chewing it after leaving the trampoline.

14. *Loose Pants.* A trampolinist bounces on the trampoline wearing a baggy pair of pants with extremely elastic suspenders and weights hidden in the pockets to make the pants drop down below the knees on each bounce on the trampoline. A loud pair of swim trunks or underpants add to the humor of this stunt.

15. *Magic Rising Stunt.* Have a small person lie on his back on the bed with the instructor standing in a straddle position over him. On the count of one, two, and finally three, the instructor gives the bed a push with his feet, which sends the small individual up swiftly into the instructor's arms.

16. *That Girl Is Bothering Me.* A performer bouncing on the trampoline stops and calls out to the emcee (coach or whomever) and says, "That girl is bothering me," (and points in the direction of a specific girl). The emcee says "That girl is bothering you? Why she isn't even watching you." The performer then says "Yea, I know—that's what's bothering me!"

17. *Triple Butterfly.* After the trampolinists have done several big tricks the announcer says "You've seen the triple back, triple twist, triffis, and so on, . . . but this young man (woman) will now do his (her) own creation—a Triple Butterfly. Silence in the auditorium if we may while this daring young man (woman) tries his (her) trick." The performer then bounces several times getting higher and higher with each bounce and finally at the top of the last bounce he or she places his/her hands under the armpits with the elbows to the side and then thrusts the elbows up and down in a flying manner, thus doing the "Triple Butterfly."

17

Warm-Ups, Flexibility Training, and Conditioning

Gymnastics is the type of activity that benefits from warming up and conditioning, through which flexibility and strength can also be developed. A proper warm-up may reduce the possibility of injury and should form the basis of a minimal conditioning program. Some development of flexibility and strength takes place during the learning process as each move is repeated over and over again, so that in a sense these two items are inherently built into the sport. However, for the gymnast who seeks high levels of performance, additional work on flexibility and strength is necessary.

WARM-UPS

To be most beneficial, warm-ups should cover all muscle groups and should not be done lackadaisically. The exercises should start off with jogging to warm up the body generally. This should be followed by a general stretching and loosening of the body joints. Varsity gymnasts

who have an extended period of time for practice may want to use a longer warm-up period. This warm-up could consist of stretching and loosening of parts of the body as indicated above followed by some of the flexibility exercises described later. For a physical education class in gymnastics with limited time, the following set of exercises may well provide a satisfactory warm-up:

The (School Nickname) Warm-Up and Conditioner

1. *Side Stretcher.* Stand with the legs spread sideways and the arms at the sides. Bend to the right, stretching the left arm overhead with the palm down. Return to the starting position and repeat to the left side. Keep alternating from right to left.

2. *Windmill.* Stand with the legs spread sideways and arms stretched out horizontally. Bend and touch the right foot with the left hand, keeping the knees straight. Return to the starting position and alternate to the other side.

3. *Arm Thrust.* Stand with the legs spread sideways and arms reaching overhead. Bend forward until the upper body is parallel to the floor. Reach the hands between the legs and touch the floor as far back as possible. Thrust the arms forward and upward without straightening the body (keep the chest parallel to the floor).

4. *Sitting Tucks.* Start in a sitting position with the legs out straight. Draw both knees into the chest, clasping the arms around the shins. Then release the arms and extend the legs to the starting position.

5. *V Flexor.* Start in a supine position (on back) with the arms stretched overhead. Raise the arms (and shoulders) and legs off the floor at the same time, assuming a V position touching the hands to the toes. Return to the starting position.

6. *Push-Ups.* Start in a front leaning rest position. Keeping the body straight, bend the arms, and touch the chest to the floor. Push up to the starting position.

7. *Leg Extensor.* Start in a squatting position with the hands on the floor and the knees together and between the arms. Extend the legs backward to a front-leaning rest position. Return to the starting position.

8. *Straddle Hop.* Start in a squatting position with the hands on the floor and the knees together and between the arms. Jump to a straddle position with the legs while keeping the hands on the floor. Return to starting position.

9. *Hamstring Stretcher.* Start in a squatting position with the hands on the floor and the knees together and between the arms. Slowly straighten the legs while keeping the hands touching the floor, then return to the starting position.

10. *Jumping Jacks.* From a standing position, jump to a straddle stand, and at the same time raise the arms sideways and upward, ending by touching the palms of the hands together. Return to the starting position.

Note: Each exercise should be done a minimum of ten times.

Warm-Downs

It has been found to be beneficial for each gymnast to go through a short warm-down after each workout. This basically consists of loose stretching, shaking, and rotation of each joint area. This seems to relax any muscle groups that have tightened up during the workout session.

FLEXIBILITY TRAINING

In the past, emphasis has been on building strength, endurance, and speed. However, flexibility is now being recognized as an important factor in training gymnasts, and today coaches and gymnasts alike are often heard to comment about the great flexibility of this or that champion.

If an athlete has flexibility the benefits are many:

1. Less chance of injury in spite of maximum effort.

2. Efficiency of body effort when particular movements are executed.

3. Correct execution of the many exacting skills of the sport.

Since flexibility is recognized as a paramount factor in championship performance, all gymnasts should work specifically on developing it. It has also been found that with adaptations the flexibility movements can further be used to develop strength, speed, and endurance as well as flexibility itself. Muscle power takes into account all four of these components, and, when all of them are used properly, the various joints of the body will move freely and efficiently through their natural range of movement. Gymnasts should therefore work hard on developing optimum flexibility along with strength, speed, and endurance. Some general rules to follow in training for flexibility are:

1. Flexibility must be worked with the same intensity as if it were one of the six events.

2. The warm-up is *not* the flexibility training session; it is not the time to work specifically on increasing your range of motion, although it does help in that purpose. Treat the warm-ups as a means of preparing yourself mentally and physically for the training session ahead. Naturally, some stretching is included in the warm-ups, but it will be more efficient and effective if flexibility is treated in a separate training session.

3. When stretching, be sure to stretch in both directions. If a gymnast stretches in one direction only, there is a tendency to tighten the antagonistic muscle groups, and thus a complete range of motion is not developed. For example, if you sit on the floor and stretch forward touching the toes as one set of exercises, be sure to do back bends or wrestler's bridges so the full range of motion is established.

4. While seeking ultimate flexibility, or the ability to open or close an angle at maximum range, it also is important to control the motion and to hold static positions.

5. When working a flexibility exercise, do not bounce forcefully into the positions, but instead move steadily into the position and hold for a period of time.

Specific Flexibility Exercises

It is suggested that before beginning flexibility exercises the gymnast run long enough to work up a good sweat. For this it is helpful to wear warm, loose clothing. The following exercises are only suggested ways of developing flexibility. Many gymnasts have their own favorite exercises, which may differ from these.

1. Jump in place and swing the body loosely in all directions. Then do leg swings by grabbing a bar that is shoulder height. Do ten swings to one side, finishing with a ten-second hold with the leg in maximum lift position. Then do ten swings in the opposite direction, finishing with the 10-second hold. Also, do the ten swings forward and backward with the same 10-second hold. Repeat with the other leg.

2. Lie on your side on the mat with the arms and legs extended in a straight line or resting on one elbow. Raise the upper leg to a vertical position, hold for a few seconds and return to place. Do this several times and then roll over and raise the other leg.

3. Sit in the regular split position. With one leg in front and the other in back, assume as deep a split as possible and hold for a short period of time. Then turn the body so the other leg is forward and again assume as deep a split position as possible and hold. Follow this by facing forward with the legs extended side-

Leg Raise

Forward Stretch

Split

Straddle Split, Forward Lean

4. Sit on the floor with the legs stretched straight ahead and the back straight. Lean forward and grab the ankles with the hands and bring the chest to the knees, keeping the legs straight. Hold for 20 seconds, shake the legs a little and then repeat for another 20 seconds. Do this three times.

5. Stand on a bench with a stick underneath the bench. Grasp the stick with a hand on each side of the bench and, leaning forward, straighten the legs and pull against the stick and the bench, placing the chest on the knees. Hold for 20 seconds. Repeat three times.

6. Sit on the floor with the legs stretched out straight ahead and the hands on the floor in back of the hips a considerable distance. Lift the hips off the mat and hold for 20 seconds, resting on the feet and hands. Try to reach as far back with the hands as possible each time. Then sit down, shake the body, and repeat. Do three times.

7. Sit with the soles of the feet together, knees bent and to the sides. Push the knees down toward the floor and hold for a few seconds and relax. Do three times.

8. With the use of a rope or towel do twenty dislocates and twenty inlocates

ways in as deep a straddle split position as possible and hold for a period of time. Finish by leaning forward with the chest as close to the floor as possible and hold. Do this complete circuit of splits three times.

Bench Stretch

with straight arms. Try to place the hands as close together as possible. Do three sets of each.

9. Hang in a skin-the-cat position on the high bar for 20 seconds. Do three times in both regular ad reverse grips.

10. Do a hand balance against a wall similar to a yogi handstand with the hips against the wall and the legs at a 90-degree angle and the chin on the chest. Hold for 10 seconds and do three times.

Hip Lift

Inlocate, Dislocate Stretch

12. Hang from a horizontal bar lowered to about 6 feet. Have a partner walk under you, placing his back against your back, pushing you away from the bar. Hold this position for 10 seconds. Repeat three times.

13. While on hands and knees on the mat, reach forward with one hand, dropping the same shoulder and stretch toward the mat for 30 seconds. Repeat with other shoulder.

Shoulder Stretch

Skin the Cat

Back Stretch with Partner

All-Fours Shoulder Stretch

11. Grab a lowered parallel bar or a balance beam with the upper body parallel to the floor. Stretch the shoulders downward or have a partner gently push downward against the back. Try to hold for 30 seconds.

Inverted V Stretch

Stretching Using Parallel Bars

14. Inverted V Stretch. With the body in an inverted V position, keeping the legs straight, press the head and shoulders toward the floor, thus stretching the shoulders.

15. Stretching using the parallel bars

a. Stand on the parallel bars and bend forward, grasping the bars with the hands in front of the feet. Keep the legs straight and lean backward, thus stretching the shoulders and legs.

b. Stand on the parallel bars and bend forward, placing the hands outside the legs and grasping the bars behind the heels. Keep the legs straight and lean forward, thus stretching the legs.

Resistive Partner Flexibility Exercises

With a partner's assistance a few resistive flexibility exercises may be beneficial in developing a full range of motion for two crucial point areas: the shoulders and the hips.

Shoulders. It is a good idea prior to starting the resistive flexibility exercises to have a gymnast in a sitting position with a partner standing behind, massaging and generally loosening up the shoulders.

1. Have the arms out to the side and parallel to the mats. Lift them straight overhead and then down to the sides of the body with the standing partner grasping the wrists, providing some resistance to the up and down motions. Repeat several times.

2. With the arms parallel to the mats bring the hands backward behind the back trying to touch the fingers together. Then, with your partner's assistance, pull the arms together so the fingers touch. The partner should provide assistance and resistance to the backward and forward motions of the arms. Repeat several times.

Hips:

1. Lying on your side, lift one leg up and down with your partner (stand-

Partner Stretch Exercises

ing behind) providing resistance to the upward and downward motions. Repeat several times.

2. Lying in the prone position (on the stomach), lift one leg and then both legs up and down with partner resistance and assistance in the up and downward motions. Repeat several times.

It is suggested that for maximum flexibility a gymnast should stretch twice daily. The morning stretch should be preceded by a running and general loosening up, since after sleeping the body responds slowly to a thorough flexibility workout. You will feel good for it, however, and your warm-up prior to your apparatus workout later in the day will become noticeably easier and more efficient.

Shower-Room Stretching

It has been found by some athletes that it is good to do stretching exercises while taking a shower because the muscles and ligaments become relaxed and pliable under the warm water. (Caution should be used, of course, in view of the slippery condition of many shower-room floors.) Almost any stretching exercise directed toward any part of the body such as the shoulders, back, sides, hamstrings, and even the wrists and ankles can be beneficial, using a program of holding a particular stretched position for 6 seconds, followed by a short relaxing period, and then holding again for 6 seconds, and so on. Do each stretching exercise from three to six times.

CONDITIONING AND STRENGTHENING

Time-Element Method of Training

A system of training that has proven successful is that of doing a set number of moves or combinations on each event within a specific time limit and is called the Time-Element Method. The gymnast and coach identify in advance a series of five moves (or combinations) for each event and each move is then tried six times with about a minute between each try. During the minute between attempts the gymnast should be thinking and analyzing how the move should properly be done. The five different moves tried six times each with a minute between each attempt will consume 30 minutes. If a gymnast works six events in one afternoon the elapsed time would be 3 hours; if only four events, 2 hours.

The chief benefit of the Time-Element Method is that it keeps the gymnast alert and efficient during workouts and allows no wasted time. Hopefully, it will eliminate a lot of excessive "chalk-talk," "tea party conversations," or other outside interferences and should result in a productive and beneficial workout. Obviously, as the gymnast becomes stronger, better conditioned, and more proficient an increase should be made in the number of moves or combinations for each event within the same time restrictions.

On a weekly basis, every day should not be the same. A good schedule would be: Monday a fairly heavy day; Tuesday only moderately heavy; Wednesday another fairly heavy session; Thursday a very light day; Friday a moderately heavy day; Saturday a very heavy day; and finally Sunday off.

The principles of this system of training could be adapted to a physical education class or for a beginning varsity team. Moves or combinations would be selected to fit the ability of the students and could actually be different for each person. Instead of a set time period between repetitions, the period would be the time it takes for each member of the squad to perform his or her move in rotation. The system would be more beneficial if the squad were not larger than four or five students. Obviously, either the number of moves or the number of events worked per class period would have to be altered to fit the length of time of the normal class period or team practice session.

STRENGTHENING (MUSCULATION) EXERCISES

A strengthening plan worthy of consideration consists of doing a series of strengthening (musculation) exercises after completing a regular workout. This plan calls for moving around to from five to eight different stations, performing at each station a strengthening exercise a specific number of times, and upon completing the entire round, repeating the program two more times to make three full circuits. The coach or instructor should carefully consider the order of the exercises so as not to overtire any particular muscle group, and the plan should also be changed periodically. The strength moves selected should fit the capacity of the performer, keeping in mind that the coach or a team member can help the gymnast in some of the particularly difficult strength exercises. Some examples of musculation exercises are:

Rings: (Assisted by coach or team member.) 6-second cross; 6-second front lever; three muscle-ups (or forward rolls or backward rolls) to L; three presses to shoulder balances or handstands; inverted hang, down to front lever, back up and over to back lever, and return to inverted hang. Repeat five times.

Parallel Bars: Five front uprises with the bars wide; five swinging dips both front and back; three presses to handstand; wide bar push-ups (fifteen); two hanging front levers (5 seconds each).

Pommel Horse: Two to five loops on end of horse; ten circles; a scissor combination; stoop through to L position, hold for 3 seconds, and return. Do three times.

Horizontal Bar: Hanging from hands, do five leg lifts to bar (V-ups); ten pull ups; hang and straight-leg, stoop-through skin-the-cats (five times).

Floor Exercise: Ten handstand push-ups; five straight-arm pulls to support (prone position, pull to front leaning rest position); twenty push-ups; ten push-ups with hands together; lift legs in each scale position and hold for 6 seconds each; V-ups (fifteen); walk on hands, 10 to 40 feet.

An Example of a Musculation Plan:

1. Pommel Horse. Rear support stoop-out to a straddle L then stoop back through (three times).

2. Pommel Horse. Ten to fifteen circles.

3. Rings. Three muscle ups into press to handstands (or shoulder stand).

4. Rings. 6-second cross with inner tube or partner assistance.

5. Parallel Bars. Three swinging dips, front and back.

6. High Bar. Five leg lifts to bar (V-ups).

7. Floor Exercise. Ten jump tucks.

8. Floor Exercise. Walk on hands.

Note: The above circuit should be done three full times.

18

Judging Gymnastics

Judging gymnastics can be a very complicated and sophisticated duty, as those who have tried to pass judgment on a gymnast's performance at any level will attest, whether the competition is elementary, intermediate, or advanced. Many facets of the performance must be considered in awarding a score. Present-day judging has been greatly improved over that of a few years ago when the awarding of points was completely subjective. Improved standards and objectivity have resulted primarily through the efforts of the International Federation of Gymnastics (F.I.G.). Its official *Code of Points* was first adopted in 1949, and constant revision has improved the code considerably to its most recent edition. Several articles and books have been written on the art of judging, including an excellent dissertation called *Judging Guide and Course,* by Frank Cumiskey of the United States Gymnastic Federation. This book, along with the latest *Code of Points* by the F.I.G.

can be obtained from the USGF office, Box 12713, Tucson, Arizona 85717. A copy should be at your side while either judging or coaching.

Judging can be divided into two main types of competition: Compulsory Routine Competition and Optional Routine Competition. Men's judging differs from women's judging and will be treated separately.

OPTIONAL ROUTINE COMPETITION

Judging Men's Gymnastics

As you prepare yourself to judge your first or 99th meet, remember that you will basically be working from a maximum score of ten points divided into four categories: (1) difficulty of the exercise; (2) combination or construction of the exercise; (3) execution of the exercise involving form and correct technique; and (4) bonus points for moves,

Judging a Gymnast's Performance

Code of Points. An *A* skill is one of minimal or lower difficulty and is worth a numerical value of .2 points. A *B* skill is one of intermediate difficulty and is awarded a value of .4 points. A *C* skill is listed as one of superior difficulty and is awarded a value of .6 points. To receive the full 3.4 points in a dual meet, a routine must have at least one *C* move, five *B* moves, and four *A* moves. Since every routine must have eleven parts, one more move of either *A*, *B*, or *C* grading must be executed to total the eleven parts. If any of the required moves mentioned above are missing, an appropriate deduction must be made. A *B* move can substitute for a *C* move but will result in a .2 deduction since the *B* is worth only .4 points. An *A* move cannot substitute for a *B* or *C* move, but, in a routine consisting of only *A* moves, a maximum of five may be counted for a difficulty rating of 1.0 (5 x .2 = 1.0). Otherwise, a maximum of four *A* moves can be counted. Some examples are as follows:

A routine of four *B* moves and seven *A* moves would have a difficulty of 2.4, determined by a deduction of .6 for no *C* move and .4 for the *B* move that is lacking. (It could also be figured by four *B* moves times .4 plus four *A* moves times .2.)

A routine of six *B* moves and five *A* moves would have a difficulty of 3.2, determined by a deduction of .2 for the substitution of a *B* move for a *C* move (or by six *B* moves times .4 plus four *A* moves times .2).

combinations, and/or routines that show risk, originality, and virtuosity (commonly referred to as R.O.V.).

Difficulty of the exercise is determined by the performance of a certain number of skills or moves of graded difficulty. If a gymnast has full difficulty, as spelled out by the F.I.G., he must be awarded 3.4 points. Each routine must have eleven parts or separate skills, and each skill is graded accorded to its difficulty. These are identified in the official F.I.G.

In Competition III, which is used in championship individual finals, the requirements increase in that the gymnast must perform three *C* moves, three *B* moves, and two *A* moves plus three other moves of *A, B,* or *C* value to make up the eleven parts.

Combination is the second factor upon which judgment is passed. The judge awards 1.6 points to the gymnast if he performs his routine according to the requirements covered by the F.I.G. Each event has its specific requirements, and these are covered at the beginning of each chapter of this text. As an example, on the pommel horse the required moves are that a performer must execute clean swings without stops, forward and reverse scissors, and all parts of the horse must be used. The primary reason for combination requirements is to ensure good usage of correct movements on each event. Deductions for combination errors are generally up to .3 for each error or omission.

Execution is the third factor in judging a gymnastic performance and involves deductions for errors of general and technical executions up to 4.4 points. Items that warrant deductions as general execution faults are: poor position of the feet, legs, hands, arms, open legs, and so on (all of these are thought of as form); and things like touching the apparatus; stops or hesitations; and a complete sit-down or fall. A part of execution is called technical execution and calls for deductions for incorrect methods of executing each part or parts. Deductions can occur for hesitations or restarts in upward movements, strength moves executed with swing or vice versa, not maintaining a hold position long enough or in an incorrect position or posture, and a poor stand upon dismounting from the apparatus.

Risk, Originality, and Virtuosity (R.O.V.) is the fourth factor in judging

a routine. Up to .6 points can be awarded if the gymnast displays risk, originality, or virtuosity in a routine. No more than .2 points can be awarded for any of the three items mentioned.

To summarize judging of men's gymnastics, the following factors are considered in awarding a score:

Difficulty of the eleven parts: 3.4 points

Combination (construction of the routine): 1.6 points

Execution (good form, technique, and continuity): 4.4 points

R.O.V. (risk, originality, and virtuosity): .6 points

Total possible score: 10 points

In the brief time that it takes the gymnast to complete a routine, the judge must determine whether the gymnast showed eleven principal parts; whether there was at least one *C* move, five *B* moves, and four *A* moves; whether the combination requirements were met in the construction of the routine; the number and severity of errors in form and technique; and whether the routine demonstrated any risk, originality, and virtuosity. Then in a few seconds the judge must mathematically make the deductions and issue the score. Needless to say, it is a difficult and exacting job, but very important to the gymnast and the team.

Vaulting is judged differently than are the other events in that the gymnast is performing an isolated stunt. Difficulty is set by the tables in the *Code of Points* and indicates the maximum score a gymnast could receive if everything were perfect in performing the vault. The angle of the body in going from the beat board to the horse is called pre-flight and is one of the factors considered. This angle is different for various vaults. Post-

A Gymnastic Meet in Progress

flight or the height of the body and the distance upon landing after the gymnast has left the horse is another factor considered. A fourth factor would be the form and execution throughout the entire vault and includes items such as poor position of the legs, arms, body, touching of the horse with feet, bending of the arms when leaving the horse, and so on.

Judging for interscholastic gymnastics is similar but with some modifications. The National Interscholastic Rule Book can be obtained from the National Federation of State High School Athletic Associations, 400 Leslie St., Box 98, Elgin, Illinois 60120.

Judging Women's Gymnastics

Judging of women's optional gymnastics involves the following factors: difficulty; originality and value of connections; value of general composition of exercise; execution and amplitude; and general impression.

Full difficulty is worth 3.0 points and must include three superior parts that are valued at .6 each and four medium-difficulty parts that are valued at .3 points each. It should be noted that a superior difficulty part can replace a part of medium difficulty, but, if only medium difficulty parts are used, the maximum score for difficulty would be 1.2 points (four times .3). The difficulty rating of the moves may be found in the *Code of Points for Women* of the F.I.G.

Originality and connections is worth a maximum of 1.5 and composition adds another .5 points. Some of the items for which deductions may be made are: lack of originality; lack or excess of one type of movement; a masculine appearance of the exercise; combinations' being too difficult or unsuitable; performing the superior parts at the beginning of the routine; and not using the entire area (pertaining specifically to floor exercise).

Execution and amplitude is worth 4.0 points. Deductions can be made for: unintentional bending of arms, legs, or body; spreading of the legs; lack of continuity between movements; overall jerky execution; falling on the floor or apparatus; and landing on dismounts without suppleness or with loss of balance.

General impression is worth 1.0 points and includes items such as: appearance of lightness; dynamic expression; beauty, grace, and elegance; fluency, body coordination, and suitable posture.

There are some so-called neutral deductions that are not specifically included in any of the above categories. These include: falling from the balance beam; falling from the uneven parallel bars; physical assistance; talking by the coach; the gymnast's stopping due to personal fault; the music's not following the regulation of only one instrument; turns in only one direction on the beam; combinations and movements too advanced for the gymnast; and overuse of one particular skill.

Judging of women's vaulting is rather specific, and the following factors are considered in making deductions: difficulty, established by F.I.G.; pre-flight; post-flight; and the form and execution throughout the entire vault. Some of the common faults and errors of execution are: insufficient pre-flight; insufficient post-flight; bending the arms in support; touching the horse with the feet; landing on a dismount in a heavy and uncertain manner or touching the hands to the floor or landing on the seat.

JUDGING COMPULSORY ROUTINES

Judging compulsory routines consists of evaluating a set of prescribed routines determined by a gymnastic committee. This committee could be of local, state, national, or international origin. Since the routines are prescribed in their difficulty and combination, the judges need only be concerned about the execution. No judgment has to be made on difficulty of the routines or combination requirements since all gymnasts will be doing the same routines. In spite of the fact that most compulsory routines do not have full difficulty, judgment is made on the basis of 9.8 points with up to .2 allowable for virtuosity.

Selected List
of Reference Materials
and Visual Aids

BOOKS

ARONSON, RICHARD, ed., *The Art and Science of Judging Men's Gymnastics.* Lowell, Mass.: Lowell Technical Institute, 1970. (Available from Nissen)

BENGTSSON, NILS, *Beginner's Gymnastics.* Palo Alto, Calif.: National Press, 1969.

BOWERS, CAROLYN, et al., *Judging and Coaching Women's Gymnastics.* Palo Alto, Calif.: National Press, 1972.

CARTER, ERNESTINE, *Gymnastics for Girls and Women.* Englewood Cliffs, N.J.: Prentice-Hall, Inc., 1969.

COOPER, PHYLLIS, *Feminine Gymnastics,* 2nd ed. Minneapolis: Burgess Pub. Co., 1973.

CUMISKEY, FRANK, *Judging Guide and Course.* Tucson, Ariz.: U.S. Gymnastics Federation, 1973.

GEORGE, GERALD, ed., *The Magic of Gymnastics.* Santa Monica, Calif.: Sundby Publications, 1970.

HARRIS, RICH, *Introducing Gymnastics.* Napa, Calif.: Physical Education Aids, 1963.

HENNESSY, JEFF, *The Trampoline . . . As I See It.* Lafayette, La.: International Pub. Co., 1969.

HUGHES, ERIC, *Gymnastics for Men.* New York: Ronald Press Co., 1966.

JOHNSON, MARVIN, *Programmed Basic Gymnastics Routine.* Published by the author at Eastern Michigan University. 1976.

JUDD, LESLIE, et al., *Exhibition Gymnastics.* New York: Association Press, 1969.

LADUE, FRANK, and JIM NORMAN, *Two Seconds of Freedom. (This is Trampolining).* Cedar Rapids, Iowa: Nissen Corporation, 1959.

O'QUINN, GARLAND, JR., *Gymnastics for Elementary School Children.* Dubuque, Iowa: Wm. C. Brown Co., 1967.

RYSER, OTTO, *A Manual for Tumbling and Apparatus Stunts,* 6th ed. Dubuque, Iowa: Wm. C. Brown Co., 1976.

SALMELA, JOHN H., *The Advanced Study of Gymnastics.* Springfield, Ill.: Charles C. Thomas, 1976.

SCHMID, ANDREA, and BLANCHE DRURY, *Gymnastics for Women.* Palo Alto,

Calif.: National Press Publications, 1977.

SPACKMAN, ROBERT, JR., *Conditioning for Gymnastics.* Springfield, Ill.: Charles C. Thomas, 1970.

SZYPULA, GEORGE, *Tumbling and Balancing for All,* 2nd ed. Dubuque, Iowa: Wm. C. Brown Co., 1968.

TAYLOR, BRYCE, BORIS BAJIN, and TOM ZIVIC, *Olympic Gymnastics for Men and Women.* Englewood Cliffs, N.J.: Prentice-Hall, Inc., 1972.

TONRY, DON, *The Side Horse.* Northbridge, Mass.: Gymnastic Aides, 1966.

TONRY, DON, *Gymnastics Illustrated.* Northbridge, Mass.: Gymnastic Aides, 1972.

PERIODICALS

The International Gymnast
P.O. Box 110
Santa Monica, California 90406

Journal of Health, Physical Education, and Recreation
1201 Sixteenth St., N.W.
Washington, D.C. 20036

Athletic Journal
1719 Howard Street
Evanston, Illinois

Scholastic Coach
902 Sylvan Avenue
Englewood Cliffs, New Jersey 07632

The Physical Educator
3747 N. Linwood Avenue
Indianapolis, Indiana 46218

Acro Sports
Box 7
Santa Monica, Calif. 90406

GYMNASTICS RULE BOOKS

International Gymnastics Federation
(FIG) Code of Points for Men

International Gymnastics Federation
(FIG) Code of Points for Women
available from either:
Amateur Athletic Union
3400 West 86th Street
Indianapolis, Indiana 46268

United States Gymnastic Federation
Box 4699
Tucson, Arizona 85717

The Official NCAA Gymnastics Rules
349 East Thomas Road
Phoenix, Arizona 85012

D.G.W.S. Gymnastics Guide
c/o Amer. Alliance for Health, Phys. Educ., and Recreation
1201 Sixteenth Street, N.W.
Washington, D.C. 20036

National Federation Rules Publications for Boys and Girls Gymnastics
National High School Federation
7 So. Dearborn St.
Chicago, Illinois 60603

"A", "B", "C" Parts of Men's Gymnastics
U.S. Gymnastic Federation
P.O. Box 4699
Tucson, Arizona 85717

INSTRUCTIONAL CHARTS

Charts of various kinds and activities are available from the following sources:

American Athletic Equipment Co.
Jefferson, Iowa 50129

Gymnastic Aides, Inc.
P.O. Box 475
Northbridge, Mass. 01534

Nissen Corporation
930 27th Avenue, S.W.
Cedar Rapids, Iowa 52406

Physical Education Aids
P.O. Box 5117
San Mateo, California 94402

Porter Equipment Co.
9555 Irving Park Road
Schiller Park, Illinois 60176

Program Aids Company, Inc.
No. 1 Physical Fitness Drive
Garden City, New York 11530

AUDIO-VISUAL AIDS FOR GYMNASTICS

Loopfilms

The Athletic Institute
705 Merchandise Mart
Chicago, Illinois 60654

Men's Gymnastics (Consultant: Newt Loken)
1. Balancing—2 loops
2. Tumbling—9 loops
3. High Bar—12 loops
4. Rings—9 loops
5. Floor Exercise—8 loops
6. Side Horse—8 loops
7. Vaulting—3 loops
8. Parallel Bars—11 loops
9. Trampoline—12 loops

BFA Educational Media
2211 Michigan Avenue
Santa Monica, Calif. 90404 (These loops are the NCAA-AAHPER-Ealing ones and are available from NCAA and AAHPER, also.)

Men's Gymnastics (Consultant: Bill Meade)
1. Rings—4 loops
2. Tumbling—4 loops
3. Floor Exercise—5 loops
4. Side Horse—3 loops
5. Long Horse—3 loops
6. Parallel Bars—6 loops
7. Horizontal Bar—4 loops
8. Trampoline—4 loops

Women's Gymnastics (Consultant: Ernestine Carter)
1. Basic Techniques—2 loops
2. Tumbling—4 loops

3. Floor Exercise Routines—2 loops
4. Balance Beam—3 loops
5. Uneven Parallel Bars—3 loops
6. Vaulting—2 loops

Champions on Film
745 State Circle
Ann Arbor, Michigan 48104 (They also handle the NCAA-AAHPER-Ealing loops.)

Gymnastics Fundamentals (Consultant: Newt Loken)
1. Basic Rolls
2. Basic Tumbling Techniques
3. Basic Balancing Techniques

Women's Gymnastics (Consultant: Linda Morton)
1. Uneven Bars—3 loops
2. Balance Beam—3 loops
3. Floor Exercise Tumbling—3 loops
4. Vaulting—1 loop

Motion Pictures

The Athletic Institute
705 Merchandise Mart
Chicago, Illinois 60654 (Consultants: Jackie Fie, Delene Darst, Linda Metheny, and Dale Flansaas) Each is 20 minutes, in sound, color, Super 8 Cassette or 16 mm. reel.

National Compulsory Routines (Women)
1. Beginning Level
2. Intermediate Level
3. Advanced Level

NCAA Films
P.O. Box 2726
Wichita, Kansas 67201 (Official NCAA Championship meets.)

Pyramid Films
Box 1048
Santa Monica, Calif. 90406 (Gymnastic Flashbacks. 10 min., sound, b & w. Gym-

nastic action over the past 50 years.)

Film Marketing Center
Syracuse University
1455 E. Colvin St.
Syracuse, New York 13210

Tumbling & Floor Exercises #1
23 min., sound, b & w
Tumbling & Floor Exercises #2
18 min., sound, b & w
Side Horse Vaults & Support Exercises
17 min., sound, b & w
On the Parallels
32 min., sound, b & w
Hi-Low Uneven Bars
18 min., sound, b & w
Basic Horizontal Bar
25 min., sound, b & w
Beam-Nastics
17 min., sound, b & w

Aerials—Tumbling—Floor Exercises
22 min., sound, b & w

Jeff T. Hennessy
Box 672
University of Southwestern Louisiana
LaFayette, Louisiana (Trampoline Championships Films)

Champions on Films
745 State Circle
Ann Arbor, Michigan 48104

NCAA Gymnastics Highlights
16 mm., sound, color
Teaching and Spotting Hints for:
1. Uneven Bar (1000' long)
2. Floor Exercises (600' long)
3. Balance Beam (900' long)

In addition to the above sources, it is suggested that equipment companies and area college coaches be contacted.

Index